MW01118627

TIGRES
OF THE NIGHT

Enjoy the
adventure

Bob Howe

TIGRES OF THE NIGHT

The true story of
Juan and Amalia Arcos,
naturalists and lay missionaries
in the jungle of eastern Ecuador,
1922-2003

Robert W. Howe

Copyright © 2003 by Robert W. Howe.

Cover art by Galen Stevenson.

Library of Congress Number:		2003094050
ISBN :	Hardcover	1-4134-1503-2
	Softcover	1-4134-1502-4

All rights reserved. No part of this book may be reproduced or transmitted in any form or by any means, electronic or mechanical, including photocopying, recording, or by any information storage and retrieval system, without permission in writing from the copyright owner.

This book was printed in the United States of America.

To order additional copies of this book, contact:
Xlibris Corporation
1-888-795-4274
www.Xlibris.com
Orders@Xlibris.com
19488

CONTENTS

AUTHOR's NOTE 15
INTRODUCTION 17
THE FIRST TIGRE OF THE NIGHT 21

THE EARLY YEARS
CHAPTER ONE: Manuel 41
CHAPTER TWO: Friends in Two Cultures 46
CHAPTER THREE: Love in the Selva 49
CHAPTER FOUR: Gold and Death 52
CHAPTER FIVE: A Place of Love 54
CHAPTER SIX: Tragedy 60
CHAPTER SEVEN: The Mission of Gualaquiza 63
CHAPTER EIGHT: The Mission Grows
     and Wars Begin 68
CHAPTER NINE: Juan's Power is Recognized 76
CHAPTER TEN: Maria 79

MENDEZ
CHAPTER ELEVEN: The Mission at Mendez 85
CHAPTER TWELVE: Education Minister's Challenge 86
CHAPTER THIRTEEN: Working for God,
     But not as a Priest 95

YAUPI
CHAPTER FOURTEEN: A New Life 103
CHAPTER FIFTEEN: Amalia Tuitsa 106
CHAPTER SIXTEEN: Courtship 108
CHAPTER SEVENTEEN: You Married a Jivaro 112
CHAPTER EIGHTEEN: Children of their Own 114

CHAPTER NINETEEN: The Mission Grows 117

CHAPTER TWENTY: The First Vendetta 120

CHAPTER TWENTY-ONE: Will the Wars
    Never End? 126

CHAPTER TWENTY-TWO: Priests, Soldiers
    and Slaves 129

CHAPTER TWENTY-THREE: Arrested as a Spy 138

CHAPTER TWENTY-FOUR: At the Door of Death 150

CHAPTER TWENTY-FIVE: The Challenge 156

CHAPTER TWENTY-SIX: Deadly Measles 157

CHAPTER TWENTY-SEVEN: Changes at Yaupi 160

SANTIAGO

CHAPTER TWENTY-EIGHT: First Mission 169

CHAPTER TWENTY-NINE: Mission Life 178

CHAPTER THIRTY: Melinia 188

CHAPTER THIRTY-ONE: River Travel 192

CHAPTER THIRTY-TWO: Jungle Dogs 197

CHAPTER THIRTY-THREE: The Dangerous
    Old Ways Return 202

CHAPTER THIRTY-FOUR: Student Soldiers 207

CHAPTER THIRTY-FIVE: Shamans and Soldiers,
    Both Good and Bad 213

CHAPTER THIRTY-SIX: Leaving Santiago 218

MIASAL

CHAPTER THIRTY-SEVEN: Where the Tsuirim
    Meets the Mangosiza 223

CHAPTER THIRTY-EIGHT: Miasal, the Beautiful Site 229

CHAPTER THIRTY-NINE: The Mission Grows
    and the First Challenge Arrives 232

CHAPTER FORTY: Army Ants Attack,
    to Amalia's Delight 238

CHAPTER FORTY-ONE: The Radio School 240

CHAPTER FORTY-TWO: Hiking with Children
    to Aguas Termales 242

CHAPTER FORTY-THREE: Tukup, the Big Man 246
CHAPTER FORTY-FOUR: Amalia is Healed
   by a Shaman-Like Doctor 279
CHAPTER FORTY-FIVE: Bringing the World
   to Miasal 286
CHAPTER FORTY-SIX: The Valiant Death
   of Mercedes Masuink Entsakua 289
CHAPTER FORTY-SEVEN: An Old Good Deed
   Saves Today 291
CHAPTER FORTY-EIGHT: Cattle in the Selva 295
CHAPTER FORTY-NINE: Pepe the Pilot 297
CHAPTER FIFTY: Shamans and the Little People 301
CHAPTER FIFTY-ONE: Pets 315
CHAPTER FIFTY-TWO: Christmas Celebrations 318
CHAPTER FIFTY-THREE: Earthquake and the
   Vanished River 324
CHAPTER FIFTY-FOUR: Fishing for Pirarucu 327
CHAPTER FIFTY-FIVE: Challenges of the
   New Century 330

LANGUAGE NOTES 341
GLOSSARY AND BIBLIOGRAPHY 343
BIBLIOGRAPHY 361
APPENDIX: The Shuar and their Homelands 363

This book is for Juan and Amalia Arcos,
whose lives of dedication and service
have touched so many
in the Shuar Nation, lifting them to knowledge
of the outside world and to protect their rights as citizens
of Ecuador. The way was seldom easy
and the Arcos family
has always lived in relative poverty,
but these two wonderful people have never shirked
the goal for which they strived.

This book is also dedicated around Carlos Tuntiak Arcos,
their son who died in 2002.
He loved to laugh and sing with his family
with his children gathered around him.
A tireless, thoughtful companion and worker
for the Shuar people, if he promised something he did it.
His friends, who are scattered throughout the
Ecuadorian jungle and the world, will miss him.
He shared so much in his short life.

Juan Arcos at 80

Amalia Arcos at 70

As told to Robert W. Howe and Justin R. Howe

AUTHOR'S NOTE

Juan and Amalia Arcos are Catholic lay missionaries who have lived in the jungle of eastern Ecuador since the early 1920s. She is a Shuar Indian, a tribe famous as the "Jivaro," head-shrinkers of the Amazon. Juan was raised with the Shuar people on a mission at the edge of the Amazon rain forest, so he was one of the first whites to speak their language as a native. The book is the story of their life—parents, missionaries, anthropologists and naturalists.

The Arcos's stories of life with one of the world's most famous warrior tribes will inspire the reader who is interested in them from the missionary's standpoint. The nature enthusiast will thrill at the depth of detail—walking through the forest with Juan—facing single-handedly and unprotected—two dozen armed warriors who want to kill him; leaving the side of his wife in labor to deal with a boa constrictor in their chicken house; and watching after an earthquake as the river by his house disappears, only to return days later in a brown wall of water carrying hundred-foot-tall trees and four-ton boulders.

A special thanks to Juan Arcos and his son, Carlos, who took the time to help us to comprehend the immensity of the experience. Juan at first was reluctant to tell his story, for he is a humble man. When he finally agreed we gave him a portable recorder and a dozen ninety-minute tapes, which he filled with different stories and details. My son, Justin, who had lived for months with the Arcos family, took on the job of translating those tapes into English. He did a remarkable job, especially in retaining the cadence and thoughtful wording of Juan's speech and the book would not have been possible without his work and dedication. We hope that Juan will feel that we have been true to the trust he has placed in us. Carlos was always nearby when we did formal interviews, urging his father to expand on various stories, providing additional details and adding a wonderful humor to the long afternoons. Father Ralph Wright of the St. Louis Abbey read the story and helped us to interpret the stories from the Catholic viewpoint. We appreciate his thoughtful comments and the long hours he spent both reading and interpreting for us.

This story, therefore, is true. Because of the Arcos's natural humility, however, we have been able to describe certain events from a combination of references they have made and our knowledge of them and their jungle home. In the stories of Juan's decision not to become a priest, Amalia's hunt and the trip to see Tukup, the incidents are, in fact, a combination of several incidents they mentioned. Quotes are in all cases directly from Juan's tapes translated from Spanish to English.

INTRODUCTION

It rained for four days without stopping, sometimes a gentle mist and moments later a thundering flood from the sky. The rainy season, "winter" here in the rain forest of eastern Ecuador, usually begins late in April, but this year it began two weeks early. My son and collaborator, Justin, and I arrived in the frontier village of Macas four days ago but had been wandering around town waiting for the clouds to lift, so we could fly the fifty-five minutes to the remote village of Miasal in the Cutucu Mountains, where Juan and Amalia Arcos live. We strolled to a viewpoint over the Upano River, looking east toward the green escarpments of the Cutucus. The trip can be made on foot, a strenuous four-day walk, so we'd taken our chances that the rain would pause and allow our flight instead. The second day we'd loaded our gear into the four-seater Aero Misionario plane and as the pilot was revving the motor for takeoff, the clouds suddenly fell again. By the third day it was too late to hike, and we just had to hope for dry weather.

A hole finally did open late in the afternoon of the fourth day, and the little plane charged down the long military airstrip, circling the edge of Macas, lifting up over the Upano and flying straight over the Cutucus. Green valleys with gray and brown cliffs and silvery waterfalls opened below us. In the mist of another gathering storm, a circle rainbow formed over the primary jungle below. Scattered clouds began to re-form so the pilot skirted their edges, avoiding the updrafts as much as possible. When the clouds separated again the forest was still below, in a thousand shades of green. From a plane flying over a primary tropical forest where lumbering has never taken place, the trees look like a close-up of the broccoli display in a supermarket, punctuated with occasional *chacras*, small farms cut from the jungle, used for a few years then abandoned as the soil gives out.

After more than two years away, we've been back in Miasal for two days now, talking with Juan about his life and adventures as a missionary. On our last visit he delivered us twelve ninety minute tapes on which he'd recorded his story. We wanted more time with this remarkable man, and he'd agreed to reminisce.

Our "office" was a typical Shuar dwelling, oval-shaped and about thirty feet long. The earth floor was uneven, cracked and hard, swept clean of debris and loose bits of gravel. The walls were built as they had been in the old days when a house was a small fort, its walls made from hard and rigid split chonta palm, set vertically and about six feet high. Chonta wood is rot resistant and beautiful when polished, a deep black, with yellow and brown tones sprinkled through the fibers; but these walls had been left raw and splintery. A small cooking fire sizzled lightly on the far side of a split bamboo wall that divided the room. Thick smoke filled the open upper end of the roof and drifted out of the house through the thatch and an eighteen-inch opening above that six-foot-high outer wall. The Shuar, who average five and a half feet tall, move around in a smoke-free zone. Those of us with more height were forced to lean over or just get used to the continuous haze. The smoke has a useful purpose though. As it drifts around the roof, it coats the inner ceiling with a dark varnish at the same time that it kills the insects and other vermin that try to move into the thatch. A smoke-cured roof can last four or five years.

When the rain began an hour before, we could hear it moving through the forest from more than a mile away. Most of the forest leaves are small and tapered, with thin "drip-tips" that flush off the raindrops quickly. The rain fell on them with a soft murmur. Away from the little house, the big leaves of philodendron and breadfruit—and the giant leaves of the "poor man's umbrella"—resonated drum-like. As the downpour continued, a soft light filled the house, and the thatched roof muffled the sound of the rain as we talked, laughed and sipped lemon grass tea.

Juan Arcos turned eight-two in 2003. All his life he has lived in the jungle, what the people here call *selva* or *oriente*. When I first met him almost eighteen years ago, I was impressed with his strength—both physical and spiritual—and the ways in which he expresses both with gentleness and smiling, patient love. Today, he wears a hat with a narrow brim, covered with pale green flowers and leaf patterns. He wears a scarf around his neck because he's cold, even on this eighty-degree day. Still energetic, his eyes are bright with intelligence and interest in those around him. When he speaks of his family and of the Shuar, his animation is like that of a twenty-year-old. His skin is light chestnut color, but where it has been exposed to the sun, it has mellowed to dark walnut. Except for the corner of his eyes where crow's feet have formed from laughter, his face is unlined. His cheeks glimmer from health and sweat. Even in the forest, he's clean-shaven, which accentuates his high cheekbones. Juan's light-colored eyes are bright, and varied in color from pale blue to hazel brown, depending on the sunlight. When he speaks, his expressive hands motion with gestures varying from gentle waves to staccato-like jabs, and even an inadequate Spanish-speaker is able to understand him. Those remarkable eyes sparkle with the fire of love for people. At five feet eight inches, he's no giant, but next to his wife, Amalia, Juan looks huge. Years on jungle trails have slowed his gait and he hunches forward slightly from arthritis, but his balance is good and he's in control. Juan's hair, once jet-black, is salt and pepper colored, and thinning on top. Each day begins with a prayer, then some stretching exercises and light calisthenics, "*Hacer el fuego del sangre,*" (to start the fire in the blood), he says.

As we talk, Justin and I sit on a *putang* (a bench with a back, hewn from a single log at least four feet in diameter).

Juan perches on a *chimbi* (a traditional Shuar stool with a slightly concaved seat top and shaped like an animal—his is a turtle). He settles onto the *chimbi* and leans forward slightly, his wrists relaxed and almost touching, hands down and waiting for the questions. His laughter comes often, and he does it well from decades of practice.

This is the story of Juan and Amalia Arcos.

THE FIRST TIGRE OF THE NIGHT

Juan Arcos nervously watched the sunlight fading over the Cutucu Mountains. As howler monkeys shrieked their last territorial calls and a great curassow grunted in the distance, frogs began their "tink" calls, and the night air cooled. The rain forest of this last mountain range of eastern Ecuador was beautiful, the place where Juan had grown to manhood and decided to follow a life for God. Just 26 years old, he sat in the darkness with a shotgun cradled on his lap. Although not a smoker, he chain-smoked cigarettes without inhaling, for the tobacco was believed to keep jungle spirits at bay. Still, he wondered whether he would live to see the sun rise again or lie dead in the jungle as food for the *tigre* (jaguar, say teegray) prowling in the darkness a few feet away.

Juan and his two Shuar Indian friends, Puhata and Tsentsak, faced the first night of a four-day trek from the mission of Yaupi to the white town of Sucua. Earlier, as the tropical night fell and the men prepared camp, Tsentsak shouted, calling the others to where he stood gazing fearfully at the ground. At his feet lay the fresh territorial mark of a *tigre* scraped in the leaf litter of the jungle trail, which reeked of cat urine. The leopard-like cat, a male, had scraped the leaves away to reveal the damp soil, then pressed its pawprint into the damp earth. The huge footprint was half again the size of Juan's outspread hand. Puhata, the hunter, guessed the *tigre* weighed almost 350 pounds.

The men hastily built a traditional Shuar *aak*, a shelter with open sides and front. Six poles leaned against a single support pole in front, draped with freshly cut palm leaves to keep out rain and create the back of the shelter. Using wax-dipped waterproof matches, Juan built a fire in front for light to watch for the *tigre* and to provide smoke to keep mosquitoes somewhat at bay. Juan volunteered to take the first four-hour watch after dinner. The two Shuar spread palm branches under the *aak* for beds, set their feet near the fire for warmth and pulled their chonta palm spears close and ready, then went to sleep as though their lives were not in danger.

An aak, built as a temporary shelter for traveling
or at waterfalls for vision questing.
(drawing courtesy of of Abya Yala, Quito, Ecuador)

Whenever the Shuar traveled through the jungle, they carried tobacco, for it warned the *tigres* that there were humans around. In most cases this prevented the cats from attacking. But the leaves moving gently as the *tigre* circled their camp told the men that this one was not afraid of people. Staring intently into the darkness, Juan's mind wandered back to how he had come to this place, and of the decision that now weighed heavily on his mind.

Juan loved the little mission of Yaupi, nestled beside the clear Rio Huambiza and surrounded by the *chacras* (farms) of several dozen Shuar Indian families. About five miles from the little mission, the river dropped five hundred feet in a series of thundering cataracts to join the Rio Chapiza, where the two formed the Rio Yaupi. The Yaupi is a short river, joining a few miles south with the Rio Santiago at the southern end of the old Cordillera of the Cutucus. Juan was born in 1922, only a hundred miles downstream at the little gold-rush town of Gualaquiza, between the Cutucu Mountains and the north end of the majestic Cordillera of the Condor.

The war with Peru had been smoldering for two years when Juan Evangelista Cigarra Arcos, arrived in Yaupi a few months earlier. Until then, he had taught for two years at the little village of Mendez, working with the Salesian Missions and studying for the priesthood under Father Peter Vosa, the man who had guided him for the past fifteen years of his life.

Juan had decided in Mendez not to be a priest and as "punishment" he was sent to Yaupi to serve. The decision had been difficult, with much prayer and listening for guidance. But in the end Juan felt he could do more good for the Shuar people as a missionary with a wife and children. Then one afternoon, as he worked with the children in the garden, his answer came. Next morning he went to the nearby river to pray and to listen to whether his decision was right. That evening he went to see Father Peter. They chatted amiably for a few moments, then Juan said, "Father, I have made an important decision and need your blessing."

"Yes," the priest said, "I have noticed that you have been

more quiet lately. Tell me what is on your mind." He smiled broadly at his favorite student.

"Father, I have made an important decision. It was not made lightly. I believe that God has guided me to be a teaching missionary, not a priest."

The priest's smile disappeared, replaced by a barely disguised scowl. Father Peter leaned back in his chair and asked, "How have you reached this decision?"

Juan described his thoughts and prayers over the past months while Father Peter listened impatiently. Finally, Juan finished by summarizing. "Father, I know how hard you and the other priests work for the people. I think that God wants me to work with the Shuar because I learned their language as a child and can speak it like I was born to it. They may trust me more than most. I think, too," he continued, taking a deep breath, "that if I were married to the right woman the work we could accomplish would be doubled. And if we have children, they can help as well."

Most missionaries worked only for a few years then left the service. From the time Juan was fifteen, Father Peter had been grooming him to be a priest. Father Peter's anger began to rise, but he held it in check. Well, if this ungrateful upstart was going to cast aside all the guidance he had been given just because he wanted to sleep with a woman, Father Peter would give him what he wanted, service in a mission with the Shuar. Father Juan Guinassi had been asking for help at that awful mission, Yaupi, where the Shuar were continually fighting and killing each other. He put on his most sincere smile and said to Juan, "Well, there may be a way you can be of service as you request. Pray and sleep. Tomorrow we will talk about your future."

The next morning Juan was relieved of his teaching duties and assigned to Yaupi. The other teachers, mostly priests and nuns, were strangely cold toward him, but he thought they would get over it. Fifty years later, the animosity persists.

He gladly left the school that day and found companions

for the four-day trip to Yaupi. His only colleague at the mission was Father Juan Guinassi (who had been the friend of his parents at Gualaquiza), a good-natured man with a wild white beard and shoulder-length white hair. Father Juan had been present to baptize young Juan and his brother and sister, and to pray over the graves of Juan's family members when their times came.

Juan had long ago learned to love the Shuar people: at age four he began to learn their language as he played among them at the Gualaquiza Mission. Father Guinassi himself had lived with the Shuar for forty years and was one of the first non-Shuar to learn the Jivaroan language, but he learned it as an adult and still struggled. He continued to study the Shuar language and welcomed Juan's help.

The two made an excellent team. They had one *interno* (boarding student) and eighty students, all boys, who came to the school each day for lessons. The students dressed in their traditional clothing, and neither of the Juans tried to change that. Young Juan taught his classes in Shuar and continued to study religion with Father Guinassi each night.

They ate *yuca* (manioc, a tuberous, starchy root), any fish they could catch, some bananas and *platanos* (plantains, a fruit similar to bananas but not sweet), but little else. To make the children feel at home, the priest requested that their helpers make *chicha* each day, which everyone drank.

Chicha is a traditional drink and food for the Shuar. The complex recipe is very old, and only the women are permitted to make it. The peeled *yuca* tubers are cover with water and boiled until tender; then mashed with a stirring stick; after it has cooled, the women sit by the pot and pick out the fibrous bits one by one; they chew them until the fibers are broken and it begins to taste slightly sweet, then spit them back into the pot—the salivary enzymes change the starch to sugar, and the mix begins to ferment slightly. In a few hours it creates a creamy, acidic-tasting brew that is served at, or even for, all meals and whenever visitors arrive. Like coffee, it is a social drink, but to the Shuar, it is more. To refuse coffee is no problem, but to refuse a bowlful of *chicha* would be a dangerous social slight. A woman unable to make good *chicha* is doomed to a life of spinsterhood.

The diet at the mission was completely Shuar. But neither man complained. Father Guinassi said, "When you work for God and have a love of your neighbor, you do not see any of your own suffering. You become more content because of the power of God." Young Juan agreed, but after so many years of working to become a priest, his mind was finally opening to new possibilities. At Yaupi, Juan Arcos still dedicated his life to God, but now he was ready for the next step, to find a wife.

As the darkness of the jungle still cloaked the *tigre*, Juan recalled his preparation for the trip.

Although Yaupi was near the border with Peru and a grass airstrip had been built for the warplanes, civilians could travel there only by foot. While the mission in the twenty-first century is remote, in 1948, when Juan and his friends started their trek to Sucua, it was perhaps *the* most remote.

Sucua was fast becoming a center for the Shuar tribe. It lay about thirty-five miles away as the condor flies, but it was impossible to follow such a line. So it was a dangerous zigzagging, up-and-down, hot-and-wet four-day walk through the jungle. In reality, it was more nearly sixty miles away. The trails were slippery and very steep, so after several miles of walking they would have traveled very little of that distance. Unfortunately, Sucua was the nearest place to get supplies for the missions.

A jungle trip required much preparation, and three or four men would make the trip together, each armed. Sometimes they had a gun, but always the men carried their seven-foot-long *chonta* palm spears. The strenuos trip required them to carry a large supply of food for energy. The women prepared several gourds and leaf packets of *yuca* that had been cooked and chewed then stored in the container without water. This concentrated *yuca* would make *chicha* at night simply by adding water. Juan also carried garlic cloves with him because he liked the taste, and because it made a good snake repellant. "Perhaps," Juan said to Father Guinassi, who always wrinkled his nose at the pungent odor, "the snakes don't like the odor either." He also carried lemons and salt to mix with the garlic. The mixture was excellent for dipping bread, when they had it, or sprinkling on bits of bland *yuca* or boiled *platanos*.

Despite the humid air, hunger wasn't their main problem; it was thirst. They always paused at the rivers, so Juan could drink and refill his water gourd. The Shuar almost never drank water straight, but rather mixed it with their concentrated *chicha*. At noon the travelers sipped the *chicha* and ate dried or smoked *yuca* or meat.

Their departure that morning seemed so long ago to Juan. Puhata and Tsentsak were eager to go to the city; they had been several times before and anticipated "seeing the sights." They wore traditional hairstyles, their long black hair cut straight at the ends then twisted in intricate patterns. For the walk they wore no body decoration but carried little gourds with red *achiote* powder. Before entering Sucua they would clean themselves and decorate their faces. Puhata, at 19, was the elder of the two. He was energetic and smiled easily. Tsentsak, at 18, was serious-minded and always knew his purpose. He intended to trade for a new machete and an aluminum pot. He would present them to the parents of the woman he wanted to marry. At five foot eight inches, Juan stood a head taller than the brothers, but where he was lanky they were broad.

After a hearty breakfast and several bowls of *chicha*, they started into the jungle. Juan always liked the early morning in the forest. Even on a clear day the evaporation clouds filled the valleys and swirled gently over the mountaintops. Distant hillsides were thick with trees, including the giant, two-hundred-foot-tall ceibas, Juan's favorite, which were pale shadows in the cool air. Walking along the edge of the Huambiza River, they watched swallows flying low over the water catching insects and dipping their beaks into the stream for an early-morning drink. Before long, the men left the main trail and started up a barely discernible pathway through the trees, continuing upward for most of the morning.

Each man carried a weapon—Juan a shotgun, the two Shuar their chonta spears—and a stretchy palm fiber *shigra* bag filled with food, including *pilche* (calabash) gourds full of the concentrated *chicha*. And, of course, they carried machetes. In the heat they sweated profusely as they climbed the slippery trail, using tree roots for footholds. Lizards, some more than a foot long, scurried into the undergrowth as the men passed. The trail edged around rocks and boulders, and the men carefully inched their way along to avoid falling into the foaming rivers far below.

Suddenly Tsentsak, who was in the lead, shouted, "*Culebra!*" (snake) and began chopping aggressively with his machete. He grinned triumphantly and raised the writhing headless snake on his machete tip—it was a deadly four-foot-long golden-colored eyelash viper.

The Shuar considered all snakes dangerous and killed any they found. This one, stretched across the trail, had indeed been dangerous. Juan noticed the severed head lay on the ground and was still twitching, its fangs—with drops of venom attached—still biting into the air. He used his machete to flick it into the jungle. Tsentsak flipped the golden carcass into the air, its muscles still flexing as it landed among the leaves where meat-hungry ants found it almost before the men continued their trek.

The trail followed the spine of a nameless mountaintop with sheer drop-offs on each side and which wound through the trees for a mile then dipped downhill. It was so steep that the men climbed down the mountain as if it were a ladder. Juan, wearing shoes, slipped and was about to fall when one of his shoeless friends, his toes gripping the trail, grasped Juan's arm so he could steady himself. Three hours later they were at the bottom of the valley. At this point they had walked six hours. A bird could have flown the distance in ten minutes.

Now they walked along a little stream, careful to avoid the thorn-covered stilt roots of the "walking palm." Thorns grew from nearly every plant, long, short and fat, still others almost hair-thin—but all of them sharp. Puhata paused to pull a thorn from his foot, joking that it was a good excuse to stop and rest a minute.

The men often followed little streams, wading in the thigh deep water and even small streams like this might eventually lead to a waterfall. To the Shuar, waterfalls are sacred things. The swirling waters and drifting vapors, host the spirits of powerful warriors and animals. A man seeking strength, an answer to a vexing problem or his right path in life will visit a waterfall for a vision. At the waterfall he builds an *aak*, drinks special potions and prays for an *arutam* spirit to reveal itself to him. After several days in which he eats nothing, drinks the potions and bathes in the waterfall several times, he may see the spirit of a *tigre*, an anaconda, a caiman or another powerful animal. This *arutam*, or "totem," becomes a special protector throughout the man's life. When he gains an *arutam* spirit, it is evident to all who see him. His confidence increases. His bearing becomes that of a leader. He is optimistic, and others begin to see and respect the change.

When they passed by the waterfall where Tsentsak had sought his *arutam*, they paused in awe of its beauty. Where the rivers flowed off the mountains they often plummeted from clifftops in huge waterfalls whose roars filled the valleys. But Tsentsak's waterfall was not so grandiose. It was surrounded by dense jungle and in semi-darkness, a stream burbled down a black rock into a small pool then turned slightly and flowed into another, finally dropping over a ten-foot-high rock into a dark basin fifty feet across. The water poured with a sizzling middle tone, not the basso of a cataract or the tinkle of a spring. A rocky outcrop surrounded the pool on three sides. Feathery moss dripping with water covered much of the cliff and filled the air with a heavy moist-soil aroma. Flowers in pink and orange and little tart-tasting iridescent-blue berries grew alongside the water. Trees—palms and legumes and a tree fern with three slowly unrolling leaves that looked like brown monkey tails—leaned over the pool. In the calm air under the forest canopy, the pool reflected green and brown and silver lights. The men gazed in respect at this place of spirits, where a man might find his own strong *arutam* spirit guide.

When the already faint trail disappeared at a rock fall, the men dropped their *shigras* and walked in concentric circles. The jungle had grown over the trail and the men took almost an hour to find the way. Even the Shuar were confused.

In the dusky light of the forest, there was little undergrowth, but here near the streams where one of the big canopy trees had fallen and where the sunlight spilled onto the jungle floor, the plants created impenetrable green doors, and the machete was their key. The men cut their way through in classic "jungle movie" style, using the machete to slash a narrow path. Ants and other insects fell onto them. Self-defensive plants sprayed stinging white rubbery sap onto their legs. They cut even the beautiful passiflora (passion fruit) vines that bore almost plastic-looking flowers. Sometimes the passiflora had ripe granadilla dangling from them. In that case they gathered the three-inch-long watermelon-like fruits and ate them on the spot, for the centers were filled with a tart and refreshing grayish-green jelly speckled with tiny black seeds.

Once back on the trail, they walked without speaking. The only sounds were those from the forest and the occasional *chink* of the machete as the leader cut a branch or young tree partway through. The plant, sagging but not broken, would mark the trail for their return.

In mid-afternoon they entered the old forest, where humans had not lived for a hundred years or more. There, it was always dark, as if night were approaching. Roots, varying in size from the thickness of a hair to that of a man's body, grew in mats across the poor soil of the forest floor. The light was low, a dusky green even with no clouds overhead, for dense layers of tree crowns overhung the men for dozens of meters.

Emergent trees rose to forty meters and more above the rest of the forest, their bases four to twelve feet in diameter. Lianas, woody vines from the size of a string to that of a ship's hawsers draped from the trees and tied the forest together, supporting the giant emergents. When the wind blew, the forest swayed in unison; if one big tree fell it would often pull down a dozen others. Any sane person quaked at the thought of being in the forest during a *tormenta* (thunderstorm).

One emergent, a *ceiba* or *sangrillo* for example, might shade half an acre or more of forest. In the cool arbor they created, the temperature was a comfortable eighty-five degrees. But when the men crossed a light gap half the size of a football field, where a giant had fallen and pulled down a dozen or more of its companions, the temperature rose to almost a hundred degrees.

In those light gaps, the smell of rotting wood permeated the still air as fungi and ants devoured the prostrate giants. Thousands of plants in dozens of species grew thickly struggling for the light, to be the one or two that would survive. In one of the sunny gaps, the lianas had spread over the open land in only a few weeks' time. The blanket of vine stems was impenetrable by the struggling tree seedlings, which shriveled under the shaded mass. Skirting around the edges of the green mounds, watching for snakes, the men picked up the trail again. Only the few light gaps and the slow movement of bright white light across the leaves told the travelers it really was mid-afternoon, not evening.

Early on the morning of the second day, the men heard a storm approaching. They cut a dozen six-foot-long palm leaves and used pencil-thin lianas to lash them to a tree with the leaves pointing upward. They leaned against the tree, under their shelter, and tried to stay dry. For more than two hours, the downpour roared over them with the sound of billions of water drops on billions of leaves. Dense curtains of water gushed from overhead, cutting visibility to only a few feet. Even in the storm the cicadas trilled. And the frogs, thinking it was night, joined the orchestra.

When the rain slowed, the men continued. A mile farther they came to a stream. What had been a small watercourse was now a muddy torrent, too treacherous to cross. Again, the men sat down to wait and, after several hours, the water had flushed on downstream. They had barely crossed the stream when the rain began again, this time light and warm, so they continued, ignoring their wetness.

As he walked, the raindrops ran from Juan's short-cropped black hair and dripped from his narrow nose like a downspout. He breathed deeply and sighed, thinking, "This is hard, but it is beautiful too, and I would not want to be anywhere else."

In this place where it never freezes, trees drop their leaves throughout the year, but it is also eternally spring. On many trees the new, barely unfurled pale green leaves mixed with old and tough ones that were moss-coated and insect-chewed.

As he sloshed along the muddy trail, Juan watched the little *colibri* (hummingbirds) flitting through the rain to drink the nectar of two-foot-long *heliconia* flowers. Related to the banana, the yellow *heliconia* flowers have huge red tapering bracts. Juan noticed that, even in the rain, most of the birds wore little loads of *heliconia* pollen on their foreheads.

In the lowlands now, they waded through a swamp, alert for anacondas. Some of the snakes were more than twenty feet long, and they lived in the swamps, where they lay curled on floating logs, watching for peccaries, caimans, capybaras (giant guinea pigs) or people. Sometimes, the Shuar believe, these "water boas" (another name for the anaconda) are shamans in animal form, or perhaps even forest spirits hungry for human flesh.

Because they walked about twelve hours from first light to almost dark, hunting was out of the question. At the edge of the swamp, however, a stream flowed into the still water and the men saw an *uyu* (nutria, a large rat-like, web-footed rodent) fishing. The Shuar never eat the *uyu*, which tastes fishy. But the men decided to see if the animal would do their fishing for them. They hid and watched as the nutria caught a fish, killed it, set it on the stream bank and continued to fish. When it caught the second fish and laid it by the first, Puhata smiled and quietly took the second fish. The *uyu* continued to fish, and Puhata kept taking the fish, until they had enough. If he had taken the first fish, the *uyu* would have stopped its work and left, but by taking the second fish, the *uyu* never saw any problem, and the men had ample fresh meat for that night's meal.

They hurried through a relatively open area where most of the leaves were covered with moss or fungus. On many trees, insects had eaten away the green part of dozens of leaves. The leaves still clung though only their skeletal veins remained intact. Layers of moss felt soft underfoot, and as the rain stopped, the air filled with the scent of molding leaves and dripping water.

Tsentsak found a rotting palm and cut it open, retrieving a dozen butter-flavored *mukuint*—palm grubs—which the two Shuar ate raw. Juan saved a few of the thumb-sized treats for roasting over the fire later.

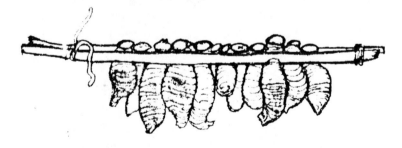

One method of roasting the nutritious palm grubs.
(drawing courtesy of Abya Yala, Quito, Ecuador)

A handful of mukuint.

At times they traveled very slowly. But upon seeing even a semblance of a trail, they traveled quickly, for the Shuar on trek walk faster than most people jog. Juan, who had lived his life with the Shuar, kept pace easily.

As night approached, they kept alert for a place to set up camp. It had to be away from the buttress roots of the giant trees, for snakes would be hiding there, as would the solitary hunting *bala* ants, with their painful and often deadly venom.

It was here that Tsentsak had paused and pointed to the ground a few feet in front of him. There in midtrail was a two-foot-long cat scrape, and in the middle, a freshly made paw-print of the huge *tigre* marking his territory.

Time stood still as the men raised their weapons to the ready and scanned the forest around them. Animals in the forest have learned to make good use of camouflage. Some of the butterflies have clear wings, so they blend with the leaves. Some insects look like sticks. The paca is a rodent the size of a·

house cat whose spots enable it to disappear in plain sight in the splotchy light of the forest floor. Juan thought of the time he had noticed a slight movement on a tree trunk. Looking closely it was difficult to see anything until an anole lizard reared slightly and flared a little orange skin-flap under its chin as a warning. The flap and its long, tapering tail sweeping alongside its body gave it the illusion of greater size, although it was no more than seven inches long.

And a *tigre* was the ultimate camouflage master.

Suddenly the air was filled with hoots and the curious, grinding warning call of a family of spider monkeys overhead. The men looked up as a dozen dark-brown monkeys tore off leaves, branches, even whole epiphytes, and threw them down at the travelers. The animals seemed to have five hands each as they leaped and hung by arms, legs and their prehensile tails. One of the males urinated downward threateningly then threw the husk of a fig he'd been eating.

The men breathed in relief. If the *tigre* had been nearby, the monkeys would have been threatening it instead. "Let's camp here," Juan suggested. The others agreed quickly.

As they cut a clear place in the forest to build their *aak*, a vermillion flycatcher perched at the end of a dead branch high overhead, poised. When a moth or large insect appeared, the bird flew to it in a scarlet blur, snatched it in midair and returned to the branch to eat, then posed for the next snack to fly past. The men smiled; it was another sign the *tigre* may have moved on.

Using wax-dipped waterproof matches, Juan started a fire—for warmth and to create smoke to chase the night mosquitoes away. Then he wrapped the nutria-caught fish in heliconia leaves and laid them by the fire to cook.

When a light rustling stirred the leaves by his feet, Juan stepped back suddenly. Then he smiled, for it was not a snake. It was a red and black poison-arrow frog. The deadly secretion from their skin acts in much he same way as *curare* and kills the prey quickly. Sometimes, when the Shuar have been unable to trade for *curare* for their darts, they capture a few of these tiny inch-and-a-half-long frogs. Holding them gently with a leaf, to protect their fingers from the poison, they roll the tip of a dart around the moisture on the frog's backs. When they have treated three or four darts the angry frogs are set free.

After dinner, the two Shuar went to sleep with their feet nestled by the fire; Juan took the first watch for the *tigre*. The spotted cats were common in the Cutucus. Since many weighed up to their full capacity of 350 pounds, they were always hungry. They usually hunted alone, but females with kittens were the most dangerous and aggressive; since *tigres* can have babies any time of the year, the Shuar on trek always took extra precautions. If women or children were in the group, they slept between two men. Over the years, the *tigres* had dragged more than one woman or child from an *aak* into the night. Trekkers always carried tobacco with them. The smoke from the night guard on duty kept him awake and warned the *tigre* that angry men were there to protect the sleepers.

About ten o'clock Juan tensed, for something had changed in the forest. The night birds had ceased to call. Tree frogs croaked in their normal way, and the leaves continued to drip onto each other with a light, hollow sound. But something was coming. Juan strained to hear movement, but the soaked leaves cushioned the *tigre's* footfall. Yet he sensed it was there. Should he wake his friends? No, he decided as he lit another cigarette and blew the smoke into the air. His eyes strained to pierce the darkness. Suddenly, the *tigre* was directly in front of him, less than six feet away. Instinctively, he lifted the shotgun and, without aiming, pulled the trigger. Incredibly, the cat had already moved back into the shadows, unhurt.

Puhata and Tsentsak bolted awake and squatted with their backs to each other, facing out with *chonta* palm spears poised. Juan reloaded the gun and was poised, just as the *tigre* returned. The attack came silently as the *tigre* leaped in front of Puhata and swiped at him, missing, then leaped back into the darkness. A moment later it tore through the weak palm fronds that made the roof of the *aak*, raking Tsentsak slightly with its claws. Juan shot again at point-blank range, but the cat had already gone. Despite the noise that scared it away temporarily, it returned three times more. The encounters lasted only seconds and were separated by hours of tense waiting. The two Shuar were terrified, for they believed the *tigre* was an evil shaman who had changed form to kill them. Much later, as an old man, Juan would not be able to recall a longer night or one more filled with fear.

Howler monkeys hooted at the arrival of the dawn. Sunlight danced in golden flashes along huge, round spiderwebs on the *aak*. The web owner, also golden, sat waiting for its prey. Juan wondered if the *tigre* might also be out there, waiting quietly. A flight of birds in a half-dozen varieties, a "mixed foraging flock," twittered and chirruped through the trees around them, eating insects and spiders from the leaves, seeds from the ground and fruits—each choosing to satisfy its own taste. When the walkers departed after a hurried breakfast, the birds were gone. The men, tense from lack of sleep and the necessity to be continuously on guard, carried their weapons at the ready and watched in all directions. The person last in line was most vulnerable, so they took turns.

They knew they were nearing Sucua when they passed a little farm where the people kept a domesticated red deer. Only about the size of a female border collie, it was quite tame but wouldn't let Juan pet it. The sleek, chestnut-haired creature daintily ate a piece of water apple Juan offered then skittered a few feet away on its fragile-looking legs. Its two-inches-long antler buds indicated it was a male that would be full-size in a few months. Unafraid, the deer followed them down the forest trail for a quarter mile. When they started down a steep hill, it turned and went back to the farm. After two nights of terror, the encounter with the gentle deer brought a deep sigh from Juan.

Finally, four days travel brought them to the cleared land

of white settlers and, late in the afternoon, Sucua itself. They let down their guard, anticipating relaxing and visiting with friends for a few days. But then, there would be the trip home . . .

THE
EARLY YEARS

CHAPTER ONE

Manuel

In 1916 the new frontier was to the east, in the *selva*, the jungle that was home to the wild people, especially the wild and dangerous Shuar, the head-hunters of the Amazon. The *selva* seemed full of possibility and certainly rich in resources— too much potential and too much gold to leave it for the Indians alone, the white government believed. Besides, the cities were filling with unemployed and unemployable people who needed another chance in life. So the Ecuadorian government made an offer to encourage *colonos* (colonists); families who would settle in the jungle and develop a farm, received free title to the land. Hundreds of people, most without any farming or jungle experience, began to move into the rain forests.

One of these *colonos* was Manuel Arcos, a Colombian. Born at the edge of the Colombian rain forest, unlike most colonists, he knew how to unlock its treasures. Manuel was thirty-three years of age and not yet married because all was work on his father's remote Colombian hacienda and he never had time to court a wife. Many women in the nearby village would have been interested, for Manuel was handsome. He kept his black beard neatly trimmed and his hair cut short. Although only five feet eight inches, he seemed taller, for he was slender. His muscles, while not bulging, were well defined from a lifetime of hard work.

His father, Rafael, refused to pay him, but Manuel expected that some day the Colombian farm would be his, so he never complained. When Manuel wanted to start a farm of his own and requested that his father give him a few acres now, Raphael refused. "Then, will you pay me for my work?" Manuel asked. "If I can save money I can buy some land to build a house of my own."

Raphael refused even this, pleading poverty. Although angry and frustrated, Manuel continued to operate his father's *tragoria*, where they made *trago*, a pale brown rum from sugar cane. But he began to make plans to leave and kept alert for possibilities.

Manuel's friend Victor Valenco had gone to Ecuador to claim a bit of the free land and to start a farm. One day a letter arrived from Victor. He wrote: "Our village is located on the edge of the Cuchipamba River, surrounded by green, forested hills. The soil is good, and the Shuar Indians who live nearby are accepting if not friendly, so it is a safe place. Last week I went with some friends to explore some nearby Inca ruins. There is little in the place now, but I could see how beautiful it had once been. I've heard that there are caves about fifteen kilometers away, and I may go there also, to see if they might be a good source of the bat droppings, which the people call *guano*. It is good fertilizer and I may be able to sell it. We are about 950 meters [almost 2000 feet] in elevation, so it is cooler than the jungle nearby. Before I left Colombia, we talked about you coming here too, and I can't think of a place more beautiful or full of possibilities. I have built a *tragoria*. Can you come and help me run it for a while? You could help me and start your own farm nearby." Manuel read the letter many times that day, and near midnight, he made his decision.

At dawn, Manuel packed his few belongings, kissed his weeping mother, walked to the field to say good-bye to his stiff-necked father and started to Ecuador.

After traveling for almost a month, he found himself in southern Ecuador with a lovely broad valley spread before him. At the bottom of the valley, the rivers Tomebamba, Yanuncay and Tarqui flowed through the beautiful colonial city of Cuenca. He remained in Cuenca for a month, but still planned to continue to the village of Gualaquiza. While in Cuenca he fell in with a group of men who were also traveling to Gualaquiza. By the end of the twentieth century, a bus would make the trip in five or six hours, but in 1916 the path was still narrow and dangerous, best traveled with a larger group of people.

For a week, they traversed the almost treeless, windswept *paramo*, the grasslands of the high Andes. Their only shelter was an occasional stunted thicket of *quinua* trees, filled with strange plants and the animals that fed on them. The *paramo* was also home to the shy Quechuas, Indians who lived in the highlands raising corn and potatoes on steep, terraced hillsides. They lived in simple houses made from rock, mud and wattle or rammed earth and roofed with the long-stemmed and tough *puna* grass that was the main vegetation of the high grasslands.

Finally, the trail began to drop from the *paramo*, and they found themselves traversing broad switchbacks. In the hazy, blue-gray distance, the two great cordilleras, Cutucu and Condor, tantalized them. Gualaquiza nestled along the Cuchipamba River, where the two mountain ranges met.

Trees, not grass, became the dominant vegetation, and the temperature soared as they reached the valley floor. Over the next five days they sweated over the narrow mountain trails of the Cutucus, edging their way into the *selva*. The landscape was foreboding yet beautiful, for the Cutucu Mountains were steep and green, shrouded with cloaks of dank-smelling primary rain forest.

Sheer, rocky cliffs rose hundreds of feet over their heads, and they stared in wonder at dozens of gigantic waterfalls that leaped from their stone-capped tops. A continuous wind blew the falling water into mist that filled the air with dancing rainbows. To the Shuar Indians who lived in the mountains, these were sacred places where spirits lived, and where a young man could go on a vision quest to find his *arutam* spirit or "second soul" that would guide his life. Yet at this moment,

Manuel knew nothing of the Shuar. He was going to discover his future.

The travelers finally reached the Cuchipamba River, and for several more days, chopped their way with machetes through the forest on small paths. They camped at night in little clearings they created, surrounded by the "pips" and "tinks" of tree frogs and the strange, cough-growl of hunting *tigres*. In the morning they woke to the booming calls of howler monkeys. They thrilled at the sight of hundreds of macaws passing overhead—scarlet and blue, blue and yellow, and hyacinth. Finally, the little party straggled into Gualaquiza. The first to greet them was Father Juan Vinia, a Salesian priest who was the head of the mission and who would become Manuel's friend and mentor. Some of Manuel's new friends remained at the mission for several days, but he went immediately to Victor's farm and began work.

Victor Valenco's farm was on the edge of the Bomboisa River. The beautiful spot, backed by dense jungle, offered a grand view of the river from his front porch. Victor and Manuel worked in the fields all day, then relaxed in the evening on the porch, swinging lightly in hammocks as they sipped homemade *trago* and shared their dreams. Although he had tried various cash crops without much profit, Victor now successfully grew sugar cane for the *trago*. While he was still deciding where to settle, Manuel began to operate the new *tragoria* for Victor, just as he had for his father in Colombia.

Gualaquiza was a growing community. The spiritual lives of the *colonos* were fed by the Salesian mission situated near the river like most of the farms. Large, wild grazing animals are uncommon in the jungle, and none of the *colonos* even had cattle or horses yet, though they did have a few pigs. The most important meat was fish in a hundred or more varieties were the most important meat. Each year, at Gualaquiza, the rains pushed the river back into the forest. Downstream in the lowlands the water stayed that way for months, but at Gualaquiza, in the low mountains, it drained away more quickly. So the *colonos* seized the opportunity when the rains and fish swam around the roots of trees a hundred feet tall, whose crowns were either underwater or barely above the floodwaters.

Most people along the river built their houses on stilts, four feet above the ground. This helped keep snakes out of the houses and provided additional protection from the floods. Even houses atop hillsides fifty feet and more above the normal river would sometimes be awash. Almost a hundred years after Manuel arrived in Gualaquiza it is still common for the people in some of the areas nearby to tie their dugouts to their front porches for part of the year. When the river level drops, everything is coated in rich mud. Manuel and Victor continued to plant mainly sugar cane for the *trago* but for their food they also grew yuca and corn and squash.

Over the next two years Victor and Manuel worked side by side. In that time the trail to Cuenca was improved. More people came to Gualaquiza, including muleteers carrying goods to sell. For their return trips, Manuel hired them to haul their little barrels of finished *trago* two hundred miles to the coast where it sold for a high price. Manuel staked out a forest plot nearby and built a small house on it. He was, however, still too busy to look for a wife.

CHAPTER TWO

FRIENDS
IN TWO CULTURES

Several dozen Shuar Indian families lived in the area around Gualaquiza. They lived in oval houses, about eighty feet long, roofed with palm thatch and walled with very hard chonta palm poles that made them more like a forts than homes. Because the Shuar argued among themselves—even about trivial things like, who owned which banana plant, the houses were always built at least half a mile apart.

Not living in villages, however, had saved them when the Spaniards first came in the 1500s. A village full of people was easy to attack and butcher. Hundreds of sparse fort-like houses were another matter, so the Spanish never conquered the Shuar. Although they had long ago adopted several of the white man's products—machetes and muzzle-loading guns— the Shuar lived as they had for hundreds, perhaps thousand, of years.

Most whites distrusted or feared the Shuar. They had heard stories of the Shuar uprising at Macas in 1599. Back then the Shuar had almost been made into slaves, forced to work in the gold mines. When they finally rebelled, the Shuar put aside their differences and murdered almost twenty thousand Spaniards. They saved a special death for the governor, stripping him and pouring molten gold down his throat as they laughed and asked, "Do you now have your fill of gold?" They went on to kill all of the Spaniards on many·

settlements, forcing the rest to flee for their lives. Perhaps this was when the Shuar gained the name of *Jivaro*.

Most of the *colonos* called them *Jivaro*, a derogatory name that means "savage." But Manuel accepted men as they were, not as he wanted them to be, and he was curious about these fiercely independent people who had survived in the jungle for so many centuries. One day, as two Shuar men passed by his house, Manuel called out and invited them to come eat with him. The Shuar were surprised but accepted. At first they sat suspiciously with their weapons at hand. Then as they realized that Juan respected them, they relaxed and ate the simple food he provided. They spoke no Spanish, and he spoke no Jivaroan, their language, but with signs and smiles they became acquainted. Over the next few months they returned, often with other Shuar, to meet this unusual man. Manuel gradually came to know all the Shuar from a wide area, for many traveled dozens of miles to meet him. He was a man the Shuar realized they could trust.

Even with his experience in Colombia, Manuel was unaware of special methods required to farm this part of the rain forest and made many mistakes. When the Shuar noticed his errors, they laughed at him but offered advice. They showed him, for instance, the Shuar way of planting a certain type of vegetable, or an easier way to clear an acre of jungle. Manuel listened and was grateful, for they were always right.

To their own disadvantage, however, most of the white *colonos* looked down on the Shuar—and in fact, all Indians. They ignored the centuries of Shuar knowledge gained from living in the jungle. More than one *colono* family lost a child to malnutrition because they refused to learn from the Shuar what to eat from the jungle and how to prepare it. Many of the whites tried to grow rice and potatoes, foods they were familiar with but which were generally less nutritious or suitable to the climate than the plants grown by the Shuar. Even in the twenty-first century, it is common to see *colono* children with pale or yellowish skin, and bones bent with rickets from calcium deprivation. At the same time, the children of their Shuar neighbors are healthy, with bright smiles and straight legs.

CHAPTER THREE

LOVE IN THE SELVA

White settlers and tourists continued to trickle into Gualaquiza. On their way, many of them passed through the colonial-era village of Sigsig, eighty miles northwest. Manuel and his friends also had paused in the pretty village on their first trip to Gualaquiza. But it was a sleepy place, and a local businessman, Exequiel Cigarra, listened with increasing attention to rumors of gold discoveries in Gualaquiza. He saw possibilities in a boomtown, and decided to have a look. Refusing to be left behind for several months, his adventurous wife, Raquel, demanded to go with him. Their youngest daughter, Maria, was sixteen years of age and had her mother's spirit. She was also eager to go. Raquel persuaded Exequiel that two women would be good company. Besides, who would take care of him, especially after he had spent a day tramping around Gualaquiza talking with people?

Like her mother, Maria had black eyes and long black hair. She was pretty, full of fun and very strong, but only four and a half feet tall. Just a few months before, she had finished school with excellent marks and for some years had been helping her father to keep his business records.

Manuel, who was thirty-five by then, met the family on their first day in the village and recalled a brief meeting they had in Sigsig. The men realized they were kindred spirits, becoming instant friends. Exequiel took Manuel to meet his wife and daughter. Raquel was impressed with Manuel's looks and intelligence. So was Maria. That night,

Manuel lay awake for hours, thinking about the pretty young woman.

The Cigarras and Manuel often dined together, either at the makeshift hotel where the family stayed or at Manuel's little house. At the end of a month, as the Cigarras were preparing to return to Sigsig (for there had been no gold strike yet, and the rumors of gold were just that), Manuel asked Victor to be his official go-between and to request permission to marry Maria. Exequiel and Raquel agreed without reservation, for they could see the two were in love; besides, Maria was the perfect age to wed.

Manuel and Maria married in 1918 in the little church at the mission of Gualaquiza. Although small, the wedding was a happy affair, with Maria's parents and a dozen friends in attendance. Manuel's friend, Father Juan Vinia, performed the ceremony. Everyone in the wedding party lived in poverty, but they pooled their resources and brought two gifts—a machete for Manuel and a cooking pot for Maria. After the service, they shared a toast or two with Manuel's *trago*, then returned to their homes and to work. The next day, Maria's parents returned to Sigsig. (Maria never saw her father again. Two months after their marriage another group arrived from Sigsig with a letter from Raquel. Exequiel had died in his sleep.)

Both Maria and Manuel were energetic and anxious to build their own hacienda. Manuel spent less time working for Victor and more time clearing his land, sometimes with the aid of a Shuar volunteer or two. The couple cut trees, stacked and burned the debris and gradually opened about five acres to the sky. In addition to the house garden, they planted sugar cane and built their own *tragoria*, adding their produce to Victor's as they continued to export more to the coast.

Two miscarriages disappointed Maria and Manuel, but finally their family began to grow. In 1921, Maria had a little boy they named Manuelito Arcos Cigarra. A few days before Christmas 1922, Juan Evangelista Arcos Cigarra arrived. A little girl was born to the couple the next year but she was weak and died two days later, but for the most part, their lives seemed to be on a good path.

CHAPTER FOUR

GOLD AND DEATH

Rumors of gold continued to flow outward from Gualaquiza. One day in 1926, a prospector arrived with a deep and persistent cough. In a week, an epidemic of *tosvarina*— whooping cough—swept through the area.

Exposed to few of the white man's diseases and with no immunity to them, the Shuar suffered the hardest. Many Shuar families lost both children and adults to the disease. The Arcos boys, ages four and five, were among the first to contract it. For weeks coughs shook their little bodies, and they could barely eat. Manuelito gradually lost his strength, and one afternoon he died. The younger Juan continued to be sick for another week, but his coughing slowly subsided and his strength returned. He was now an only child.

Discoveries of small pockets of gold encouraged the prospectors, and more arrived. Wandering up and down every river valley in the area, they inevitably met the Shuar and often abused them verbally and in other ways. The mission became a center for assisting the poorest of the new arrivals, some who came with their families. Father Juan often asked Manuel and Maria to assist him in caring for the green *colonos*. They were still dealing with their own loss, but Manuel and Maria reached out to the newcomers. The Arcos farm soon became a refuge, where people could stay for a few days or a few weeks. With so many whites at the farm and with so many Shuar deaths from the whooping cough, Shuar visits came to a halt. Father Juan and Manuel often talked long into the night, struggling with the question of how to give aid to both Shuar and *colono*s, for there was never enough money.

The mission school was operated by the Salesians, an order of the Catholic Church. The Salesian's main mission was to educate children and, where possible, to help train boys for the priesthood. Both the Shuar and the *colonos* sent their children to the mission school. Until the gold strike, most of the students had been Shuar Indians, but now more of the *colono* children began to attend. At the school the Salesian priests and nuns hoped they could control the children and train their minds to accept each other. In the community, however, there were problems, for most *colonos* still disliked the Shuar, admittedly a dangerous and warlike people. The *colonos* often stole the Indians' food from their gardens and harassed them when they came to town. Shuar women had even been raped by drunken *colono* men, who still thought of the Indians as *Jivaro*. Despite the best efforts of the Salesian clergy the parents continued to teach the attitude of hatred to their children.

CHAPTER FIVE

A PLACE OF LOVE

The Shuar knew, regardless of their treatment at the hands of most of the *colonos*, that Manuel and Maria were different from most whites. The couple respected the Shuar and extended their hands in friendship. When the gold fever faded as the mines produced less, most of the prospectors returned to the cities. Some, however, settled onto the free land. As fewer whites stayed with the Arcoses, the Shuar again began to visit.

Early one morning in 1928, a call came from the forest surrounding the Arcos farm: *"Tuuhey."* Manuel recognized the greeting call of the Shuar, for he had heard it many times. The call meant the Shuar were coming in peace. The greeting traditionally gave the people inside the house notice, so they could properly ready themselves for visitors.

Manuel and Maria went to the door of their house and waited eagerly, for it had been a year since they had seen their Shuar friends. Little Juan, now five, stood with his parents, tense and nervous.

Eleven Shuar walked soundlessly from the forest into the clearing. They paraded in single-file, the strutting men first, their faces painted red with achiote pod paste. All were bare-chested, barefoot and wore traditional *itips*, soft beaten-bark skirts to mid-calf. The men's pierced ears sported decorated sticks called *karis,* one centimeter thick and thirty centimeters long, which bounced slightly as they walked. The men's shiny black hair was tied back and braided in intricate patterns, each man's hairstyle unique. For protection, and in case they happened upon some animal, every erect warrior carried either a muzzle-loading shotgun or a blowgun and a sharp-barbed *chonta* palm lance. They had announced their coming, but as a further sign that they were peaceful, they had brought along several women, who walked at the end of the line, modestly looking at the ground. They carried burden baskets and gourds of *chicha* and led several children who were of Juan's age.

A typical Shuar man.
(Drawing courtesy of Abya Yala, Quito, Ecuador)

When he first saw the Shuar, little Juan hugged his father's legs in fear, crying, "Papa, Papa, look how ugly. They are devils."

Manuel knelt down and hugged Juan gently. The answer he gave that morning both allayed the boy's fear and charted the direction of his life. Manuel said, "Son, they are not devils. They are our brothers, and they like to dress that way. They like to paint themselves, and they like to wear crowns of feathers made from made birds that they kill for their food. So my son, when you see one of them do not be afraid. Go to them and say 'Hello.' Even though they may not know our language they will know you mean well. Make them feel welcome, for they are our friends."

Manuel invited the people to come into the house and eat. The Shuar women and Maria went into the kitchen side of the house and began to prepare a meal, for they had brought gifts of meat—peccary and the rich-tasting jungle rodents, the agoutis and pacas.

Neither Manuel nor Maria spoke Shuar, and the Shuar did not speak Spanish, but they managed to communicate with gestures and smiles, the men in one room, the women in the other. After the meal, as they prepared to depart, the leader of the Shuar asked Manuel if, from time to time, he would be willing to go to the store in town and buy things for them—needles, thread, a mirror, salt and such. The colonos often harassed the Shuar in Gualaquiza, and if Manuel would buy these things it would prevent problems. Because of warnings from the Ecuadorian military, the Shuar took care not to retaliate against the colonos, but they could only take so much abuse. Manuel said he would be happy to assist.

Other Shuar families began to stop by with their requests. Soon, a typical week brought three or four families to visit, and life at the Arcos farm began to change again.

No matter when the Shuar came, they were always welcomed. Most often the visitors were men only. They usually brought gifts of meat, and as the men visited, Maria would prepare a meal. At first they expected to be served *chicha*, the traditional food and welcome drink of the Shuar, but Maria did not know how to make it. Manuel did not want to appear inhospitable, so gave them water with lemon in it, which he often used to refresh himself. The men would drink a little from the gourd of lemon water, trying not to make a face. When they came again, they would bring their own long gourds filled with *chicha*, and Maria served it to them. The men never involved themselves in the making of *chicha*, for it was forbidden by their traditions, and always appreciated that she served it for them on their hour-long visits.

Quickly realizing what they would need, Manuel bought a little supply of mirrors, matches, needles and thread. The appreciative Shuar sometimes paid with a few coins they had earned, but they more often gave meat or other food in exchange.

Maria, too, was interested in the Shuar, and as time went by, more and more women arrived with the men. She noticed that if, as was common, a man had several wives, Shuar etiquette required him to make a separate visit with each wife. If they were sisters, however, he brought all of them at one time.

Juan loved the visits and he would go from the men to the women, ignored by both groups but feeling very special. Juan particularly looked forward to visits when the Shuar brought their own children. Visitors with children usually stayed overnight, and Juan delighted in playing their games with his new friends. Without effort he began to learn their language, and soon he was translating for his parents.

In order to honor his guests, Manuel made visits to Shuar homes, where he learned how the Shuar sleep. To make the visitors to the Arcos home comfortable, Manuel built a small bedroom beside their own house. Manuel's guest house featured Shuar-style beds of springy split-bamboo platforms raised about two feet above the floor. At the end of each bed, an open footrest held the sleeper's bare feet over a small, smoldering fire. The Shuar used few or no blankets; if their feet were warm, the rest of their body would be as well.

A typical Shuar house

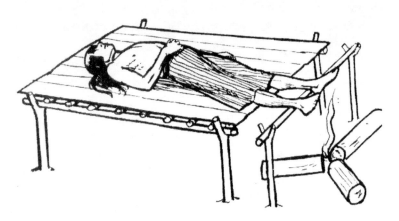

A typical Shuar bed complete with small fire at the foot to keep them warm.
(drawing courtesy of Abya Yala, Quito, Ecuador)

Sometimes the group of visitors consisted of seven or eight people plus the women's hunting dogs. Most of the women loved to hunt, using the dogs to track agoutis, pacas and the hard-shelled armadillos. While at the Arcos farm the scrawny jungle dogs were docile. In their own territories, however, at the Shuar houses, they earned their keep, snarling and attacking intruders, both human and animal.

By the time he was seven, Juan was comfortable in both the white and the Shuar worlds, but his life was about to change again.

CHAPTER SIX

TRAGEDY

Despite their hard work and the sale of the *trago*, the Arcoses had little money to afford such luxuries as mosquito nets to cover their beds. When the mosquitoes became unbearable, Manuel put damp leaves on the cooking fire, and the smoke kept most of them at bay. One of the Shuar taught him to cut down a papery, clinker-looking ant nest or a termite nest and burn the smoky, smoldering heap, which was more effective. But, unless it was raining, the whining mosquitoes returned each night, and in the morning the family itched from dozens of new bites.

One day Manuel returned to the house very tired, with a raging headache and aching muscles. By nightfall a fever was building. He alternately shivered and sweated with waves of chills and heat. A dozen or more of their neighbors had come down with malaria, and Maria was afraid. When even one person gets the disease, it means more cases to come, as the mosquitoes continue to infect other people and animals. In Manuel, the signs were unmistakable. Over the next few days, Maria treated her husband for malaria, using herbs and the bark of the cinchona tree, from which quinine is made, mixed in *trago*.

Father Juan came from the mission with medicines. Shuar friends, when they discovered he was sick, brought armadillo meat, which they believed fortified malaria sufferers.

But nothing helped, and Manuel began to weaken. Then,

one morning, he refused yet another meal, for he had no appetite. Juan was playing nearby and Manuel called him to his bedside. As an old man, Juan would remember that morning:

My father hugged me. He was a strong man, and he usually gave powerful hugs. But this one was very weak, and his skin was clammy, wet with sweat. Then he said to me, "Juan, be a good person. Take good care of your mother. Always remember that I love you both so very much." I remember he held out his hand to my mother. He could barely lift it from the blanket. Tears filled Mother's eyes and fell onto his hand as she held him close, kissing his forehead. I could barely hear him as he spoke to Mother, but he said, "Maria, my love. Take care of little Juan. Please don't leave him, but know that I hope you will remarry and that your new husband will love you as I have loved you."

Then, unable to speak more, he laid his head back onto the pillow, closed his eyes, and slept.

The next day Manuel's skin and the whites of his eyes turned yellow as jaundice set in and his red blood cells weakened. Maria wept as she applied cool cloths to his feverish head. Father Juan arrived and decided it was time to give Manuel the last rites. When he finished, he leaned over and whispered, "Die peacefully my friend. I will take care of Maria and Juan as you have cared for your neighbors."

Later that day, Manuel quietly slipped into a coma. The next day his heart stopped. He was forty-six years of age, and Juan was only seven.

Father Juan invited Maria and Juan to come live at the mission. Maria was still young, only twenty-seven. Perhaps she would remarry. But in the meantime, Father Juan said, "It will be better for you and Juan to come live under the protection of the mission and help with its goals. There is too much work on this farm for you to do alone. Besides, at the mission Juan can be educated. He can get to know the Shuar better, and you can be a big help to us in our mission."

Within a week they abandoned the farm—for no one would buy it when there was free land all around—and moved to the mission. As promised, they found support in their grief, and little Juan continued his formal, and informal, education.

CHAPTER SEVEN

THE MISSION
OF GUALAQUIZA

Father Juan kept his word and took special care of Maria and Juan. He was well known to the church community and respected by the Shuar, who seemed grateful that Maria and Juan were cared for by someone who also respected the Indians. Father Juan became the mentor and protector of young Juan and Maria.

Father Juan Vinia was powerfully built and stood six feet four inches tall. About fifty years of age at the time, he always wore a white, broad-brimmed hat, which protected his balding head, and loose-fitting black clothes instead of a robe. Father Juan's energy and enthusiasm radiated from him, dedicated to improving the spiritual and daily life of the people at Gualaquiza. He had been among the first white men to learn the Shuar language and diagrammed the Shuar grammar, which became the basis for the language instruction used six decades later. (The Evangelists created a Protestant Bible for the Shuar, but there never has been a Catholic Bible, which Father Juan hoped would come from his work. He was also the first to assist the Shuar in an effort to gain official title to their own lands, preventing its theft by the *colonos*. Unfortunately, he never lived to see the idea come to fruition.)

Picnic along the Rio Gualaquiza. Father Juan Vinia is at the left wearing a hat and white scarf, leaning on a staff. Maria Arcos is standing to the back right, wearing a hat. The photo was taken a short time after she and her son, Juan, moved to the mission following Manuel's death.

Young Juan moved in with the other boarding students, all of them Shuar, and Maria joined the nuns. Juan started school and, with the other children, helped with chores around the mission. Maria did all kinds of work. She was very energetic but earned only about twenty or thirty sucres a month, less than twenty-five dollars, so she and Juan had even fewer luxuries than before.

Juan attended school in the morning and in the afternoon joined the mission's other boarding students at work in the garden. Even the young children carried machetes, and by that time Juan was a good help as he weeded. Although his machete might have been rusty, he learned how to sharpen it several times a day because he knew a sharp tool that works more easily and is less dangerous than a dull one. In the gardens, the machete was used like a hoe, to chop the large weeds. However, it was not an easy or comfortable implement to use; the gardener had to lean forward at the waist for hours at a time. Juan became strong as he worked the brown-yellow soil and learned to cut the roots of weeds just below the surface by grasping each end of the machete and pulling it back and forth like a saw.

The other children taught him the Shuar technique of cutting the weeds then piling them around the edge of the garden. Some weed walls at the garden were more than three feet high. When they rotted, which was quickly, they improved the soil. The weeding removed competition for the garden plants. More important, it cleared areas that would otherwise provide shelter for snakes.

Father Juan planted the mission gardens in the traditional Shuar manner, with plants growing in clumps, not straight lines. The children and priests planted yuca, pelma, squash, corn, bananas and plantains, hoping the mission could be self-sufficient someday.

Their most important crop, however, was manioc, with its pretty, non-glossy green leaves and scarlet-colored stems. As they weeded, the children picked up the withered leaves below the manioc, which they called *yuca*, for as it grew, the plant would shed its lower leaves. Because the leaves were large, they left big, nubbled scars on the stem. At the base of each scar grew a tiny bud, where a new plant would grow if the stem were replanted.

Father Juan had learned from the Shuar how to grow yuca and in time taught little Juan the important skill. As the children harvested the elongated potato-like yuca tubers, they immediately planted the next crop. They first cut the stalk into sections twelve to eighteen inches long then pulled the tubers from the ground. Some of the vegetables were almost a meter long, and the boys stacked them like firewood, then planted each of the stems. In a few weeks new plants sprouted from the leaf scars. In another month, Juan and the other boys cut away the weaker stems and within six months the next harvest was ready.

The girls usually carried what the boys harvested, using stretchy woven palm-fiber bags called *shigras*, or stiff palm baskets with "tumplines," broad bands across their foreheads, which bore the main weight. Much of the time, for coolness and as a cushion, the girls tucked banana leaves between their backs and the forty-pound packs.

One day when Juan was eight, they paused by a little lagoon after harvesting and waded in to cool off. In minutes, laughter echoed across the lagoon as everyone, including Father Juan, joined in a water fight. Then Juan and the other boys sprawled on the stony beach admiring the cruising fish trapped in the shallow water behind the dam they had built the week before to contain the vital food source. The girls stood in a circle, laughing and talking as they used their machetes to peel the two skin layers from the dark brown tubers the boys had pulled from the ground. The outer is thinnest and brown. The inner layer, white and brittle, broke away easily. Then, after a brief rinse in the river, the girls tossed the white tubers into the baskets or the *shigras* for the rest of the trip to the mission kitchen.

In the gardens, the Shuar children worked together harmoniously. It was different when the white settlers' children joined them for the morning classes. There were about fifty students in all, half Shuar and half white. Although the priests tried to teach the children to respect each other, every day fights broke out in the schoolyard. Years of work, had finally begun to earn the Shuars' confidence, but the *colonos* continued to make it an uphill battle.

Because he lived at the mission all the time, young Juan spent most of his time with the Shuar, though he was accepted by both groups. Sometimes, however, he was forced to take sides. The *colono* students would taunt the Indians and call them *"Jivaro."* Juan would ask the whites, "Why are they *Jivaro?"*

"Because that is what they are," the white children retorted.

Remembering what his father had taught him, Juan said, "No they are not. They are like us. Do they not also have two ears and a nose? They are our brothers. They are saved people. How can they be *Jivaro?"*

For the first year or two the white children beat Juan up at least once a week. Although most of the students were young because the school went only to sixth grade, there were some eighteen—and twenty-year-olds, and they were the worst. Maria worried because Juan wore bruises and black eyes most of the time, yet he never hesitated to support his Shuar friends. Padre Juan preached equality and respect. He punished the boys who abused the younger ones and even sent one or two home, refusing to educate them further. The Shuar respected Juan for standing up to the *colono* children and eventually the white children respected him for his lack of fear. Gradually the taunting decreased and finally, when Juan was almost ten years of age and bigger than the other students, it stopped.

CHAPTER EIGHT

THE MISSION GROWS AND WARS BEGIN

At this time there were no religious teachers, so the students walked fifteen minutes from the mission to a public school where Miss Elena Carrion gave instruction. Young Juan studied with her for two years before Father Juan found the helpers he needed to organize a school at the mission.

Teaching priests began to arrive. Father Louis Vosa and Father Jose Peter first, then Father Gardinni and Father Conrado Darde. With Father Juan they began to enlarge the mission.

The three original buildings formed one side of a rectangle. One building was a kitchen and eating area, and the second were two dormitories—one for the boys and the priests, the other for the girls, the nuns and Maria. The team of priests gathered Shuar and *colono* workers in a series of *mingas*, community work projects, to help build classrooms of split palm trunks, thatched with palm fronds.

The two groups, Shuar and *colono*, refused to work together, so they worked on separate days and each built a separate classroom. Invariably, the Shuar-built structure was the best made. In three months, working a day here and a day there, they had completed the mission. As noted above, it was in the shape of a rectangle with the perimeter comprising buildings that included a little church. The central plaza became a playground for the children, with a small altar and cross set at its center. Father Darde carved a little wood plaque quoting from Mark 10, verse 14: "Suffer the little children to come unto me."

Despite the fact their children were being educated by the Salesian Mission, many of the *colono* men forgot their Christian responsibilities outside church. Each month they perpetrated more injustices against the Shuar. First there were robberies, as the ill-prepared *colonos* stole food from the Shuar gardens or chickens from their yards. The Shuar and Father Juan reported these problems to the white authorities, three ineffectual white policemen. They would agree that it was a problem, nodding their heads solemnly, saying, "Yes, yes, we will see what we can do." But they had no intention of doing anything, "forgetting" almost before Father Juan left the room.

One morning, a fifteen-year-old Shuar girl went to her garden to pick food for breakfast. A drunken miner sprawled on the path, feigning sleep. As she edged slowly past him, he "awoke" and grasped her ankle. She struggled, but the miner— who was not as drunk as he first appeared—pulled her down and raped her. Afterward he let her go, and she ran home. Her father was outraged and ran back to the place with his lance. He tracked the man to his house, but there were others there also who protected the rapist, then broke the father's lance and beat him. The policemen still refused to intervene.

When the Shuar girl became pregnant and had a baby boy, the outraged Shuar family put no blame on the child but accepted him as full Shuar. There were many more rapes, for the whites knew there would be no punishment. Although Father Juan preached against the outrages, they continued.

He wrote to the head of the Salesians, who sent Father Londasoli. But Londasoli hated the Shuar and not-so-secretly undermined Father Juan's efforts, so the robberies and rapes continued, now spreading to the *colono* community as well. Londasoli returned to Cuenca but instructed Father Juan, "Do not preach against the whites." The Shuar kept even more to themselves and were always on guard. But they respected Father Juan and against their instincts, did not retaliate.

The priest refused to remain silent while such injustices continued. One Sunday he preached an especially vehement sermon against the criminals. After church, almost two dozen of the *colono* men gathered near the mission to devise a plan to kill Father Juan the next day.

Not all the *colonos* were evil though, and one of them warned Father Juan, who hurried half an hour away to a small hut that housed the mission cane press. He spent all that day and night in prayer by the Rio Gualaquiza, listening for any pursuers.

When the mob arrived at the mission, Father Gardini, who was Father Juan's assistant, was very calm. He invited the people into the kitchen house and offered them coffee. They accepted but continued to shout and threaten as they ate and drank. Gardini remained calm and spoke with them quietly. Several hours later they calmed somewhat and left. But the threat remained. Each day Gardini brought food to Father Juan, and they talked about what to do. Finally, after two weeks of exile and prayer, Father Juan returned to the mission.

Father Landasoli, who had received reports in Cuenca, realized what his actions had led to. As head of the Salesian Missions for this zone, he bore a large part of the responsibility for the continued rapes and violence. As much as he disagreed with Father Juan, Landasoli knew he must do something to protect him. So he reassigned Father Juan to the mission at Sucua. It was fast becoming a center for the Shuar, and the priest could use his growing language skills. Perhaps with Father Juan gone, peace of some sort could return to Gualaquiza.

When he heard that he was to leave immediately, Father Juan went to Maria Arcos. Would she and little Juan want to move to Sucua to help at the mission there? No, Maria said. She and little Juan were happy at the mission near Gualaquiza,.

and while she appreciated his care, she released him from his promise to care for them. He left the next morning.

Father Carlos Simoneti, a Spaniard with dark hair and blue eyes, arrived from Quito to become the new head of the mission. Father Simoneti was an excellent communicator and soon developed friendships within both the Shuar and *colono* communities. His sense of humor seemed undimmed even when things were at their worst, and he began to rebuild the mission community. In 1931 Peruvian troops attacked the border area in a rough line from Gualaquiza south almost a hundred miles to Zamora. Suddenly, the little village of Gualaquiza became a military camp. It quickly grew overcrowded and filthy, a bad place for soldiers to bivouac, so the captain in charge visited Father Simoneti.

The mission, in his view, had a large and unused building, which actually served as the community hall, so important to the Shuar. Could he rent this building so his men could stay there? Father Simoneti realized that the Shuar needed a place to gather for visiting parents as well as for all-important Shuar councils. He tried to refuse, but the captain said: "I'm sorry but I must have that building for my troops. Have it prepared, and we will move into it tomorrow morning."

Father Simoneti's own father was a general in the Spanish army, so he knew it was useless to try to stop the army; he reluctantly agreed. Soon there were forty soldiers at the mission. In the days of waiting that soldiers must endure, the men played with the mission children, teaching them soccer and even helping in the gardens. The war had turned into a stalemate, and after several months of living together at the mission, many friendships developed.

But some of the *colonos* continued to abuse the Shuar, and a few of the soldiers joined them. By this time, Juan was ten years of age. His duties were expanded to include sweeping the classrooms at the end of each day. One afternoon, as he swept little clouds of dust out the doorway of a classroom, the father of one of his Shuar friends arrived to talk to him.

Juan had visited his house many times and knew him to be a thoughtful and patient man.

"Juan," he said in Shuar, "You are different from other white boys. You understand our language very well, but more important you are as much Shuar as you are white. We have a problem, and I need your help. The *colonos* continue to steal from us and to hurt our girls. Father Juan and now Father Simoneti preach that we should not take vengeance against them, but we can no longer tolerate this treatment. Will you go to Father Simoneti and tell him this?"

Amazed that this Shuar warrior would trust him with such a message, Juan promised to speak with the Father and with the captain. Leaning his broom against the wall of the classroom, he hurried to the priest's house, where the captain happened to be visiting over afternoon coffee. Juan stood respectfully before the two men and told them what the Shuar had said.

When he finished, the captain thumped the table with his fist and stood up so violently that his stool fell onto to the floor. "That is totally wrong," he declared to Father Simoneti and to Juan. "If those people are going to commit those abuses, the Shuar need to defend themselves. If they are defending and not attacking, there can be no claim against them."

The captain spoke perhaps too quickly and from passion rather than reason. For whatever reason, his statement, which Juan reported faithfully to the Shuar man, opened the floodgates of hatred. The Shuar smiled slightly and said simply, "This we will do."

For two months more, all was quiet. Then news came to Gualaquiza that Peruvians had attacked a group of miners near Zamora. Between twenty and thirty *colonos* were massacred. The captain mobilized his troops, and Father Simoneti prayed for them as they left on their mission against the Peruvians.

Three days passed before the soldiers returned. The killers had gone from the massacre site but the soldiers could tell·

that they were not Peruvians but Shuar who had murdered the miners. In their anger the soldiers spread out and captured all the Shuar men living near Gualaquiza. They brought them to the mission and held them under guard in the school plaza until their superiors could determine what was to be done. "Father Simoneti," the captain said, "tell the children and your helpers that it is their responsibility to feed the Shuar. If you do not feed them they will not eat, for I will not feed murderers like them."

"We will feed them," Father Simoneti said, "but they cannot be the people who killed the miners for they were here when the miners were killed at Zamora. If you insist on capturing the guilty Shuar, go back to Zamora and capture the ones who are the killers. I tell you, the killers are not from Gualaquiza. They are from Zamora."

But the captain would not listen, and he seemed to have forgotten his statement that it was all right for the Shuar to defend themselves. He seemed intent on organizing a death squad to kill the Shuar being held in the plaza of the mission. Father Simoneti called the other priests together and asked for volunteers to go to Limon with a special letter. All volunteered, but Simoneti chose only two to take the letter the next day at dawn. Fourteen exhausting hours later, they arrived at Limon and demanded to see Father Juan Vinia, now head of the Salesians, replacing the deceitful Landasoli. In the letter, Simoneti pleaded with Father Juan to come to Gualaquiza because he feared that the soldiers were going to kill the Shuar.

Although they were exhausted from their hurried walk from Gualazuiza, the two priests insisted that they return the next day with Father Juan. At dawn the three of them plus two more priests returned. Late that night they arrived, and, while the others rested, Simoneti and Vinia drank hot coffee and discussed the situation.

Early in the morning Vinia sent a messenger to the captain, inviting him to Simoneti's house. When he came in, Simoneti offered food, and the three began a conversation Vinia hoped would be civil. He sipped his cup of thick, sugary coffee and asked gently, "My captain, what are you doing here? Why have you captured all of these Shuar? We all know they are not the killers and should be set free."

"What am I doing here? I am doing my duty," the captain shouted defensively. "Do not interfere with me, for I have the responsibility to punish those murdering Shuar."

Vinia's eyes widened at the unexpected outburst and his voice boomed out angrily, "You have the responsibility to punish the murderers. I am telling you, you must *do* your duty, and that is to protect the innocent and punish the guilty."

The shouting grew louder on both sides, startling a flock of parrots, which circled overhead adding their own garbling to the din. A mob of *colonos* began to gather again, many of them the same ones who had wanted to kill Padre Juan only the year before. As the shouting increased, they surged into the room, yelling, "Priest, we are going to kill the Shuar, but we are going to start with you!" Vinia stood his ground with Simoneti beside him as the captain turned pale and stood motionless. The situation was fast spinning into an uncontrollable mob. As the captain seemed to shrink, Vinia stood a head height taller than the tallest *colono*, shaking his fists violently and threatening back. Simoneti stood beside him, his black robe billowing as they pushed the attackers out of the room.

"Good," Vinia bellowed. "I am here. Kill me! Kill me! I may be dead, but God himself will deal with you." Then, something happened. The mob realized they were threatening "God's messenger." They were suddenly afraid, and silence replaced the shouts. Looking at each other nervously, they backed away slowly, murmuring to each other. In a moment, the room was empty except for the two priests and the captain, who slumped onto a stool and leaned onto the table, pale and shaking.

"Captain," Father Juan said quietly, "I am going to Quito to get instructions for you. It is your responsibility to protect your prisoners and if they are harmed in my absence, you will literally have hell to pay."

Fearing excommunication, the captain merely nodded. Then, as Simoneti offered to assist him to his feet, he waved the aid away and stood up. He straightened his uniform and ran his hand over his hair to smooth it. Then without a backward glance he walked stiff-backed from the house.

Vinia called his companions, embraced Simoneti, and left for Cuenca. He rested there a few hours then pushed on to Quito to report the situation. At the mission the captured Shuar lived in miserable suspense for almost a week. They were permitted food and chicha but were kept under guard in the central plaza of the mission, open to the sun and forced to scrape holes in the ground to defecate in full view of any passersby. Young Juan always volunteered to deliver the food and messages from the families to the captured men. Sometimes he even smuggled little gifts to them. Juan had never before seen such injustice, and he would never forget it.

On the sixth evening, an official arrived from Quito with a small platoon of soldiers to back him. He declared that the Shuar were to be set free. "If there are any reprisals against these men," he said, then turned a stern gaze toward the captain, "the guilty *colonos*—or soldiers—will be punished."

The official remained at the mission as a guest of Simoneti for ten days, to be certain that peace had truly settled. In a month, the mission routine returned to almost normal although tensions between the Shuar and the *colonos* remained high for nearly a year.

The *colonos* felt betrayed by the missionaries, and many refused to help them or even sell them food. At the same time, the missionaries had strengthened their reputation in the eyes of the Shuar, who more than made up for the aid the *colonos* withheld.

CHAPTER NINE

JUAN'S POWER
IS RECOGNIZED

Father John Shutka arrived at the mission as the healing began. A man who truly loved the Shuar, he had learned their language and, on his many trips to his homeland of Czechoslovakia, obtained aid for the Shuar—medicines and money. When he first saw Father Shutka, Juan stared, for Shutka was white blonde, taller even than Father Vinia, and held himself very erect as he walked.

Shutka believed that the only way the Shuar could protect themselves was to organize themselves into a federation. But the Shuar, always independent-minded, resisted it.

In 1932 Shutka invited about a hundred Shuar to Gualaquiza to discuss organizing. The soldiers had departed, so Shutka and the Indians gathered in the community hall, which filled several hours before the meeting with Shuar men and their families. Everyone from the mission joined as well, for they wanted to hear the outcome. Ten-year-old Juan and his friends leaned against the palm walls, listening and sipping *chicha* as it was passed to them. Shutka rose and explained what he thought should be done to protect the Shuar's rights. When he finished the room erupted. Some of the men agreed with Shutka, but most adamantly believed a federation would steal their freedom.

Their voices rose now against Shutka, who leaned back in shock and listened. Suddenly, he became lost and confused by the abuse and threats against him. For more than an hour he sat on a *chimbi* stool with his elbows on his knees, his head bowed as first one man then another threatened him. The shouting continued for more than an hour, and Juan became increasingly tense as he sat watching. Finally he could stand no more. He ran forward and stood by Shutka.

Juan was already as tall as most of the Shuar, who knew him as a friend of their children, and in his ten-year-old voice, he began to attack them back. The Shuar were so surprised that they stopped shouting and listened to Juan as he shouted at them, then as they quieted he lowered his voice and spoke in the Shuar method of addressing, quietly and forcefully. He spoke in Shuar, "Why are you abusing Father Shutka? He can gain nothing if the Shuar join together. Why will you not listen to him? He is white like me and loves the Shuar people. His life has been dedicated to your service. He wants to protect your rights, not take them away." For more than ten minutes, he yelled questions at them, never waiting for an answer, for he expected none.

He finished his tirade, and silence reigned. A man coughed. Another shuffled nervously then whispered something to his neighbor. Suddenly the silence was broken as wild applause and cheering echoed through the building. The tenor of the meeting had changed and Juan had learned a valuable lesson: The Shuar appreciated a man of power, and despite Juan's age, they respected what he had to say and the manner in which he said it.

The Shuar agreed to consider the matter in more depth, so the meeting ended well. Shutka, as surprised as the others by Juan's outburst, solemnly shook his hand and thanked him.

The Shuar surrounded Juan, insisting that he go with them to the bar in Gualaquiza so they could buy him a beer. Shutka at first refused to let him go, but the Shuar insisted. Juan, too, was nervous—not just that he had never had a beer before but because he was afraid they might try to poison him. Shutka knew that Juan had made a powerful showing that night, and that it would worry some of the Shuar: if Juan spoke so powerfully as a young boy, he could be dangerous as a man.

At the tavern, Shutka and Juan sat down, and the Shuar set glasses of beer before them. The Shuar patted Juan on the back and congratulated him, urging him to drink. Juan had often seen Simoneti make the sign of the cross over any drink, so, as the beer was put before him, he did the same. Several men pressed forward eagerly but leaped back in fear—when Juan picked up the glass it shattered in his hand. The beer, indeed, held poison and would have killed Juan had the glass not broken. The men who had leaned forward turned pale as they realized he might already be a great shaman whose anger could be turned upon them. They left the room. Later, as Shutka and Juan walked to the mission, Shutka explained what had happened. The boy learned his second lesson of the night: it is dangerous to work with the Shuar, even if you are their friend.

But there was one more lesson yet to learn.

Shutka had made enemies among the Shuar. And now the colonos were angry that he given aid to the Indians before them. While Juan's life was changing at the tavern, the colonos laid their plans. Later that night, as Shutka lay in bed, a dozen men crept to his house with buckets of gasoline. Shutka's house was three stories high, so he could have a kitchen on the lower level and children on the second. His bedroom was on the third level, where he had a good view over the mission. Shouts and the smell of burning palm woke him, and he ran to the second floor. The stairs were already burning, so he began dropping children from the windows to waiting missionaries. When the children were safe, just as the roof was about to collapse, he leaped from the second story to safety.

Juan had been sleeping in another house and came to help. He was one of many who saw the arsonists watching from the shadows, men he had often seen in church and at the mission. That night he learned the full power of hatred, even among good men.

CHAPTER TEN

MARIA

Maria and Juan spent time together every day. Sometimes he helped her as she worked in the garden or kitchen, but often they talked about his father, so he would not forget him. Over the years Maria had been proposed to many times, but she always said, "I had a great love and need only one like that in this life."

She was a quiet but friendly woman and respected by the *colonos*, for she never took sides. It was from his mother that Juan learned diplomacy.

Because the mission was isolated, she realized the importance of good relations with both Shuar and *colono*. So in her quiet way she began to work for change. As she traveled to the farms to buy food, she talked with the women and made many friends. Inevitably, they would discuss the mission and the school the children attended. Always poor, the people needed money and were glad to sell the food. But the mission had little money so she was forced to ask for donations or very low prices. Over several months, as she visited, they gradually gave more food—plantains, yuca, raspadura, honey. The message in her conversations was lightly spoken but serious and carefully delivered. She said, "What has happened is in the past. It is neither Shuar nor *colono* who is to blame. If there is someone to blame, however, perhaps it is we as the mothers. It is our children and husbands who are injuring the community, and we have the power to improve their thinking.

"Slowly, through her patience, without threatening, the community began to heal.

By the time Juan was fourteen, he and Maria had lived at the mission for seven tumultuous years. Almost every week the children had either witnessed or heard of some abuse against the Shuar. But finally, thanks to Maria and the subtle influences of the *colono* mothers, tensions eased. Life was beginning to feel normal and safe. By 1934, whites and Shuar who met on a narrow trail would greet each other, often in a friendly way.

Fathers Simoneti and Shutka left the mission, replaced by Father Jose Peter, Father Alvino Gomez Cuello—an Ecuadorian—and Father Gambiracio. At the time, Father Alvino hated being in the *selva* because his family in Quito had problems, and he was always worried about them.

Part of the problem the new priests faced was that none of them could speak Jivaroan. When they realized that Juan could translate for them, they often called him in to help at meetings or to explain what they saw as strange Shuar customs.

One day, as he stood with the men in the meeting house, Juan's body thrilled at the good that was being done. He realized that this was his life's mission. He would be a priest.

Years later, Juan would recall:

> I went to Father Peter and told him that I wanted to be a priest. He did not seem surprised. In fact, he said, "I have been hoping you would make that decision. There are many things for you to learn and to share, but your love shows in what you do already."
>
> From that day, Father Peter became my mentor. I was fourteen years of age at that time and almost finished with school, so he gave me other responsibilities. I became a small leader at the mission, and when the school year began I taught classes to the first and second graders. The days began to pass very quickly, and I was very happy to receive instruction in the religious life from Father Peter. My mother's work

continued to bear fruit, and the bad feelings between the colonos and the Shuar seemed to be healing.

Maria.

Maria continued to seek food for the mission, often traveling great distances alone over rough trails and carrying a heavy *shigra* filled with food. Returning to the mission one afternoon, as she crossed a log that had been laid over a ravine as a bridge, she slipped. Her legs straddled the log, and the seventy-pound *shigra* on her back drove her onto the log with such force that it injured her vagina.

Bleeding profusely, she inched her way to the edge of the log and set the *shigra* onto the ground. After she recovered her breath, she tried to stop the bleeding but could not. Recognizing blood-clotting plants nearby, she gathered a handful of leaves and lay on her side as she pulverized them with a stone. Forcing the moist wad into her vagina, she lay back on the trail to wait.

An hour later the blood had stopped but the pain had increased. She picked up the *shigra* of food and slowly walked to the mission, where her friends cleaned her and sent for Juan. Over the next weeks the wound would seem to heal, but then begin bleeding again. Father Alvino, the medical priest who had taken charge of overseeing her care, decided to send her to Sigsig, where her mother and sisters could help.

At Sigsig a doctor found that the wound had become a malignant tumor. Within two months she could no longer walk. Juan worked in the family's garden and did odd jobs around town to help earn money, but each day he spent hours talking with Maria. Her pain grew, and he could see her strength fading, though her smile and laughter did not.

Juan remembered:

> After one year of suffering, my mother stopped and died. She was also young like my father, only thirty-seven years of age, and I was fifteen. She had been a wonderful mother and friend, but now I was alone.
>
> So, I became an orphan of mother and father. What was I to do? At fifteen I was considered a man but had no place in Sigsig. So I returned to the only home I had known, Gualaquiza, and worked again, helping with teaching and overseeing the younger children. There I worked with the little children and finished the school year.

Father Peter asked him one day, "Juan, what would you like to do next?"

They had talked about possibilities, and Juan knew that he could not be a teacher with only a primary-school education, so he said, "I think I should learn a trade. Then perhaps I will have something I can offer later if I can become a priest." Father Peter grinned broadly, as he did each time Juan made a good decision that seemed to be leading him toward God's service. They discussed possible trades, and Juan chose tailoring. Father Peter made arrangements for Juan to live in Cuenca, and for the next two years he served as an apprentice. He missed his discussions with Maria and Father Peter. Totally alone, Juan began to expect that tailoring would be his life. But God had other plans for him.

MENDEZ

CHAPTER ELEVEN

THE MISSION
AT MENDEZ

Juan recalls:

The fathers had seen that I was good with people and had an inner fire to help them. At the mission in Mendez, they were having problems with the teachers because none of them could speak Shuar and would not stay long. Besides, the Shuar were more difficult there. The superiors knew that I understood Shuar well because of my time in Gualaquiza, so they suggested that I put down my studies in Cuenca and go down to Mendez, to be a teacher there. At age eighteen I became a teacher, instructing pre-school and first graders, and discovered that I loved it.

So, I spent three years there giving classes and spending time with the Shuar children. The years there were not difficult for me because I had the key. I could understand and speak the Shuar language, and I loved and respected them. Because of this key, I was happy all the time.

CHAPTER TWELVE

EDUCATION MINISTER'S CHALLENGE

The Ecuadorian government considered the Salesian missions and other religious groups to be indirect allies of the state. They shared the goal of educating the children. If possible, the Indians were to be converted to Christianity, and at the very least they would provide an available source of cheap labor. But in an era when communication was at best difficult, at worst impossible, the government heeded rumors and rumor told them that things at the missions needed inquiry.

Questions began to arise regarding whether the Salesian missions were truly meeting the goals of the government or even providing education. Although it gave the missions little aid, the government still wanted a role in their operation. Juan had been at the mission in Mendez for two years when the latest in a series of questions arose. The education minister at the time was a hard man who wanted proof that education was going on, lest the missions be closed. He demanded that the Salesian missions bring children to Quito for his personal testing. He challenged the teachers, "If you are truly educating the children, show me."

The distance was great and the travel was difficult. Each mission brought along ten to fifteen boys. The women had prepared baskets of food for everyone, and each carried a *shigra* with food and their best clothes. It was to be a very long bus ride. Mendez lies in the lower foothills, covered with dense rain forest. For hours the bus ground its way slowly through a landscape where they could never see past the edge of the road. Then, as they climbed higher, the air thinned and dried. Each steep slope shimmered with silvery waterfalls, and their thunder rose even into the noisy bus. Soon they were replaced by sweeping vistas and wind that howled around the bus and whistled through the grass.

These high lands, called *paramo*, nurtured ample clumps of *puna* grass three or four feet high. The Indians who lived there wore woolen shawls and harvested the grass to feed their animals and repair the thatch on their houses. Most of the houses looked as if made of adobe bricks but Juan began to notice scattered, squarish holes cut into limestone hillsides, where the local people had cut out slabs of soft rock that were broken into bricks and used to make the walls of their houses. They also cut out the soft rock, pulverized it with hammers and mixed it with water to make whitewash. The bus labored past three families using it to whitewash their houses, which they often did twice a year. The locals knew that the lime paint would brighten their houses, softening the sharp angles with layers and layers of powdered stone, as well as kill most of the vermin living in the walls.

The *paramo* was the place in the Andes where Europeans were introduced to potatoes. With centuries of experience, the people had developed many varieties and ways of growing them. Whole hillsides near villages were terraced for fields, even on almost forty-five-degree slopes. The bus driver stopped to give a Quechua man a ride and the man proudly told Juan that there were more than eighty varieties of potatoes, just in this area they were passing.

Juan and the students, all boys, pressed their faces to the windows to absorb the scene, so different from their home fewer than a hundred fifty miles away. "Tidy tips" flowers grew in dense clumps with yellow, five-petaled flowers around orange centers. And there were blue lupines. "Where are the trees?" the boys asked. Only the gullies contained groves of hickory-looking *rivase*. Their rich, brown trunks grew twisted and gnarled and though picturesque, they would never make good lumber. Still, the Quechua used them for fence posts and firewood.

These mountains differ from other ranges, such as the Rockies in the North America. Much higher, steeper and greener, the Andes rise past nineteen thousand feet. Juan watched in wonder as brown, silt-laden rivers dashed foamy and brown through the bottoms of the broad U-shaped glacial valleys. Footpaths followed many of the rivers, and small groups of Quechua people, brightly clad in homespun wool serapes, toiled along them, carried bundles of grass or firewood. The Quechua seemed very businesslike, never smiling at the boys or returning Juan's friendly waves.

The bus continued to climb, its motor whining and the gears crunching as the driver continually shifted up and down. The driver was nervous, for earlier they had seen a group of people standing at the roadside calling in concern. Juan peered over the edge and saw a truck several hundred feet down the grassy slope. It was still upright but the wheels lay on the ground because the axle was broken. Then Juan saw the driver. He was unhurt, and the people were calling encouragement to him as he slowly worked his way up the hillside, using the long *paramo* grass for handholds.

After many hours, Juan's bus entered a high valley; for an hour they drove up one gentle hill and down the next. The wind swept plain was devoid of houses or people. As the bus ground up a final hill that would take them out of the valley, they passed a dirt-smudged man carrying a huge pile of *rivase* branches on his back. Their weight bent him forward and he moved almost as if in slow motion. A little farther up the road, two equally filthy girls of about five and six each carried a branch. Farther yet, a mother, holding five arm-size branches, paused to rest at the side of the road and watched the two girls carefully as the bus ground by them. Finally, moving faster than the rest and carrying a load almost equal to his father's, a ten-year-old turned into the pathway of his house. Just like in the *selva*, every family member was doing their part.

The bus dropped down again into the valley of Cuenca. *Cuenca* is a Spanish word for river basin or watershed and was named for the three rivers that come together there. Juan brushed away a tear as he recalled his mother telling of his father's visit there on his way to Gualaquiza. He had no tears, however, for his own two years there in a dark tailor's shop. As in the days of his father, the riverbanks were filled with women washing their clothes in the clear water then laying them to dry on the grassy banks in a multicolored array while the women sat back to visit.

Cuenca was a beautiful old city with many things to see. Women of the area made handsome straw hats, called Panama hats, from the fibers of the toquilla palm. As the bus drove through the outskirts of the city it raised a rooster-tail of dust behind. People and chickens and long-haired pigs scurried out of the way, for the bus didn't slow for them. The boys watched clusters of women weaving hats as they sat chatting under red-bracted poinsettia trees, laden with more drying laundry.

Juan recalls:

It takes about three days to make one hat, for which they women receive about fifty cents, even in the 1990s. Many of these come to the U.S. to become straw "cowboy hats," which sell for fifty to seventy-five dollars.

The Mendez Mission entourage disembarked from the bus. Walking in double file past the staring Cuencans, the teachers and children walked to the Salesian school. Later that day they transferred to other buses, joining a hundred of the best students from seven other mission schools. Juan regretted that he had no time to take the children sightseeing. Ah, Juan thought, when we get to Quito we will see the sights.

One of the priests bought several baskets of "short biscuit," a favorite mountain snack, and distributed it to everyone. It had a crumbly texture like piecrust and was pale yellow, as if a little cheese were stirred into the dough before cooking. Its rather bland flavor becomes sweet as it is chewed. For several precious minutes the bus was almost silent while the boys ate and the buses continued the even longer ride toward Quito.

Juan recalled their arrival in Quito:

> The trip altogether was about four days, one-way. From Cuenca on, we had about a hundred children from eight missions. Most of the children had never been to a city before and were very excited and wide-eyed. Father Simoneti had been elected as director and, although it was very stimulating, he was becoming exhausted even before we got to Quito. But he kept up a continual good cheer before everyone.
>
> Finally, at Quito, we gathered in the gymnasium of a local school. To entertain the education ministers and to give the boys some diversion, we held dances, played music and sang. All the teachers were nervous, but we tried to hide it from the boys. For two days we laughed and had fun together. At Cuenca, the people only stared at us, but the people of Quito were crazy for the Shuar children and came to watch. They brought food and gifts.

A few days before departure from Mendez, the father of one of the Shuar boys went to Juan and said, "Our son is learning very much here at the mission, and you have been very caring for us. Do you think it would be a good idea to take a traditional Shuar family with you to Quito? That way the education minister and others can see how we have lived before and how you are teaching us to live now." Juan thought that this would be a wonderful idea but wondered who might want to put themselves in a position where people might stare at them and think, "What a primitive and savage person." The Shuar man said, "My wife and I would like to do that for you."

So they went. At Quito they did demonstrations in Shuar, for they spoke no Spanish. The man demonstrated his ability with a blowgun. Setting a banana atop a log he blew hard on the blowgun and the little dart pierced the fruit from more than fifty feet away. Meanwhile, his shy wife demonstrated how the Shuar made soft cloth from tree bark. All the children wore blue cotton trousers and white shirts, but the Shuar family dressed in traditional clothing. Juan watched carefully, to ensure that no one offended the family.

The education minister watched them and listened, then Juan acted as interpreter so he could ask the Shuar questions. The minister never smiled but he seemed interested. The people of Quito also had also been invited, and there was a constant line of visitors, many who brought gifts and food and asked dozens of questions. Everyone was impressed with the difference between the old ways and the new, but Juan wondered . . .

On their journey here, the group had already passed up many learning opportunities. But Quito offered more, and Juan refused to squander them. On the second day in Quito, while the other teachers kept their students at the gymnasium to practice, Juan gathered the seven boys from Mendez and walked around the city.

At first the boys cowered from the crowds of people walking along the packed sidewalks; they had never seen so many. Unlike the jungle, where the loudest sounds were the howler monkeys, Quito was a continuous roar of motor traffic and noisy people. Horns and shouts of drivers added to the din and created more confusion for the children who gathered around Juan with darting, frightened eyes.

A beggar with no legs perched on a padded platform only inches from the bricks of the street. He kept his eyes downcast but held up a little cup with a few coins in it, which he shook occasionally in a jingling request for help. Juan dropped a few coins into the can and whispered a prayer for the man.

An old man, almost bald but with a thick, gray beard,

slept on a bench, leaning on his hand. Barefoot, he wore a filthy gray sweater, and his pants were slit from knee to waist, exposing emaciated white legs. He never stirred as hundreds of people swirled around him.

Another old man pushed a wobbly two-wheeled cart filled with melons and green coconuts still on their stems. To keep the cart from running away when he came to a hill, a wide leather strap ran from one cart handle over the old man's shoulders and back to the other cart handle. He was *very* old, and the cart moved slowly among the pedestrians.

Also on the street, little children age two and three held their mothers' hands and gazed with curiosity and boldness at everything, especially the group of Indian children passing through their streets together.

The Shuar boys stared and laughed quietly together, as one of them mimicked a wealthy woman who passed by with a purebred dog on a leash. Even the dog walked with an air of aristocracy, its head and chin raised slightly. The woman and her dog passed two street mutts rooting in a little pile of garbage. Jungle dogs look more or less alike, but city dogs are mongrels of mongrels. A "Heinz 57" variety geometrically separates further from its purebred ancestors with each generation, creating after dozens of generations a "Heinz 1,975,257" variety—no two are alike.

Juan and his students paused at a bakery filled with cakes, bread, cream horns and cookies. Juan bought a bagful of *suspirros*, meringue cookies as light and sweet as the sigh of the one you love. He bought marshmallows, too, which none of them had seen before. Juan handed the white, roundish sweets to the boys. Instead of eating them right away, they sniffed them and squeezed them gently. They rubbed the puffy candy alongside their noses, feeling the softness. Then they bit into the sticky center and smiled at the sweetness on their tongues.

Juan was thirsty and bought a *pipa* from a vendor selling the green coconuts. The vendor used his machete to cut away an end then carefully removed a little plug of coconut meat. He inserted a straw into the sweetish milk and handed it to Juan, who drank thirstily. Then Juan returned it to the man who split the coconut in half. Juan used his knife to remove the chewy white coconut meat and passed it among the boys.

The sound of hundreds of wings and the cooing of birds filled the central plaza. Eagerly, the children watched pigeons, similar to their forest doves but more colorful. Dozens of the birds strutted around the plaza eating bits of popcorn tossed to them by pedestrians. Male pigeons, with iridescent purple necks, puffed out their chests and strutted on their toes as they pursued the females, even amid the feet of passersby. Other pigeons gathered on a fountain, beaks inserted into the water and sipping, unlike most birds, which take a beak full and tip their heads back to let the water flow down their throats.

Small groups of teenagers gathered, talking and laughing. They pointed and made comments under their breaths, some obviously not complimentary, as the Shuar walked by. The Shuar boys looked away nervously.

Night approached and it was time to return to the gymnasium, where food awaited. They walked along the darkening streets, through neighborhoods with iron-barred windows and eight-foot high walls capped with broken glass embedded in concrete. Private guards strode the streets, swinging long clubs and watching Juan with serious eyes as he led his boys back to the school.

Each day the gathered Shuar attended classes as the education minister walked around, looking stern and talking with no one. The teachers became nervous, for he was obviously not impressed. One morning, the education minister said, "Gather everyone together in one hour. I have some questions."

Many *Quitenos* (citizens of Quito) gathered to see the outcome. Juan and the other teachers were very nervous, for if they could not prove they were educating the children they would be ordered to close the missions. But they knew it was important to keep the children relaxed and unafraid, lest they might make mistakes in answering the questions. So the teachers played games with them until it was time for them to demonstrate. The dark-faced, almost scowling minister sat at a table watching and listening as each school demonstrated the students' skills in mathematics, writing and speaking Spanish. Each time a school finished, the audience applauded loudly, but the minister sat unmoved except when he scribbled a note on the papers before him.

As the eighth school finished, the minister looked around the room carefully, his forehead wrinkled into a slight scowl. A great silence filled the gymnasium for many minutes. Then, he signaled to the smallest Shuar, a boy who was no older than seven. "Please come here," the minister said quietly.

The boy went to him, shook the minister's hand, greeted him in proper Spanish and said, "My name is Puhupat."

A trace of a smile curled under the stern minister's dark moustache, as he asked, "Well, Puhupat, do you know the national anthem?"

"Of course, I do," he said.

Then the man set Puhupat on his table in front of the hundreds of people and said, "Would you please sing it for us?" Everyone stood to honor the anthem as, without hesitation and in a strong and loud voice, the boy sang the national anthem in perfect tune. When he was finished, the applause filled the room for more than five minutes. This time even the minister was applauding and smiling very broadly as he nodded to the teachers.

His decision was that the missions were not only doing a good job but an excellent one. He thanked the teachers for their service to the republic, and to the Shuar, then left the room. The children and their teachers had proven the worth of their teaching. The children returned home in triumph, but not before Juan stopped at the bakery to buy *suspirros* and marshmallows for everyone.

CHAPTER THIRTEEN

WORKING FOR GOD, BUT NOT AS A PRIEST

In Mendez, Juan began to follow the religious path more intensely than ever. The priests encouraged him, for they believed he had the right qualities to follow a religious life. He understood how to work with the children and would make an excellent teacher. So after two years in Mendez, at the age of twenty, he was sent back to Cuenca to study under Father Ormajio; he would learn to become a teaching priest.

A year later Juan had completed his novitiate, and Father Ormajio was convinced that he was ready to teach. He arranged for Juan to be sent to the mission at the Shuar center in Sucua where Juan's old mentor, Father Peter again took up Juan's education. Juan's assignment was to teach the Shuar students, who were still shy toward most whites but comfortable with him because he spoke their language. For the next three years he worked work with undiminished enthusiasm. He would soon be a priest, and at night, lying in his little room, he thought about the future. "Father Juan Arcos." He liked the sound of that. Then one night, he realized that something was not quite right.

He loved the children, but he began to realize he needed to work more with adults, to organize meetings and help guide and protect them and their families. But he had been preparing for so many years to be a priest. As a priest he would be told what to do, to go only where the church wanted him. Would that be enough?

One morning very early, he walked out of town to a place where he could pray. He sat alone with his God, by the edge of a stream, praying. Despite the recent heavy rains, the little side water was a mere trickle, for it had a steep slope and drained quickly. About 70 feet across, the stream was clear, flowing from one pool to the next. As usual for early morning, a blue-gray fog hung along the river and contrasted with the white sky. It was beginning to lift, and the distant mountains and forest appeared as if through a gauze veil. He sat on a rock and watched as a clear-winged *ithomid* butterfly landed on his arm and began to sip a droplet of sweat. It rose to flit from rock to rock then flew on. Plants crowded the shoreline in a thousand shades of green. Birds called, and things slithered and struggled as they caught something in the undergrowth, or were themselves caught as something's breakfast. He was surrounded by the trilling calls of turquoise cicadas. He waded upstream and paused at a sandbar on the inside of a curve. It was covered with the parallel tracks of a turtle, the clawless tracks of an ocelot, and even the tracks of the big rodents, pacas and capybaras. The scene was as one imagines the jungle, dense and impenetrable, wet and mysterious and filled with life.

Stripping, he waded into the clear water and swam from one long pool to the next through the water, which alternated between blue and green water, depending on whether sky or trees were above. He allowed himself to drift with the current, slow, as if the little stream were afraid to enter the bigger river. He swam upstream for a few hundred yards, watching turtles slip from logs into the seventy-eight-degree water. On the shore, long-tailed silvery-blue skinks raced across the forest litter, pausing to watch him drift by.

A green anole lizard clung upside down on a liana, flicking its orange throat patch. Juan watched it, amazed at the complexity of God's creation. He decided to catch the anole for a closer look. Like his Shuar friends had shown him long·

ago in Gualaquiza, he wiggled the fingers of his left hand slowly, a foot or so from its head, distracting it as his right hand sneaked up on it from behind. The anole never saw the danger until it was squirming between Juan's fingers, still flashing the throat patch. It calmed quickly in the warmth of his hand. When he replaced it on the liana, it scurried away, frightening two walking-stick-like young basilisks, which scurried across the shallow water and under a bush.

He turned on his back and drifted downstream, watching the canopy of trees slide by, as if he were in the vestibule of a huge, tree-filled church. Four-inch-long fish, with bodies so transparent he could see their reddish organs, nibbled at his legs and arms, creating a strange, prickly sensation. The surface was rippled blue and green, but where pools of sunlight fell on the water, it flashed golden. The light illuminated columns in the water and cast shadows next to bottom rocks eight feet below. In the brightness, little scurrying shrimp, *langustinos*, waved their antennae as they fed on bits of debris that flowed inches above the floor of the stream. It was midmorning now, and no birds moved, but the treetops swayed in the breeze that continuously flowed over the roof of the canopy.

As he listened, God gave him his answer. Juan suddenly "knew" he should be a religious missionary. As a priest he would be one person doing enormous good. If he were married and had a wife who believed in the work, they could do twice as much. And if they had children, they could help and increase the good works even more.

But how would he tell Father Peter?

The next morning he went to Father Peter's office. Twice he tried to knock before his courage came and he tapped lightly.

"Father Peter," Juan said, "I have made an important decision and need your blessing."

Peter smiled broadly at this, his favorite student, but the smile disappeared, replaced by an ill-concealed scowl as Juan continued, "I have prayed for a long time and believe that God does not want me to be a priest."

"Oh," Peter said. "What does He want you to be then, a tailor?"

Juan swallowed at the sarcasm, then continued. "No, Father. I believe He wants me to be a teaching missionary. I love the life of a missionary and would like your help in becoming one."

Missionaries seldom kept at their work for more than a few years and Father Peter suspected that Juan merely wanted to leave the mission and take up a different life. Smiling again, but still without enthusiasm, he said, "Of course I am disappointed. You would have made a wonderful priest. But the priesthood is not for everyone. It is good that you realize this now, which is part of the reason it takes so long to become a priest."

Juan said, "I am committed to leading a life dedicated to God and His people, the Shuar. I want to continue to stay here and work with you, but as a lay missionary. Will you have me?"

"Since you have made this decision," Father Peter said, "it would be good for you to start on that direction immediately. Come to see me tomorrow morning, and I will have instructions for you."

The other priests who had been his teachers were surprised at the turn of events. Many were resentful; their time had been wasted. Some refused to speak to him, as Father Peter had suspected would be the case. They were taken aback by his decision, and many of them looked at Juan scornfully, but others accepted it.

Next morning Juan returned to the office. A distant and unsmiling Father Peter gave him a letter and said, "You will go to Yaupi immediately. Father Juan Guinassi has started the mission there and needs assistance."

So the next day Juan left Sucua on the first of many dangerous treks to Yaupi. But he was to learn that the greatest threat was not the snakes or *tigres*, but the humans he went to serve, for there was more than one kind of *Tigre* of the Night.

Juan and Amalia visit the Mitad del Mundo
(middle of the world), where the equator crosses at Quito,
sometime in the 1950s.

Juan celebrates graduation day with Pepe and Esther.

Marianna's first communion. Esther, Patricia, Amalia, Marianna,
Juan with Juanito and Maria

YAUPI

CHAPTER FOURTEEN

A NEW LIFE

Juan recalls his change to religious missionary and his new mentor, Father Guinassi:

He was a wonderful old man, about sixty years of age when we first met, and with a magnificent full white beard. We got along well immediately. He spoke little Shuar at the time but was learning as well as he could and communicated with them in Spanish, which more of the people were beginning to learn. When I first saw him with the children and their families, I knew that he loved the Shuar as people, not just as humans to "save." In school he wanted to help the children to learn about their own culture, wear the clothes they preferred instead of what missionaries demanded, and to eat the kinds of food at the mission that they were used to in their own homes. I was excited about this wonderful approach to serving God and the Shuar, so in 1949, when I was twenty-eight years of age, now a "formed man," I made my first walk across the Cutucus to Yaupi. It was there that I truly began the life of a missionary.

Father Guinassi knew of my change and supported my decision. "The religious life is not for everyone," he said. "You have obviously prayed about this, and I will support your path. I hope, however, that you will want to continue to work with me here in Yaupi, because we are two men with the same spirit."

After news got around that I had decided to leave the religious life and to become a missionary instead of a priest, things changed and have never been the same. There were some Salesians who looked at with me with scorn. Sometimes I would have to go to Cuenca or

Mendez to do errands for the mission of Yaupi. At first I expected things would be the same at the missions there. After all, I continued to work for God. But the Fathers there seemed to despise me because I had left the religious life to become a missionary. Most missionaries only work for a few years, then turn to secular things. Perhaps they thought I would do the same and they no longer respected me. [He adds with a sad smile.] Although I have now been a missionary for more than fifty years they still do not believe that I will stick with it.

Not long after leaving my training for the priesthood, I was in the village of Macas, gathering supplies for the mission. I went to the religious house to request a bed for the night because I had no money to stay in a hotel.

At the door of the house, a nun greeted me, a woman I had known most of my life. She said, "What are you doing here? Go on. Go on!" I was surprised by her anger but said, "God gives us many paths to serve him. You have chosen the life of a religious woman, but I have chosen to be a missionary. We are both working for God and to help the people. Why can't I stay here?" She gave me no answer, and I was still refused a place. For several hours I wandered about town, trying to think of what to do or where to go. If I used the money I had with me for a hotel room, I would not have enough to buy the supplies. Finally, I met a friend in the plaza who offered me a place to stay at his house. I accepted gratefully. If he had not offered, I would have slept in the town plaza with the drunken ones.

At Yaupi, Father Guinassi and Juan became immediate friends. They worked every day to make the remote mission a success, and to serve the people. Juan continued to study, now in a new direction and under the instruction of a special, loving man with no ulterior motives. After long days teaching the children, working in the garden, fretting about how to meet their expenses, they sat in an *aak*—for there were no houses yet—and talked about God. Father Guinassi, in turn, was excited about Juan. Here was a young man with the fire of love for God's people. He had strength, energy and a complete faith in God's plan for him. There were books as well as the Bible for Juan to study. He had to learn dozens of prayers, the order of service, the laws of the church and more. Juan in his turn taught Father Guinassi how to speak to the Shuar in their language. These subjects they discussed by candlelight, surrounded by the darkness of the Amazon rainforest.

As one would expect, Sundays were very busy. Before the sun rose, eager Shuar families began to gather. They came from their farms many miles away to visit with friends and to hear Father Guinassi perform Mass. Juan's assignment was to teach religion to the people. Both Juan and Guinassi realized that although most of the Shuar would say they were Catholic, and religion was an important part of their community life, they still had little knowledge of formal church teachings. Indigenous or folk beliefs coexisted and mingled with Christianity.

Before noon on any Sunday, Juan had already taught a class for the men, one for the women (for the Shuar would not allow both to be in one class) and another for adults preparing to be married.

Father Guinassi appreciated that Juan spoke Jivaroan like a Shuar. The language skills Juan had learned playing with his Shuar friends as a little boy made the work of the mission much easier; but it was Juan's understanding of the Shuar thought process that was most helpful.

CHAPTER FIFTEEN

Amalia Tuitsa

At first there was only one *interno* but almost eighty day students. All the students were boys. They sat in the simple classroom with no walls, dressed as they had for hundreds of years, bare-chested and often decorated with red achiote paste. Their parents lived totally traditional—what most people would call "primitive"—lives. Juan smiled through his days, glad of the path God had shown him, and the man He had given him as a teacher. They lived in *aaks*—one for Guinassi, one for Juan, and one for the *interno* boy. Their food was simple—yuca, platanos, bananas and fish when they could catch them. But neither man complained about the bland food or lack of comforts, for they had that total love for their neighbor and the desire to serve God that short-circuited self-pity. As Juan explained, "You become more content because of the power of God."

But Juan's growing loneliness for a true family of his own somewhat tempered that contentment. Money was always in short supply. The parents of the *interno* paid only twenty sucres a month (about fifteen dollars), and parents of the day students brought food from time to time. One night Father Guinassi, after boiling away the water in the dinner pot and burning their meal, turned to Juan. Still holding the smoking pot, he said to Juan in Spanish, "We need someone to cook and help here at the mission, or I will starve us all."

They both laughed, and Juan translated for the puzzled *interno* boy, who laughed even harder. A few weeks later, Juan·

and half a dozen Shuar men went to Sucua for other supplies. As they prepared to leave, Guinassi said, "See if you can find us a helper."

At Sucua, Juan went to the head of the mission. Although he greeted Juan coldly, he sent him to the director of the girls' school, Maria Troncate. Juan knew her well from his days studying in Sucua, and she seemed unaffected by the bad feelings of the priests. She suggested three girls (Paulina, Juana and Amalia) who she thought might like to go to Yaupi.

When he first heard Amalia's name Juan realized she would be perfect, for he had known her when she was a young girl. "She attends church several times a week," Troncate said. "She is not tall, barely five feet, but possesses unusual energy and strength."

Juan recalled that when he last saw her, the twelve-year-old girl always carried the heaviest *shigras* from the garden. Now eighteen, she would probably have even more strength. When Juan studied at the mission, the Fathers had given her very high marks for her intelligence. She frustrated them from time to time, for she, unlike most of the girls, had a great sense of humor. But the priests forgave her, for she was pretty as well as earnest. Juan imagined the years would have been kind to her and that she would be a beautiful woman now.

Juan and Amalia's older brother, Pedro, had been students together and were good friends. Whenever he was in town it seemed they always ran into each other. So Juan named Amalia Tuitsa as his first choice. Thanking Maria Troncate for her kindness and help, Juan said, "I will go to find Pedro, to see what he thinks, then talk with Amalia."

Four days later, on 24 January 1948, Juan, accompanied by Amalia Tuitsa, left for Yaupi, where Amalia would be cook and housekeeper for the two bachelors and one *interno*.

CHAPTER SIXTEEN

COURTSHIP

Father Guinassi and Juan were amazed at Amalia's energy and efficiency. She worked like them, from early morning until late at night. She prepared breakfast and dinner for three, then a noon meal for almost ninety people each day, and still had time to joke with the boys she was serving. Juan recalls, "After she had been there for two months, I began to think she would be someone who would want to marry me."

Four months after she arrived in Yaupi, Pedro guided a German pastor to the mission and they decided to stay and help for a while. Pedro was an excellent carpenter, and the pastor was a hard worker, so in the three months they stayed at Yaupi they helped to build several new houses. First, they built a real house for the missionaries, so they could abandon the *aaks*, then a house for the one *interno* as well as the others they hoped would come. Finally, they constructed walls on one school building that had originally been left open-sided, and a second school building, so the children would not be so crowded.

Juan thought about proposing directly to Amalia but knew that it would be improper. So one day, as he and Pedro rested in the forest where they were cutting palm leaves to thatch the new school building, he broached the subject.

"Pedro, what would you think if I asked to marry Amalia?"

He was surprised when Pedro answered, "But my friend, you are white. Although I like you very much, and respect you, I do not think that would be a good idea."

As if the subject were a closed issue, Pedro picked up his machete and started to cut palm leaves again, stacking them atop ropes to bind for carrying them to the mission.

"Pedro, what has my whiteness to do with my love for Amalia? You know I have always lived with the Shuar, and their life is mine."

"Juan, my friend, I understand what you are saying, but it is not easy for a white man to marry an Indian." He continued, "You are a teacher and have more money than any of us. We are poor Shuar. Sometimes I walk in Sucua or in Mendez and see the abandoned Shuar women who married white men. Most of them have two or three children and no way to support them. I would not want this for my sister."

"No, Pedro. That is not true," Juan said. "I am a formed man. I am twenty-eight years old. Once I thought that I had found a white woman to marry, but she hated the idea of living in the jungle and of working with the *Jivaros,* as she called them. I knew she was not the person for me. Look, since I was a child I have lived with and loved the Shuar. My parents worked with them for many years. I love the Shuar community and the Shuar people. I would be so happy if you would allow me to marry your sister."

Pedro grunted in understanding then continued to work. For almost an hour they cut palm fronds, and the only sounds were from the jungle and the "chink" of machetes clipping palm leaves. From time to time, Pedro stood erect and watched Juan working, considering their conversation. Finally he said, "I will do it. I will speak with my sister. But also you need to speak with Father Guinassi."

Later that day, Juan talked with Father Guinassi. "I have found the woman I would like to marry: Amalia," he said. "I understand that there is another man the family expects to marry her, but Pedro tells me that the family is worried because he is very violent, an angry and abusive man who might beat her. They would be glad to have her marry someone who would love and care for her."

Surprised at Juan's revelation, Father Guinassi thought for a long time then said quietly. "Juan, you are a very good person for this mission, and I appreciate your dedication to the children. But consider this. You work very well with the children and their families here. But there are many cases in Sucua of whites marrying poor Shuar, fathering two and three children, then abandoning the woman and children. You need to think very carefully, because I do not want Amalia to be hurt."

Juan repeated what he told Pedro, and Father Guinassi said, "Very well. I will send a request to God and to the Virgin. You should do the same, and we will see what happens."

But then Pedro returned with bad news for Juan. Amalia did not want to marry him.

Juan was disappointed but thought, "If it is right, God will open her heart. If not, then He will show me another."

So Juan passed time more quietly than before. He went to the kitchen and sat down at a table. Amalia smiled brightly and asked him, "Would you like a cup of papaya juice I just made?"

"Yes, thank you."

As he sipped the cool juice, Amalia continued to prepare the evening meal. Silence between the two allowed the forest sounds to fill the new kitchen house Pedro had helped to build.

Finally, Juan broke the silence. "Amalia, we are both mature people who have a special desire to help others. I think we would be good as partners, to make a home together and work for our Shuar brothers."

Amalia smiled again, this time with only a slight upturn of the lips, and said, "Perhaps. But let us give this some time, and we will see what God has prepared for us."

Juan thanked her, took his juice and left. Each day he returned in late afternoon for a glass of juice and to talk, but he never touched on the question or her decision.

Finally, after three months had passed, as Juan sipped his afternoon juice, Amalia asked, "When do you think we should get married?"

Juan grinned and kissed her forehead. "As soon as Father Guinassi says we are ready," he said.

The state required a civil wedding but the nearest justice of the peace was in Sucua, an eight-day round trip. Neither could be spared from the mission for that long, so Father Guinassi prepared them for an ecclesiastical wedding immediately. They could be married by the state officials on their next trip to Sucua.

Pedro and the pastor built a small house for the couple, and a few days after it was completed for their home, 24 May 1948, Father Guinassi performed the simple wedding ceremony. Pedro and the pastor were the only witnesses. The eighteen-year-old Amalia officially became Mrs. Juan Arcos, and more than fifty-five years later they would still be performing the same work together. But neither was aware of the adventures they would have along the way.

CHAPTER SEVENTEEN

YOU MARRIED
A JIVARO

After the wedding mass, Guinassi invited the new couple, Pedro and the pastor to have coffee at the table in his room. They talked and laughed for about an hour, then each of them returned to work. There would never be a honeymoon.

Most of the Shuar felt the marriage was good, but many of the whites were shocked. On the first visit back to Macas, Amalia remained behind, for she was needed at the mission (they would have to wait a bit longer for the State to sanctify the marriage). At the mission, Juan discovered that what he had done was considered scandalous. For a missionary to marry an Indian was unthinkable in the eyes of many of the church people. So now he had done two "unthinkable" things— left the study for priesthood *and* married an Indian.

He discovered the depth of the church workers' feelings when he went to the mission. A nun he had known for many years asked him, "Why did you marry a *Jivaro*?

"Because I love her," Juan answered simply.

"But she is a savage. She is not your equal, and you will be dragged down to her level," the nun reasoned.

Juan, frustrated, became angry and through gritted teeth he fought to control himself as he said, "You teach that we are all equal. Why should I not marry her?"

But the nun persisted in asserting that he had made a huge mistake.

"Fine," Juan almost shouted, "if we aren't all equal, I was wrong. I'll go back to Yaupi and divorce her. And it will all be your fault!"

The nun became very nervous and said, "No, no, no. I didn't say that." The Church frowned on divorce and she didn't want this one, no matter how right it might be, on her head.

Juan realized there was nothing more he could say, so he turned without another word and left. The nun poured a glass of wine and sat down at a table, shaking.

At Cuenca, Juan found the same attitude, even among those who had known him since he was a child. Their unchristian attitude confused and frustrated Juan, but he never wavered in his love for Amalia nor did he ever regret his choice. Over the next fifty years he would be chastised often, but his answer was always the same: "There is nothing that bothers me, and there is nothing that crucifies me. I have chosen my path, and am happy in it."

CHAPTER EIGHTEEN

Children
of their Own

The newlyweds were delighted when Amalia became pregnant almost immediately. Amalia asked Juan to build a new birthing house for her. It was done in the Shuar style with a bed for resting afterward. At one side of the room he constructed the birthing support—two forked sticks, three feet tall, three feet apart, driven deep into the ground. A strong cross-member joined the two and fastened to the forks. In birthing, Amalia would lean or rest against this while kneeling on the ground atop clean banana leaves, rather than lying on a bed.

Carlito entered the world without incident and was strong and healthy. But when he was only three months of age, the *tosvarina* visited the valley. They tried the modern medicines and all the traditional remedies, but none of them worked against this foreign import, known in the United States as whooping cough. In desperation, Amalia even suggested they take the baby to a shaman, but neither Juan nor Amalia really believed in the spiritual doctors. So when the epidemic had run its course, dozens of people were dead, including little Carlito. Sadly, although a whooping cough vaccine had been used in the United States for a dozen years, none had come to the Ecuadorian jungle.

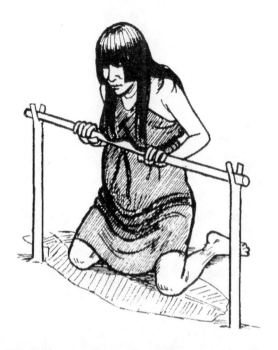

When a Shuar woman gives birth she will be upright, using some sort of vertical or horizontal support and with clean banana leaves for the reception of the newborn baby. (drawing courtesy of Abya Yala, Quito, Ecuador)

Amalia and Juan continued their selfless work. The next year Jose Hermundo Arcos arrived and was nicknamed Pepe.

Juan describes the night Pepe was born:

We had a small flock of chickens that roamed the mission during the day, and at night we put them into chicken coops, usually made from the thorn-encrusted prop roots of the walking palm. Because Amalia was in labor I asked one of the *internas* to go put them back into the coop. In a few minutes I heard her making the traditional "pshk-pshk-pshk" sound with her lips as she herded them into the coop. Suddenly the gentle sound turned into high-pitched screaming.

I took my shotgun and ran toward the screams. In the yard, a *tigrillo* (ocelet) had found easy dinners. It had killed one chicken and was ignoring the shrieking girl as it chased another terrified hen around the yard.

With a lucky shot I killed it. From the birthing house, Amalia was calling, asking, "What is going on?" I disposed of the animal, washed my hands well and returned to help the Shuar midwife who was with Amalia.

"Did you touch the animal?" Amalia asked nervously. No, I lied, for I knew that the Shuar believe that the child would be injured if I touched a dead animal during the birth. It's more likely that there are germs on the animal that are bad for the baby. Pepe was born strong and remained so.

A year later, Esther arrived, followed the next by Carlos, then Domingo a year later. Their family was half-formed.

CHAPTER NINETEEN

THE
MISSION GROWS

In the third year of their marriage, when Amalia was pregnant with Esther, Juan was preparing for the day's classes when Father Guinassi came in. After greetings, he sat at one of the wooden desks and for a moment was quiet, but Juan could tell he was excited. He stroked his beard slowly a moment, then announced, "Juan, I think it might be good to have girls as well as boys staying at the mission. Before you married there was no one to direct the *internas* (girls who would live at the mission and go to school). Now, with Amalia, there is a wonderful person to do so."

Amalia agreed eagerly, for she loved the idea of more female companionship. Juan and Guinassi began to spread the word, visiting the families of boys who were already studying with them. Within a few days the parents of fifteen girls agreed to send them to live at the mission.

With the addition of the girls, the school became even more of a community social center. In fact, it became another way for a pair of young people to meet each other and to find a mate.

Juan described their system for taking care of the older children: "Some of the missions had trouble, but our system of keeping the children together all the time except at night meant there was little mystery in seeing each other. If a pair wanted to get married they knew they could come and talk with me, and I would help them to prepare for a life together, including talking with their families about their plans."

Over time, the Salesian schools of the area evolved into a social as well as education center. In the past, when a Shuar wanted to marry, his father would send him to live with the relative whose daughter they anticipated he would marry. The boy lived with the family for a time, and the parents (often an uncle or aunt of the boy's) could see what kind of a hunter he was and how he would fit in, for once they were married he would move in permanently with the girl's family.

Juan's marriage to a Shuar opened more doors that it closed. The people trusted Juan, and with Amalia at the mission the women had someone they could talk to. For the first years, no problems arose in dealing with the Shuar at the mission; but there was no shortage of other challenges among the people themselves, and things began to worsen.

A few white *colonos* lived nearby. From time to time, they made fun of Juan for "wasting his life to work with the Shuar," but they were still his friends and even helped by shooting food for the mission, a service for which Guinassi paid them.

After Juan and Amalia had been married for two years, Amalia's parents, Juan Tuitza and Mercedes Masuink Entsakua, had decided to leave Sucua and move to the quieter life at Yaupi. They settled onto a little farm about a mile from the mission school, which was beginning to grow rapidly as more boys became *internos*. Amalia was delighted, for she loved her parents dearly.

Juan and Amalia had been married a few years when Amalia's father, Juan Tuitza, died. He was a good man who had treated them well. Amalia, as the oldest daughter, felt it was right that her mother, Masuink, should come to live with them. Of course Juan agreed. They built a small house for her at the mission so she could continue to be somewhat independent, and she moved there. Amalia was receiving a pay of about fifty sucres per month (now worth about seventy-five dollars) for her work at the mission, which she shared with her mother. She would live with them for more than four decades and eventually die a violent death, defending herself admirably at more than one hundred years of age. But more of that later.

At the mission, Masuink began to take her part with the daily life, helping Amalia with the work of cleaning and taking care of the children and of feeding everyone. None of them had any vacations at all, and their lives continued well as they worked seven days a week.

CHAPTER TWENTY

THE FIRST
VENDETTA

The mission school also became a place of refuge, a haven of peace, surrounded by a dangerous society. The three missionaries gave help when they could, but they sometimes found themselves embroiled in the inter-family and intra-family feuds of the neighborhood.

One morning in 1950, a Shuar warrior, who had heard of their willingness to help anyone in need, arrived at the mission from the Peruvian frontier. Musiek Ungutcha came to see if Father Guinassi could help him. The septum of his nose and soft palate were covered with running sores. One hand was badly burned. Because he felt no pain in his hands and feet, when he picked up a hot pot from the fire, he didn't realize it was burning him until he smelled the burning flesh. Even on very hot days, large areas of his body did not sweat, so he felt feverish much of the time. It was a classic case of *mushu* (leprosy). Most types of *mushu* can be cured easily, with the right medicines, but Yaupi had no dosages and his case was much advanced. Ungutcha had been told that Father Guinassi had successfully cured others and he implored the Father to help. Father Guinassi was willing to try, but he was unaware that Ungutcha was responsible for killing many people, including several from Yaupi. Two Shuar helpers, Shaque and Ujukma, volunteered to let the poor man stay at their house, and they did what they could to make him comfortable as Father Guinassi began his treatments.

As in any small place, word quickly spread that "Ungutcha, the old warrior," was at the mission. Those who sought revenge became very excited, for this would be their chance to catch him unguarded by his family. In the middle of one very hot afternoon, a single Shuar man from Chapisa arrived after a six-hour walk. Juan saw him, but the man came and went very quickly, without greeting anyone. Shuar often passed through without stopping to visit, so Juan thought nothing of it until later.

That night, Juan learned later, the spy and his friends laid their plans as they gathered for their revenge. A week passed, and no one at the mission suspected a thing.

Late one night, Father Guinassi and Juan sat on *chimbi* stools at a rough-sawn table in Guinassi's house, talking about their plans for the school. A humid, musky scent rose from the vegetation surrounding them and filled the air, made silvery by a full moon shining through clouds and accented by the flashes of lightning bugs. Frogs trilled and croaked their love songs. A single, thumb-sized cockroach scurried across the table in the candlelight. Careless moths, attracted by the flame, fluttered around it until they singed their wings and fell into the wax below. The men heard something that should have warned them but didn't—in the distance there was a sound like a big fruit falling from a tree with a thump, and dogs began to bark. After a few minutes they stopped, and the jungle sounds dominated again.

At about ten o'clock the dogs began to bark frantically in one of the houses, followed by gunshots in the darkness. Juan knew the shots were from the house of Shaque and Ujukma. He leapt up to run to the house, but Father Guinassi held his arm, saying, "No, we will wait. If you go out now you will only be shot by one of the Shuar."

For another ten minutes the dogs barked and people shouted from all directions. One of the *interna* children began to cry in fear for Amalia to come. First the dogs quieted, then the people, but people were now running toward their houses. Father Guinassi, who suspected what was happening, said to Juan, "It is still too soon. Have patience. There is nothing we can do now. Ungutcha is dead, and anyone who appears to be helping him will be killed as well."

In the darkness they could hear people talking loudly from the safety of their houses.

Finally, at about eleven o'clock, Guinassi and Juan ran to the house where a grisly sight awaited. Two bodies lay on the ground. Both of their heads were gone, and blood puddles seeped into the dirt floor. Ungutcha was in the room, easy to identify from the sores on his body. At the doorway, Shaque still clutched his spear. He had tried to protect the sick man and was also killed, as Father Guinassi predicted.

It was the first Shuar murder victim Juan had seen. Staring at the ugliness of the bodies without their heads, he involuntarily put his hand to his own neck as he said a prayer. All his life he had lived with the Shuar and heard of this kind of violence, but the reality stunned him. He realized, truly understood, that these people he worked with daily and whom he loved would have easily and without conscience done the same to him had Father Guinassi not kept him away.

"When the avenger's blood is rising to murder, it is best to remain neutral, and hidden from view," Father Guinassi counseled.

As was the Shuar custom, the attackers had killed the men and cut off their heads to make *tsantsas*, shrunken heads. The murders were terrible, but Juan and Father Guinassi knew that it was only the beginning. Now, as honor required, two families—Shaque's and Ungutcha's—would be on the path of war. Worse, the missionaries and the children at their school would be in the middle of the fighting. Shaque's family listened to Guinassi's words and decided to do nothing for the moment. But the family of Ungutcha was different. He had many

children. Four of them were soldiers at the frontier and went
AWOL to join their family for the return killings.

"I have to stop this," Juan said.

"There is nothing you can do, Juan. You see how they
treat people who become involved in their vendettas."

Juan tells what happened next as he started out the next
day:

Father Givinassi advised against it, but I was young and headstrong.
So I went out toward Chapisa to try and stop the fighting. When I met
a group of seven or eight warriors on the trail, we stopped to talk. They
were carrying guns and spears and were very angry as they pushed and
shouted at me and threatened to kill me. Several in the group were
Ungutcha's sons. They were the most angry, but they realized their
father had been very sick and ready to die anyway. I saw this as a point
to talk about, and as we stood on the narrow trail, I implored them to
stop the killing now. We talked for a very long time, perhaps several
hours. Finally, the oldest son spoke for his brothers, saying, "If you are
able to get back my father's head then I will return to Santiago, and
will not go to Chapisa. But if you cannot, I will go to Chapisa quickly
before they have the *tsantsa* ceremony. I want to have my father's
head back in my hands, to protect his *arutam* spirit." I told the Shuar
that I would do everything I could do to get his father's head back.

And this started the work to return the head to the sons of
Ungutcha. The warriors agreed to return home for a day or two as
I tried to help. Then I continued on to Chapisa. When I walked into the
little community, I was alone and unarmed. The men of the community
had gathered at the house of Chumpi, the chief of the Chapisa
community, who received me very badly. He jumped up from the stool
on which he sat with his gun on his lap. In seconds he had covered the
ground between us, and stood inches from me with his face almost
against mine, shaking his loaded gun and yelling, "What do you want?
Why are you here?"

I tried to remain calm, or at least make my face show calmness,
when I said, "I am here to take the head of Ungutcha back to his
family."

"Why do you want the head of this warrior who has killed so many of our brothers? Do you think you can claim his *arutam*? Do not talk to me about this or I will kill you too!"

As quietly as possible, I answered him: "Chumpi, I came to talk with you. Sit down. I do not come armed. Look, I do not come with anything; only my equipment and a little machete. But you jump up with a rifle. I heard you were a great warrior. Do you threaten unarmed men?"

The two of us were surrounded by other warriors, also shaking their weapons, but I spoke only with Chumpi. After some very long minutes, he began to calm down, and he called to his wife to bring *chicha*, a good sign. We sat for a while in his house, and began the more ritualized visit, which calmed everyone down. Chumpi was a young man, younger than I. He had become the leader in his community because he was a good hunter and a powerful speaker. Sitting on the *chimbi* stool with the rifle across his lap, he drank deeply from the *pilche* bowl of *chicha* that his wife brought then handed it to her, and she began to pass it to the other men and finally to me.

"Chumpi," I began, "you are a great warrior and a man who has the interests of your friends in your thought. But on the way here, I met the war party that was on its way to attack you. While you will certainly kill many of them if they attack, many of you will die as well. Ungutcha was old and ready to die, so his *arutam* was weakening and is not a good *tsantsa*. If you return the head, so it can be put with his body to be buried, his family will forget the whole affair. If not, they will come soon and will avenge the death, taking your heads to make their own *tsantsas*.

After a time I left, but the situation was still tense.

A month passed, and the children of Ungutcha were becoming impatient. Ungutcha had been buried without his head. So I returned to visit Chumpi, this time carrying a small gift. I was received a little more calmly. But it was difficult because the man was very strong and not afraid of the avengers. It was also difficult because all of the people of Chapisa were against me. After some hours of drinking *chicha* and talking, I left, knowing they were considering my request. It was important to their community that they not appear afraid or to have given in too easily. When I returned a month later, we had a third meeting, and as I was about to leave they gave me the dried head of Ungutcha wrapped in a small package of banana leaves.

"We give this head to Ungutcha's family at your request and because we respect you. But be careful to tell them if they return to kill any from this community, we will not tolerate the insult." So I carried the grisly package with me back to Yaupi and then on to Santiago, where I gave it to the family. After several months of tension, the mission returned to normal, but it reminded me that I was working with people who were entirely Shuar and were very primitive."

CHAPTER TWENTY-ONE

WILL THE WARS
NEVER END?

The next year a war party from across the Peruvian border went to Mendez and killed a man named Juatin, making a *tsantsa* from his head. No one could understand why they had murdered the man. The only motive appeared to be the old tensions that existed between Juatin and some other man in Mendez.

This time, the avengers reacted slowly and patiently. A full year passed as they laid their plans, and tensions increased in the communities around Yaupi and at the mission itself. In that time, Juan and Guinassi laid plans of their own. Juan had been successful the first time, and since this family was quieter, perhaps there was a chance to stop further violence. Slowly, Juan worked to gain the trust of the Peruvian Shuar who had done the killing. He sneaked over the border and visited them several times, bringing gifts. At first they were suspicious and unwelcoming, but slowly Juan began to establish a relationship with them. Then one day, on a visit about a year and a half after the murder the Peruvian Shuar's headman brought out a small, well-wrapped package. Inside was the *tsantsa* to be returned to the family. Tensions immediately released when Juan handed Juatin's head to his sons.

A few months later, the people of Yaupi became the target of vendettas, and tactics had to change. A young Shuar named Mangash was shot in the head as he sat by his house near the mission. The killers left immediately, and Mangash's mother ran to Juan's house for help. Moments later, Juan arrived at the house but it was too late, and the young man died in his arms.

So now the family of Mangash organized, and four days later they went to the head of the Yaupi River, where they killed another Shuar. That family retaliated by killing another man from Mangash's family. There had now been three killings in less than two weeks.

Because Mangash and his family were from the mission, the Shuar considered Juan and Amalia to be part of his family, and therefore they were in danger. Before the Shuar anger turned against him and his family, Juan took action. He gathered several young men from Yaupi, and they captured three men from each of the fighting families and brought them under guard to the mission.

"Why are you acting like the military authorities?" they cried angrily.

"Because we are the authorities," Juan said firmly. "But we are not military authorities; we are religious authorities my brothers. What we want," Juan continued, "is to talk. We are better than the military, because we understand you and your anger. We are not going to hurt you, but you must listen."

They freed the men on the agreement that they would return in two days with representatives so they could have a meeting. Never before tried, this tactic could either solve the problem or lead to a deadly day of blood. On the agreed upon day, about fifty Shuar arrived, each band bringing twenty-five well-armed representatives.

The meeting began badly with shouts and threats, then gradually calmed. The women of Yaupi brought large pots of *chicha* and began to pass it to the men, serving their own men first as proof it was not poisoned. The men began to relax, but no one smiled, and they held their weapons at the ready in case there should be a surprise attack.

Father Guinassi welcomed them and expressed his interest

in helping. "We are not involved in your fight but are concerned that your fighting will hurt the people here at the mission, and the children we are protecting—your children."

Juan rose to speak. "We are here to help, not to take sides." He spoke as a missionary, saying, "What are your children going to learn if all they know is fighting?" After two hours in which the two men alternated talking, they could see that the hearts of the warriors were opening. Finally, Juan asked, "Can we make this work without violence?"

The men looked at the two white men for a very long time, then one Shuar said, "Yes, I can." Another nodded his assent, and another, until all had agreed. In jubilation, Father Guinassi asked the women to prepare a meal. After a good meal and more buckets of *chicha*, the party broke up and the latest war ended with only a skirmish of words. Beginning that day, tensions among the Shuar community began to ease, and several years passed before the peace was again broken.

So the ten years in Yaupi were difficult but rewarding. Father Guinassi, Juan and Amalia worked feverishly, happy to see that attendance at Mass had increased and that the people seemed to be applying their religion to their lives. Each year Father Guinassi would perform weddings for people of all ages, even couples with children. Always, the people for whom he would perform the weddings were emotional. The three missionaries never ceased to be amazed as they watched the transformation of the Shuar people of Yaupi from warriors to peaceful people. No husbands or brothers died by war or murder, and the women smiled and sang each day.

CHAPTER TWENTY-TWO

PRIESTS, SOLDIERS
AND SLAVES

In 1954 Monsignor Coman Obispo, who was in charge of Mendez at the time, organized a trip to the north as far as Morona. One of his goals was to visit the Shuar warrior Chumpi and the Shuar of Chapiza, and because Juan had made a good impression on Chumpi he was asked to go. Although Father Peter, also one of the participants, continued to harbor ill feelings toward Juan, he grudgingly agreed that Juan could be a help to them. Father Guinassi and Amalia would be left alone to their work until Juan returned, but both of them were excited for the young man to have the additional experience of meeting more of the Shuar.

In the early morning Amalia and Father Guinassi waved as the eight men taking the journey, including the two priests, Juan and five helpers, walked into the misty morning forest. By midafternoon they had walked only one-third of the way to Morona and arrived at the Chapiza River, where a relaxed Chumpi greeted Juan warmly and welcomed the others. He went with them to Wee, where a salt spring flowed. As they rested and bought salt from two men who were boiling the spring water, the travelers and Chumpi talked about life in the jungle, the church and improving the lives of the Shuar. Although the two priests would normally have been more exalted than Juan, Chumpi recalled Juan's bravery and spoke mainly to him. Father Peter did not speak to Juan, diverting his eyes whenever Juan looked at him or spoke to him.

They returned to the house of Chumpi where he removed sections of the split bamboo wall between the men's and women's portion of his house and laid them on the floor as sleeping pallets for his guests. On the third morning they continued their walk, now with precious salt as a gift for the people downstream.

Toward sunset they arrived at a small military post where six young soldiers nervously greeted them. Juan saw their tenseness and wondered, was it the presence of priests, or something else?

Later that night, over a thin military stew, the soldiers began to open up, explaining their plight. "We have been here for almost a year now," one of the soldiers said. "The *commandante* left us here with ammunition but very few supplies. We have had to buy food from the Shuar in the area and we occasionally kill a larger animal. Just to survive has been very difficult and each day we must patrol the jungle for an enemy that is not there. None of us know when we will be relieved of our duties, and sometimes we think we have been forgotten. But we continue to do our job for the glory of Ecuador. Now you have come when we have nothing left and this meal is, in fact, almost the last of our food."

After a hurried breakfast the next morning Father Obispo gave the soldiers a few cans of food, thanked them for their hospitality and blessed them. It would take another ten hard hours of walking to the present site of Miasal and the Mangosiza River, so they wanted to get an early start. After blessing each of the soldiers Monsignor Obispo promised to report their problem to the authorities.

They started the fourth day of their walk, but as Juan looked back he saw a plant move slightly and caught a glimpse of a pair of frightened female eyes.

Near six that evening, as the sun neared the horizon, the exhausted men came to the Mangosiza River. They had traversed two steep mountains, following a faint trail or chopping their way through dense forest. Laughing, they removed their sweaty clothes and waded from the rock-strewn beach into the water to bathe and cool themselves. As they splashed and laughed they were surprised to hear voices shouting in Spanish just before eight soldiers ran onto the beach brandishing guns. The soldiers lowered their weapons in relief when they found the priests instead of a marauding Peruvian platoon. But they looked at each other nervously then stared at the ground when the Monsignor requested that his entourage be permitted to spend the night at the army post.

"We have no food to share," said the sergeant, "and we cannot provide you with a house for sleeping out of the rain."

Finally, after much coaxing the soldiers agreed but offered only protection, not shelter. As they walked to the post in the gathering darkness Juan felt ill at ease, just as he sensed the night before when the mysterious female eyes watched from the foliage. He signaled for the sergeant to hang back with him and said, "My friend, I am Juan Arcos, a missionary who is traveling with these priests and I feel that there is something wrong. I am not a priest but perhaps I can help you."

"Perhaps you can." the sergeant whispered. "The post is full because we have a number of women who are with us. They are not our wives but Shuar women that we have encouraged to join us and to work for us."

At hearing the word "encouraged," Juan paused on the path and stared at the man. "Are you telling me that you have captured these women and that they are your slaves?" Juan whispered.

The sergeant hesitated and his face became red as he looked down and said quietly, "Yes, we have four women that we have captured and that we can use to meet our needs for sex and companionship. I am afraid that your priests will report this to our commandant and we will be punished. We know it is wrong but we are afraid to let the women return to their homes because then the Shuar may kill us once the women are free."

"I think that what you have done is wrong," Juan said, "but the priests, too, are human and realize how hard it must be for you to be alone out here for so long. Perhaps they can give counsel that will help you."

"Perhaps you are right," he said. Then, raising his voice he spoke to the Monsignor. "Monsignor, I have been thinking and we will be glad to have you and your friends stay with us at the post. You can have our quarters and we will move to the smaller place for the time that you stay."

At the post, which lay alongside a little jungle river, a Shuar named Katani was passing by. In the bottom of his *canoa* was a huge *bagre* (catfish) that weighed between thirty and forty kilos (seventy-five to ninety pounds). Katani was delighted when he found that Juan spoke Shuar and he had questions about everyone. Katani recognized the names of Monsignor Obispo and Juan, having heard of them in his travels. Then recognition dawned and as he turned to Juan he asked with wide eyes, "Are you the famous Juan Arcos, who stood up to Chumpi and his family two years ago?"

Juan smiled faintly and admitted that he was indeed that man.

"I have heard how you work for my brother Shuar in Yaupi. How can I help you?" Katani asked.

"We need meat. Can you sell us some of your fish?"

"No, but I want to give it to you as a gift for you and your friends."

"And for the soldiers . . . ?" Juan asked.

"Yes, even for the soldiers if you wish," he added, but his smile faded.

At the fort Juan asked the sergeant for permission to use the kitchen to prepare dinner. The man's eyes lit with pleasure and hunger as he ordered his men to help prepare the food, cutting the huge fish into pieces and preparing it with yuca, plantain, papachina and some of the garlic clove Juan always carried. There was laughter and relaxation as the men joined in the meal.

Later in the evening the sergeant felt more relaxed and began to recount his adventures and misadventures in the selva.

"Padre," he began hesitantly, "we humans have many defects in our lives and I must confess to you one of ours. We have here four women in our power. We have kept them well dressed and fed and they have taken care of our physical needs. I know this is wrong but we have been here alone in the jungle for five months, and as you know life here is very hard and lonely. We need women to make it bearable."

Obispo's eyes glinted as they widened in the firelight. "You have you taken them from their families without permission? How could you do this? The Shuar have done nothing against you and in fact continue to feed you. They have shown you nothing but respect and this is how you repay them? This is not good sergeant. If you love and respect these women you should marry them. If not you should return them to their families before the families come and do you harm. You say you are human. That is well but you have deprived them of their families and of the right to marry. Perhaps the Peruvians are not what you should fear. Perhaps you should fear the families of the women you stole. Please, listen to my counsel and return the women."

The sergeant was silent. The specter of loneliness hovering around him was even more fearful than the possibility of attack by the Shuar. Without saying anything further he bowed slightly to the priest and left the room. Father Obispo and Father Peter looked at each other and shook their heads slightly.

Three days later, as the priests and Juan finished their breakfast of coffee and fish stew, the soldiers arrived and requested that they follow them to a small house where the women being held had been warned to be silent. The sergeant said to Juan, "Please, you can speak their language. Tell them that they are free to go. We have prepared a few gifts for them, and they may return to their people. Please apologize to them. If they want to stay we will marry them, but if they wish to return to their families we will not stop them."

Accepting the gifts and thanking Juan for his explanation to them, the women left without speaking to or looking at their captors.

Juan suggested that the priests should remain in the area for a few days more, to be certain all was well. Besides, he had not yet found any men with *canoas* who would take them downriver and return with them later. Juan had learned that Katani lived a mile away and across the river, so Juan and one of the Shuar from the expedition walked down the beach. When they saw his house they stood at the edge of the river and called "tuuhey." In minutes Katani came to the riverside, waved, climbed into his *canoa* and poled across to Juan. No, he couldn't go with them but took them to see Shakay, whose son-in-law, Domingo Chumpi, would be glad to help. It was to be the beginning of a very long friendship as Domingo built a large balsa raft and accompanied them downstream. The party started to Morona as the soldiers waved them on their journey. Only the two priests, Juan and Domingo Chumpi continued downriver. The five other Shuar from Yaupi remained behind to visit and to make trading alliances with the people near the fort.

Balsa rafts, made without nails from the soft and light wood of the balsa trees, are held together with lianas and sharpened hardwood stakes. The men sat on thin poles, holding aloft their shoes, for the water sloshed around their feet. Although the Spartan pole seats were very uncomfortable, this kind of travel was appealing after days of walking, especially to Juan, who had become more interested than ever in observing the jungle. For long stretches the river flowed smooth and glistening, reflecting the forest and birds flying over it. Domingo stood in the back, and poled while Juan perched on the front of the raft helping him avoid rocks while simultaneously enjoying the changing scene. When an Amazon kingfisher dove from a draping liana into the river and came up with a fish, Juan smiled. He wanted to cheer but knew Father Peter wouldn't approve. At rapids the passengers either held tightly to their seats or—if the rapids were large—Domingo beached the raft and the priests walked around the whitewater while Juan and Domingo rode the raft through, laughing and cheering despite what Father Peter might think.

They camped along the river that night and the next afternoon reached Morona, where Tiwiram, a powerful-looking Shuar man, welcomed them and invited them to stay at his house and farm. It overlooked the Mangosiza where a big eddy created a whirlpool that Tiwiram told them had years before drowned another priest, Father Angel Rubi, and his Shuar guide

After dinner, Tiwiram told the travelers through Juan that strange things had happened since then. Each morning footprints appeared, coming from the river and going in the direction of the jungle. In the afternoon the footprints returned to the river. No one ever saw who made the footprints and even in 2003 the footprints continue to appear from time to time.

The next morning they loaded the new raft and thanked Tiwiram for his hospitality. Father Peter offered prayers for the lost priest and they continued on their way, pushing the balsa raft into the river well below the whirlpool.

Continuing downriver they arrived at the home of Chau, a retired military drummer who had a large boat he used to ferry people across the river. Chau was a happy man, kind to everyone, and often tipsy with aged *chicha*, which he was glad to share. It had been years since he had seen a priest, and he welcomed the chance to confess. He offered his house but said, "You must go to the fort and help the soldiers there. They have little food, and one of the soldiers told me that in desperation he had gone to the Peruvian fort just downriver and asked them for food. Although they are enemies, the Peruvians gave him a little but did not have much themselves."

Juan wondered what surprises this fort might harbor. It lay then as it does now, upstream of the junction of the Mangosiza and the Morona, on a little bluff overlooking the Kankaim River. Every few years the fort must be moved farther inland as the combined forces of the Kankaim and the Morona eat away at the cliff on which the fort perches.

At each fort they had visited the soldiers seemed bereft of hope. Here it was the same. The soldiers, six young men ranging in age from eighteen to twenty, were listless and hungry, some thin to the point of emaciation. A deep sadness seemed to permeate the entire army post. Juan and Domingo were astounded for they knew that the forest was filled with food. There was no reason for this suffering. So, with Father Obispo's permission, Juan and Domingo went to gather food while the priests prepared something from their stores. Domingo shot two *guans*, beautiful and tasty black pheasant-like birds the size of small turkeys, and Juan cut an armload of palm shoots to prepare as *palmito*. They found a little pool with a dozen trapped fish that Domingo speared and Juan cleaned as fast as they could pull them from the water.

Soon, the churchmen and soldiers sat down to a fine meal that the hungry soldiers devoured as if it were the first they had eaten in months. Juan and Domingo promised to teach the men how to get food for themselves, but as importantly, Father Obispo and Father Peter wrote a letter they agreed to carry to the commandant (with perhaps a copy for the bishop) for they had now seen three military posts, all in serious need of assistance. Although two of the forts may have had captive women, the priests withheld it from the report, for they did not blame the soldiers but sought to help them to escape from the trap that had ensnared them.

Two of the soldiers accompanied them as they continued up the River Mangosiza for several hours, after which the soldiers returned to their fort and the priests continued toward the mission of the Yaupi. Toward nightfall they came to the home of Tomas Pujupat, who had never before seen a priest and was delighted to offer them lodging for the night. He had several wives, who brought chicha and served a special meal of *cuy* (guinea pig). After dinner they spent the evening sharing with Pujupat their vision of God. It was Juan's first meeting with Pujupat—but not his last and certainly the only pleasant one.

The next morning they continued their journey, now into the cordillera of Shaimi. Leaving the river they began the climb into the mountains and were delighted with the abundance of animals—for they saw dozens of bird species in the treetops, tapirs, armadillos and peccaries crashing off into the forest. Juan had a rifle and one of the others a shotgun, so they had no trouble obtaining food, which they prepared with aromatic mushrooms gathered during their walk. That night they slept in *aaks*. Even the priests took their turns at night guarding. Several days later they reached the top of the mountains and began the descent into the valley where Yaupi lay, reaching it about the middle of the afternoon by which time Amalia had prepared a delicious feast and Father Guinassi waited to listen to all that had happened on their journey.

When the priests returned to the city they wrote letters to the local commandant and soon the soldiers at the three forts were relieved. Juan was delighted when he heard, for this to him represented the best way to be of service to others, offering the hand of assistance to raise their thinking from the base to the spiritual, caring for individuals without criticizing them.

CHAPTER TWENTY-THREE

ARRESTED AS A SPY

In February 1956, a new girl arrived at the school and captured everyone's heart. Because she was beautiful, sweet and helpful to everyone, all who met her thought of her as an angel. Anna Maria Pirish was eleven years of age. At school vacation time she went to one of the *centros* (small communities) with her father, Cunambue, and her mother, Nunguiche. At the *centro* she caught the eye of an older Shuar, Tomas Puhupat, who was forty years of age and already married to two women. He declared to Cunambue that he wanted to marry Anna Maria. Not really wanting her to marry at such an early age and needing to stall, Cunambue said, "I need a few days to think about this offer."

"You think it over. Then in three days I will return to take my new wife with me."

Cunambue and Nunguiche went to see Father Guinassi at the mission, explaining their predicament. When they were finished, Guinassi asked, "You do not want your daughter to marry this man. Is this right?"

"No, he is too old and already has more wives than he can properly take care of," Nunguiche answered, speaking for her husband.

"Then simply tell him he cannot marry your daughter," Guinassi offered.

"Puhupat is a very violent man. If I refuse there could be trouble," Cunambue said.

Guinassi sighed. He could see their peace beginning to

fade. But fast action was needed. He called Juan to him and explained the situation. Together they agreed on a plan to save the little girl.

"Cunambue and Nunguiche, go home and bring Anna Maria back to the school," Guinassi instructed. "If Puhupat comes for her, we will not permit it." The parents smiled and breathed deeply with relief, returning with the girl that afternoon.

"Guinassi was in the gardens when Puhupat came to the mission and demanded the girl from Juan, who calmly but politely refused. "She is too young to marry and is receiving an education here." Puhupat became angry and threatened Juan, who stood his ground. "She will not leave here," Juan said firmly.

"If that is the way you want it white man, then you will have much trouble."

With that he turned and stamped angrily from the mission.

Unknown to Juan or Father Guinassi, Puhupat had expected their denial and began to act on a deceitful plan. He went directly to the army post downriver and reported to the officer in charge. "Sergeant Sepeda, I have information you need to know." Then he began his lie. "Juan Arcos pretends to be a missionary but he is actually a spy for Peru. I have been told that he reports to them each day, using a radio he has hidden at the mission."

The sergeant listened and said, "It's okay, I will handle it." The next day he selected a man who had just arrived at the post, so most of the locals didn't know him. The sergeant assigned him to go to the mission and discover what he could about Juan and a hidden radio.

He was understandably nervous about his assignment and tried to fit in with the visitors to the mission. But the Shuar, who were themselves expert at spying, recognized his task immediately as reconnaissance—only later would they realize he was sent to "spy on the spy." With no training, the soldier was clumsy in his approach, asking questions of everyone who would talk to him. Many eagerly spoke, because they wanted to know what he was trying to accomplish—perhaps he had been sent by another Shuar group to check out their vulnerabilities. He even went to Juan's empty house and slipped in, he thought unknown, to search it.

The spy found no radio or other evidence that Juan might be a spy. Everyone he talked to in the area had only good things to say about the missionary. Still, the not-so-undercover agent felt threatened. If he found nothing, Sergeant Sepeda would think he did not do his job, so he reported that he thought the accusations were true.

Next, the sergeant sent a dispatch to Colonel Toman Naranjo in Limon, reporting that Juan was a spy. The colonel read the letter and angrily sent for Father Luis Carrolo, the head of the Salesian Missions for that area and an old friend of his.

As he read the dispatch, Father Carrolo was incredulous. "I have known Juan Arcos since he was a boy. He is a hard worker for the Church, although he is not a priest, and he is focused on assisting the Shuar. I do not believe he would ever be a spy for Peru."

"The evidence appears otherwise," the colonel said coldly.

Although Carrolo requested the colonel's patience while he investigated, the colonel refused. He was angry that a man would use the job of missionary to hide his true role of spy.

But Colonel Naranjo was also an astute man and sensed that something was wrong. He sent a second squad to bring Pujupat (the man who had accused Juan) and four others whose names he had been given as possible witnesses. The witnesses, who arrived first, were questioned as Naranjo waited for Juan's arrival. All confirmed Pujupat's story.

Carrolo returned to his office and immediately wrote a letter to Father Guinassi, describing the accusations and requesting both that Guinassi investigate and that he watch Juan to be sure he was at the mission when soldiers arrived to apprehend Juan. In charge of the squad of ten sent for Juan would be Sergeant Castillo, who had once been in charge of the fort near Yaupi and who knew Juan and Guinassi. Yet, he put aside his friendships to do his duty as he was instructed.

Meanwhile, carried by special messengers, the letter from Carrolo arrived within two days, before the soldiers had shown up. Father Guinassi sat down at his table to read the letter, for he seldom heard from Carrolo and he always appreciated the good news and information in his supervisor's correspondence. Adjusting his glasses, Guinassi began to read. But the smile quickly faded from his face. When he finished, he let his hand drop to his lap, still holding the letter and staring unseeing at a red-rumped black tanager feeding in a tree by his house as he pondered what to do.

An hour later, Juan returned to the mission, still sweating from his work in the gardens.

Guinassi waved Juan to him. "I have some important news from Father Carrolo."

At first Juan, too, thought it was good news, but he noticed that Father Guinassi was not smiling.

"Juan," Guinassi said, "you are accused of being a spy. They say you have a secret radio hidden here at the mission and that you report each day to the Peruvian soldiers."

His eyes darting right and left, Juan tried to think how someone would ever get an idea like that. "Father," he said finally, "you know that I would never be a traitor to my country. Besides, when would I do it, and how? When the soldiers at the fort use their radio, everyone around the place can hear the conversation, for the radio operator has to shout to be heard."

"True, my friend. But I have been told to search for the radio, and to keep you here. Let us first go to your house and while you talk with Amalia I will go and look. I expect to find nothing, but that is my instruction."

"As you must," Juan said quietly. Then he had an idea. "Do you remember that rather clumsy spy who was here last week? Do you suppose that he reported this to Sergeant Sepeda?"

"An excellent thought, Juan," Guinassi said, brightening. "We must make our own offensive. Have one of the Shuar men come to see me quickly. I will invite the sergeant to a special party here at the mission tomorrow. We will do our own bit of spy work before the soldiers arrive."

The next day, Sergeant Sepeda, scrubbed and shaved, arrived at noon for the special lunch. Amalia had laid out a wonderful meal for Guinassi and the sergeant. The two laughed, discussing their jobs and the various rewards and trials of service to others. Guinassi carefully guided the conversation to those who helped them in their work, the sergeant's soldiers and Guinassi's friends, Amalia and Juan.

"It is important to protect your soldiers isn't it?"

"Of course. I would be nothing without my men."

"I feel the same way about Juan and Amalia, my soldiers for God. It appears my friend that we are united in many ways. Right now, I have a problem and need your help."

The meal had been good and the conversation relaxed and friendly so the sergeant leaned forward earnestly and said, "Of course. How may I be of help?"

"This is very difficult for me to say," Guinassi said diplomatically as he seemed to hesitate. "I have heard that you have been spreading bad rumors about the teacher at the Yaupi mission, Juan Arcos."

Without considering, the sergeant spoke his true feelings when he said, "No, Juan Arcos is a great person, a very hard worker!"

"Fine," said Father Guinassi with a broad grin. "Will you please put that into writing to affirm that you believe that?"

"Certainly," Sepeda agreed.

So Father Guinassi took out his ancient typewriter and asked the sergeant about each of the six or seven accusations that Father Carrolo reported were leveled against Juan. To each the sergeant said, "No, that is false. In fact, I know nothing about the charges. Juan Arcos is an excellent man and certainly not a spy, for I know him well."

He then signed the letter.

The sergeant had no idea that the priest was taking the notes to send to higher officials, to show them that the sergeant had changed his story. Using the same mission-to-mission-only communication, he returned his response to Father Carrolo.

So, with Guinassi's letter still in transit to Father Carrolo, Sergeant Castillo arrived at Yaupi with ten soldiers. Arriving at midday, he went immediately to Father Guinassi's house, where he was greeted somewhat stiffly, for Guinassi knew why he had come.

"I am sorry my friend," Castillo began. "I must take Mr. Arcos to Limon tomorrow. Although my companions do not know Juan and believe he is a spy, I know the truth. But I am I soldier, and must do as I am told."

Juan was called, and sergeant Castillo asked, "Can you get together what you need tonight? I must take you to see colonel Naranjo in Limon. We will leave tomorrow."

Juan saw that it was hopeless to do otherwise, so he promised, "I will prepare."

Father Guinassi offered the community house to bivouac the soldiers, and they quickly set up camp. But from the looks they gave Juan, it was apparent they would sleep little. They believed he was a spy and that he would try to escape despite the word he had given. All were nervous and kept their loaded guns nearby, for only a few weeks before there had been shooting skirmishes with Peruvians.

Before the soldiers arrived, Juan had planned to go hunting the next day, and Amalia had already prepared his gun and cartridges. The humidity of the jungle would dampen the gunpowder no matter how carefully it was stored. So the cartridges had to be carefully dried ahead of time. Before the arrival of the soldiers, as usual, Amalia placed the cartridges in a basket a few meters above the fire in the kitchen, then pushed the logs together so the extra heat would dry the powder. Ordinarily this would not have been a problem, but on this night the wind blew into the house and fanned the fire. It became unusually large. Amalia and Juan were at Guinassi's house, discussing how just two people would care for the mission and children while Juan was gone, when suddenly the powder overheated, and shots rang out in the night. The cartridges went off as if a little war had begun.

The Arcos house was about half a block away from the community house in which the military men bivouacked. As the first shots began, the soldiers thought they were under attack by an enemy. They quickly dispersed into the darkness, leaving their guns behind. Sergeant Castillo stood his ground, but the troops would not rally until the shots ceased. Finally, the soldiers crept back to retrieve their guns then ran to Juan's house. They advanced cautiously into the smoke-filled kitchen only to find that lying on the floor of the kitchen were about forty cartridges. There had been a small war in the kitchen, and the cartridges had been in quite a fight!

Guinassi and the Arcoses apologized for the noise and danger but laughed in relief. The embarrassed soldiers, however, were angry. The next morning Castillo made the official arrest and with Juan under custody led his party back through the jungle. More than once as they hurried along, Juan, walking amid the ten sullen soldiers suddenly felt his feet caught up and fell across a root with a thump. Or he "lost his balance" on a narrow trail and fell a dozen feet into the forest and crashing against trees, as each time a soldier would look at the sergeant, feigning that he was innocent of pushing Juan.

Three days later they arrived at Limon. By this time Juan was filthy from so many falls. His wrists hurt, and his face had several bruises. The sergeant either never saw the soldiers trip or push him; or perhaps he chose not to say anything. Perhaps he also believed Juan was guilty despite what he had told Guinassi.

At Limon, Juan was taken to the mission, for the jail was full. Father Carrolo greeted them and promised to bring Juan to the post as soon as the colonel was ready for him.

Carrolo greeted Juan with a confident smile, "Juan, Juan, what's happening? Come here my son, come. You are very tired. Sit and eat." As food was being prepared, Carrolo poured each of them a glass of wine.

"Have you received a letter from Father Guinassi?" Juan asked.

"No, only the news you were to be brought here."

There was a knock at the door of the office, and another priest announced, "A soldier is here to take Juan Arcos to the colonel, and he insists that he leave now."

Carrolo went along to introduce Juan, and together they sat on hard chairs in an anteroom, waiting and praying. A stern-faced soldier stood nearby as if to warn Juan not to try an escape. An hour later, a voice called from the office. The soldier opened the door and ushered them in.

Colonel Naranjo spoke kindly to Father Carrolo, but to Juan he said, "Stand there and be quiet." Then the soldier left the room and stood outside by the door, which he had left ajar.

After a few minutes of polite conversation, Naranjo said, "Thank you for bringing Mr. Arcos to me. Now I must speak with him alone." Colonel Naranjo allowed Juan to accompany Carrolo to the door then return to the front of the desk where he stood without speaking. The room was bare except for the desk, a chair for the colonel, and a calendar with a picture of a snow-covered Swiss mountainside. Minutes passed as colonel Naranjo ignored him, continuing to write and shuffle papers. Juan studied the colonel, a tall and broad man with a black, drooping moustache that made his unsmiling face even more foreboding. Naranjo studied Juan too, peering at him periodically as he pretended to be busy with the papers. Ten minutes passed in silence, then fifteen. Finally, Naranjo looked up and said with a sneer in his voice, "So this is the famous Juan Arcos."

Then the questions began, about the mission and Juan's personal history. How had he learned to speak the Shuar language? Why had he chosen to go to Yaupi when he did? What was his work each day? How did he feel about the war with Peru? Where did he have his radio hidden? Why was he supporting Peru in the war against his own country?

Finally, the colonel tried a different tack. Juan describes the change:

> After some time of questioning, the man's face changed. He looked with me with much caring. He called for a chair and asked me to sit down. He said that we must now speak man to man. We talked about the Shuar and about what I did as a missionary. I told him that I spent all my time with my wife and teaching the children at the mission. I was practicing the law of God. He said, "Mr. Arcos, we are speaking man to man. You must have some secret." "No," I repeated. "I do not have any other things. I am always working for my mission, for my work. You do not work against the laws of the military. I do not work against the laws of the mission."

To each of the questions, Juan answered simply but truthfully. "There is no secret radio sir, and I am not a spy for Peru. I am at Yaupi to serve God and the Shuar people. If you ask the people of Yaupi, you will know that these are false accusations. I am too busy at the mission to be concerned with politics except to assist our soldiers when they need religious guidance."

The colonel continued questioning, courteously now, asking many of the same questions several times, obviously hoping to catch Juan in a lie.

Then he sent Juan back to the mission, telling him to return the next day. At the mission Carrolo fed Juan, had his injuries treated again and asked what had happened. Juan told him what he knew but that what might happen next was a mystery.

As Juan again stood before him the next day, Colonel

Naranjo continued his interrogation. Two hours passed, filled with dozens of questions and repeated questions. Gradually the demeanor of the colonel changed. He ordered a chair for the missionary and asked him to sit down. Juan was never sure what he said that had made the difference—perhaps it was his simple and straightforward manner. But suddenly, Naranjo smiled broadly and rose from his chair. "Guard," he called. "Bring some food for this man. He has done nothing wrong."

Just then Carrolo returned with the letter signed by the sergeant. Colonel Naranjo read the letter and became angry that his time had been wasted. Ordering the four Shuar to be brought to him, he offered coffee for Juan and Carrolo, and they talked as they waited.

Juan again:

He [Colonel Naranjo] said he understood that all of my problems and that all of my problems were caused by the Shuar man, Pujupat. He [the colonel] did not like the Shuar, which worked in my favor, because he felt that I was sacrificing myself for the savages and that they were not respecting that sacrifice. My accusers also had come to town and had spent the past day celebrating. Now the colonel asked them to be brought to him and they came eagerly, expecting to be congratulated for their fine and patriotic spirit. When they came into the room I recognized the man Pujupat as the one who wanted to marry little Anna Maria. The colonel did not smile when he asked the other Shuar what they knew of me. Their smiles faded and you could see the fear spreading through their bodies as they pretended that they did not understand what the colonel was saying. They stood there with their heads down because they could not answer. The colonel began to shout and declared that they were all in trouble because they had worked to slander me. They were all slanderers. "We are going to arrange a strong punishment for you," he shouted angrily. "There will be many days in prison."

They all looked at me with sad eyes as I translated. I remembered the Lord's words—to return good for evil—and said to Naranjo,

"Colonel, with your permission, I would like to pardon these men for what they have done."

His eyes widened in surprise but the colonel stood and shook my hand, saying, "Mr. Arcos, I am happy because if it had been me I would not want to pardon these Shuar. You have been suffering because of them. Are you certain I should do this?"

I said "I could never forgive myself if I did not follow that path."

So he let them go. Then he sat back at his desk and wrote a letter to his superiors in which he certified that I was not guilty of the accusations and gave me a copy. "You are free to go and return to your work," he said. Outside the office Pujupat and the others gathered around me to shake my hand and thank me, then scurried away quickly, afraid that I might change my mind.

I went back to the mission, where I told Father Carrolo what had happened. He smiled and congratulated me. He said, "Rest tonight, and tomorrow return to Yaupi."

Father Carrolo ordered Juan's cuts to be cleaned again, for they were festering badly. The next morning he gave Juan a little of his own money, wished him Godspeed and sent him on his way to Yaupi. But the ordeal was not yet over.

Juan found three Shuar men who also were going in the direction of Yaupi and joined them on the three-day trek. They traveled up a trail to the Zamora River, where it began to rain. Then another trail led up the Paute River as it continued to rain. Juan and his friends stopped at a military post. At first the soldiers were unwilling to help, for they still thought he was a spy, but when Juan showed them a copy of the colonel's letter they allowed Juan and his Shuar friends to sleep in one of the houses, finally out of the rain. The next day they departed, again walking in the rain.

For most of the trek it poured. Juan was unprepared and was constantly cold and wet. His untended wounds from the original trek to see the colonel again continued to fester. By the time he arrived in Yaupi, Amalia and Father Guinassi were ecstatic and welcomed him with love. But his head was already throbbing with fever and as he walked he staggered with dizziness. Amalia put him into dry clothes, fed him hot soup and put him to bed, then watched and prayed as Juan slipped in and out of consciousness.

CHAPTER TWENTY-FOUR

AT THE DOOR
OF DEATH

The illness lasted for more than two weeks, as Amalia and Father Guinassi cared for Juan and continued to do his work. He became delirious and called out day and night, speaking gibberish as the fever climbed. They tried to keep him in bed but he wanted to be back at work. Each time he tried to walk, his weakness overcame him and he fell back onto the bed as if drunk.

Juan's Shuar friends thought he had been cursed. Puhumata and Shiika, two powerful shaman friends, came to visit and offer their help. They talked of little things for a while, then Puhumata, the older of the two, said, "Juan, you have been witched by the people of Limon. Let us help you by sucking out the arrows of enchantment. We know you do not like us to use *natema* (a hallucinogenic drink used to contact the spirits for healing) or chants, so we can do it with smoke."

Juan smiled feebly. "My friends, I cannot thank you enough for your care and kindness, but I must refuse. My life is in the hands of God."

Shaking their heads sadly, the two shamans left, promising to return if he changed his mind.

As the third week began, Father Guinassi gave Juan the last of the antibiotics, and prayed again for God to intervene. All this time Juan had eaten little and drunk but small amounts of broth. Each day he became thinner and his skin turned waxy and gray. Then one night the fever rose again and his skin turned red with the heat. Juan prayed silently, "God, if my work is done here, I will go willingly. But if you think I can do your people good, please save me for the sake of my family and for your children, the Shuar."

That night two owls called from each side of the house, an omen that the Shuar believed was very bad. When they began hooting, Amalia became very nervous and watched Juan earnestly, fearing they had come to take his soul away. When they finally flew off, Amalia sighed deeply in relief, then sat down on the bed and caressed Juan, grateful that he still lived.

Juan recalls:

Father Guinassi came into my room early on Sunday and told me that this was the last week that I had, and that I had to get better now or I would not live. I felt very thin and very weak. I still had a fever and was acting crazy. Father Guinassi said that he had confidence that I would end the week without a fever. I smiled and looked at him and said, "Whatever God wants. If he wants to have me work more with the Shuar then I am here." Then he went back to the church because there were many Shuar waiting for Palm Sunday. So, the next day, Monday, he came back and I was the same. I could not eat. Only like a bird. I could only drink.

The next day, it was the same. I told him that I was preparing to meet God. I had a child at this time. His name was Jose Hermundo Arcos. My first child. I told my crying wife—poor woman—"If God wants, I will leave this earth, but you must stay and work with your fellow Shuar." She was very sad and she dropped her head and cried. All those nights I had not slept well, as I had been acting crazy. I was talking in my sleep. After lunch on Wednesday I had a very restorative sleep. I felt that my fever was dropping. My wife thought that I was dying, but when I awoke, I said, "Amalia, get me some food. I am hungry."

When I said this Amalia got very sad because she thought that I was asking her to bring me food to fill my stomach, so that it would have something in it after death. (The Shuar believe that after death, the real soul wanders through the forest and is always hungry, so when a person believes he is dying he tries to eat a lot of food.) She began to cry harder, and I had to repeat what I had said. I told her that I was feeling better and that I was very hungry. I told her that I did not think that I had a fever. So she touched me and it was true. My temperature was normal. She ran to get Father Guinassi. He came also running and I told him that I was feeling better. He said that my suffering had passed with Jesus during Easter week. He told Amalia to prepare some food, but only a little soup that I would eat slowly. "Do not eat a lot because you have not eaten in days," he said. First I ate soup and then I slept and slept. I slept Thursday too, but was hungry whenever I awoke. Each hour Amalia would give me a little soup and a little yuca, or a few oritos, tiny thin-skinned bananas with a slight lemony taste and that were one of my favorites. Finally after a few days more, she brought me a little meat.

Juan's thoughts now turned to giving proper thanks to God, who had healed him. Father Guinassi was leading Mass, and Juan wanted to go to it to let the people know he was beginning to recover. He felt better, but with his face unshaven, his hair awry and his pale-gray skin stretched as if over a skeleton, he looked frightful. Amalia cautioned him, "Juan, you look very bad. People will be afraid and think that you are going to die, perhaps in church."

But he insisted and she helped him wash and put on clean clothes. Then they slowly walked to the little thatch-roofed church. Sad, scared eyes followed them, and two of his Shuar friends came to help support him on the way. In the church, he asked to sit in the front row, where he listened with a smile on his face. Then as Father Guinassi led the Lord's Prayer, Juan bowed his head and quietly thanked God for his deliverance. When it came time to receive communion Amalia helped him to stand, and he took the Communion. From that Sunday on, Juan began to improve, but his sickness did not stop there.

The balsa trees were blooming then, scattering their fluffy seeds to the wind. Amalia gathered a *shigra* full of them and stuffed the soft fibers into a cotton bag to make a bigger pillow, for now Juan could sit up and needed support. His strength slowly returned, but gradually a painful tumor began to swell across his lower back, just above the hips and extending from one side to the other. He could sleep only while lying on his stomach. One morning very early, he felt it break, and in minutes the bed linens were soaked with a horrible yellow pus. Father Guinassi was afraid that the fever would return and made plans to send Juan to Quito for treatment.

Four Shuar volunteered to go with Juan and Amalia to Sucua. The journey took almost a week, because Juan needed help every step of the way. His oozing wound caused special concern, for it might have attracted a *tigre,* but they saw none. At Sucua a missionary airplane took them to Pastaza, and from there another plane flew them to Quito.

Father Guinassi had sent with them a letter to the head of the Salesian Mission, asking the Salesians to give them a place to stay. But the Salesians refused. Amalia used the little money they had to get a small and filthy hotel room. Amalia made Juan comfortable then spent hours cleaning the room. But help was on its way.

A few years earlier, Alonso Rampon had been asked by the Salesians to check on Juan and had spent several weeks at Yaupi to report on how Juan was working out in his role as a missionary. Guinassi, Juan and Rampon often sat together at night talking about the church, Yaupi and the Shuar. When Rampon left after a month, he had a good report to make, and the three men had become friends.

Now living in Quito, Rampon heard of their need and invited them to stay at his house. Rampon suggested a doctor he knew, and they began daily trips to his office. The first day, the white-coated doctor looked at the growth, poked it, sniffed it, felt its temperature and declared it a "soft tumor." Then he lanced it, and for several days yellow pus drained from the growth, soaking the bandages and leaking onto the bed sheets. At the doctor's office each day, the doctor's assistant helped Amalia to clean the wound, but after more than a week it continued to ooze the foul fluid.

The puzzled doctor treated Juan with various medicines, but he continued to lose strength. To keep Juan hydrated, Amalia made a drink from *cania agria* and *mosote* branches, which she gathered from wild areas in the neighborhood. She cut the leaves off and crushed the stems, then put six stems of each into a gallon of water and let it steep overnight. The next morning she put a little honey into a cup and filled it with the liquid, which was now the texture of thin rubber cement. The drink was refreshing and revived Juan for a while, but the pus continued to soak the bandages.

This continued for several weeks. One morning Rampon said, "I have been asking around, and I think you should give up on that doctor. I just met a man from Chile who is a doctor of natural medicines. We talked about your case, and he thought that he could help you." So the next morning, instead of going to the usual doctor, they went to see the Chilean. Juan was very weak so Rampon sent them in his car with his driver.

The Chilean doctor saw them immediately and began a long evaluation. He told Amalia, "You are doing a very good job of cleaning the growth, but now we must make sure he is eating very carefully."

He continued. "Juan should take no alcohol, not even a little. He should not have meat of any kind, not even fish. For a little while he should eat only fruit—papaya, banana, grapefruit, lemon, hearts of palm." The cure, he said, would take a long time, six months or more. With no other hope and no money left, they thanked their friend Rampon and returned to Yaupi. By this time, Juan had been sick for almost six weeks.

Three times each day, Amalia heated towels with very hot water and laid them on Juan's back. After the hot towels, he eased into the Rio Huambiza for a cold bath. When he was again lying on his stomach in the bed, Amalia patted a compress of clay mud around his waist, to help draw out the fever. Strangely, the fever was only at his waist.

But Juan ate as the Chilean doctor had suggested and felt better. From time to time he would be hungry for protein and would eat a little fish, but each time he did, he had a recurrence of the pus flow. After a few setbacks, Juan concluded that the doctor was correct and that fish was an irritant to his system, so he ate only fruit and vegetables.

Then one morning in the seventh month, the pus stopped flowing and the tumor slowly began to shrink. In another month Juan was back at work. The ordeal left an indentation in his back, but there never were other side effects, and no recurrence. All this from one vengeful lie.

CHAPTER TWENTY-FIVE

THE CHALLENGE

It was hard work to encourage the Shuar to become Christians. Many of them were touched by the Holy Spirit, but many also came to church for the wrong reasons. Sometimes, though, the Shuar were hesitant to become men of God because they *did* take the sacrament very seriously. If they were baptized, they would have to do without the help of shamans and even without the advantages of polygamy, which was important in a society where the women outnumbered the men by two to one. Above all, they would have to renounce vendettas; to "turn the other cheek" was unthinkable for a Shuar. Many also refused baptism because they believed that only when they were baptized would the eternal punishments the Christians promised be brought down upon them.

Compared to the Shuar, the whites appeared to have many more material goods, more evidence that God was on the side of the whites. For this reason, many Shuar came to church in an attempt to just get closer to the whites, who possessed those goods. Juan and Guinassi realized this and worked hard to show them that God's way held more than a material benefit.

CHAPTER TWENTY-SIX

DEADLY MEASLES

Every year Father Guinassi left for Cuenca to buy things for the mission. One year he took a young man with him, a sixteen-year-old whom everyone loved for his good humor and intelligence. It would be the first time he had been to the city, and the boy was very excited. While they were in Cuenca, there was an outbreak of measles and he caught the disease. Like most Indians, he had no immunity. While Americans and Europeans had years of contact that gave them innate immunity to the very bad but not fatal children's disease, among the Indians it was different.

For an Indian, death by measles is horrible. The words, *Tu tienes sarampion,* "You have measles," are a pronouncement of their coming death. As with children from the cities the disease begins with a fever, reddish pimples on the skin and sensitivity to light. But for the Shuar it progresses. The fever would climb toward 105 degrees, for the red pimples on the skin were only an outward sign of what was going on inside the body. Soon red sores called Koplik's spots would appear in the mouth then spread to the throat, lungs and eventually the eyes and intestines. Hemorrhaging would follow, and the patient would bleed from the nose, mouth and anus. Even if the patient were in a hospital, their chances to survive were limited.

When Guinassi told them, the parents began shouting and threatened to kill him. Tensions were very high, and Guinassi knew they were serious, so Juan hid him in the jungle. In a few hours, a dozen armed men came to the mission to kill the Father.

Juan tried to calm them, speaking patiently and quietly, but after several hours they were at an impasse. Finally he said, "Father Guinassi did all he could to save the boy, and it was not his fault. If you kill the Father, you will be murderers, and you will die too, for that is what happens to people who kill missionaries."

The father of the dead boy became afraid and said, "Give me something."

"What do you want," asked Juan.

"I want the padre to talk with me."

Juan told him to return the next day, alone, and he could talk with the padre.

As the sun rose, the parents were at Juan's house, and so was Father Guinassi. "Why did you kill my son?" the father asked sadly.

"I did not kill your son; measles did. I took him to a hospital, and we did all we could, but the disease was too strong."

Finally reason won out, and the parents calmed, realizing the truth. Father Guinassi gave them a few gifts, and they went away.

A few months later, measles came to Yaupi from Mendez, and many of the children in the school became ill. The missionaries told the parents, "Stay away from the school, or you will carry the disease home and into the homes around you. If that happens, many will die." Some fearful parents came anyway and took their children home. One morning, on the way to a nearby farm to offer assistance, Amalia found their neighbor dead on the trail. Measles had come to Yaupi with the force of a jungle thunderstorm.

At the mission most of the *internos* stayed, and all but one survived. For three weeks, night after night, the missionaries carried water to the sick students and went to the nearby houses to help, but more than 110 of the people in the area died. Each day two or three more died and were buried in little group graves over which Father Guinassi prayed.

Measles was a problem periodically. One man related how he had gone on a week-long hunting trip with his uncle and aunt. They returned, paddling up the river, and saw vultures circling above their farm and the farm of the man's parents. Everyone was dead. Some bodies were in the river where the sick ones had gone to cool themselves and died. Those bodies were not buried; the three poled across the river and sat in their dugout, looking at the awful scene for an hour or more, then slowly drifted downstream to start their lives over.

Finally the epidemic at Yaupi faded. Life would not be the same, but it continued.

CHAPTER TWENTY-SEVEN

CHANGES AT YAUPI

For almost eight years, Father Guinassi, Juan and Amalia had been able to handle the mission. But with the growth of the mission, the Salesians decided they needed more help and sent Father Peter to help. A month later, Father Juan Sana and Father Salvai arrived. It was ironic because Father Peter had been the one to send Juan to the isolated mission at Yaupi as what to him seemed like punishment for becoming a missionary instead of a priest. Father Peter was still somewhat angry with Juan, especially since he had married a Shuar, and made his life miserable.

Father Sana didn't work out because he fell in love with one of the girls at the school. When it was discovered he left discretely after only two months in Yaupi.

Father Salvai became very tired of the meager food that was always served at the mission. "Can't we at least have something other than fish sometimes?" he asked.

Juan told him, "No, the chickens lay eggs we can eat for many months. If we kill a chicken it gives one meal."

One night Father Salvai went into the chicken yard and killed a chicken. In the morning he brought it to Amalia and asked her to cook it for him. "An animal killed it," he said.

Amalia went to the chicken yard and saw that no predator had been there. In fact, when she looked at the chicken she discovered that its neck had been broken. Father Peter realized the truth, too, but told Amalia to cook it for him. The chicken was dead now, and Salvai was obviously desperate for meat.

Unable to speak with the Shuar, lonely, and always hungry, Father Salvai left too, after only four months.

Before Father Peter's arrival, the mission workers enjoyed mutual support and the belief that they were a family of workers. Now under Peter's leadership, which he shared with Guinassi, tension increased.

Father Peter brought two white girls from Gualaquiza to help Amalia with the girls at the mission. Rather than helping, however, they caused problems. They did not understand the Shuar and tried to bend them to their own white rules. In the conflicts that arose, Juan supported Father Guinassi because, to him, Guinassi was the true head of the mission and because they had worked together successfully for so long.

Father Peter complained that Juan was negative, a bad teacher and not helpful with the children. Guinassi tried to refute him, and soon he and Peter were arguing in public, even in the dining room and before the children. Finally Father Guinassi told Juan, "I cannot work here any longer. I must leave, or I will die from the stress."

One of their recent projects was clearing a small landing strip, and they had only about a thousand feet completed. But Father Guinassi was growing older by the day and so weak that he could not walk out of the jungle—the landing strip was their only option to save him.

The only plane that could land at the short strip was one from the Summer Institute of Linguistics, and when they heard of the need they immediately sent a plane to rescue the priest. Bad weather kept the plane grounded at Yaupi for a day so Juan and Amalia invited the pilot to stay and to eat with them. During that time the pilot delivered to Juan an offer. He had been authorized by the leaders at the Summer Institute to offer Juan a job at Macuma, working with the evangelists. He and his family would be flown there and he could work alongside them, still helping his beloved Shuar. Juan politely refused.

"I appreciate your kindness but I could never leave my religion for all the material riches of the world."

Still, things were not good at the mission, so the offer did plant a seed that there were other options he should investigate.

Dawn arrived with a cloudless sky. Juan and Amalia helped Father Guinassi to the airstrip. Juan was almost in tears as he received a blessing from his old friend. Then he and Amalia watched as the little plane roared down the airstrip and climbed into the sky. Juan had a foreboding that he would never see his friend again. Two weeks later Father Peter told Juan that he had received the news that Guinassi had, indeed, died. Some said it was from a broken heart. As no other man before or since, Guinassi had helped Juan become the man he was. For many months afterward, Juan found himself weeping for the loss of his friend and mentor.

As the tension at Yaupi increased, Juan went to Father Peter's office room. Juan faced his former teacher and said, "I must leave the mission and ask that I be sent to another, because I do not like the way things are working anymore."

Father Peter's face became red and he stood up. Standing only a few inches from Juan's face, he berated him as if he were still one of his students. "Do not say such things," he yelled. "You will go to bed now. And tomorrow you will go to work as usual."

Surprised at the level of Peter's anger, Juan said nothing. The next day he went to work. God would place him where He wanted him.

But the tension and accusations began to affect the Shuar.

A new priest, a little Spaniard named Aparicio, arrived to replace Guinassi. He worked hard, but he hated being in the jungle and started drinking in the middle of the afternoon, so by evening he lay passed out on his bed. The two new white girls resented Juan's attempts to teach them the ways of the Shuar, considering it criticism of the way they worked with the girls. In Aparicio they found a sympathetic listener.

Although he tried to be fair to Juan, he tended toward believing the girls.

Things came to a head when a new student arrived at Yaupi, a fourteen-year-old named Leonella. Amalia tried to make her feel welcome but the white girls who ran the dormitory criticized Leonella and shouted at her in front of the others. She was unhappy and wanted to return home, so she ran away.

By this time, Juan had built a new house for his family a few hundred yards from the school. It was built in the "white style"—square rather than oblong—but with walls of palm, like a Shuar house. He and Amalia had recently moved there to give themselves a little more privacy with their children. They loved its location beside a little lagoon where the frogs sang most nights. Juan had just completed a little birthing house nearby, for Amalia was pregnant again.

The peace of their little home was disturbed early one morning when one of the Shuar girls came running to the house to report Leonella's disappearance. When Juan arrived, Peter and Aparicio were already there and listening to the white girls.

One of the white girls said that she had seen Leonella go into the Arcos house at about 5:30 in the morning, which was a lie. She said to the Fathers, "Go and look inside their house. They are probably making her work for them and abusing her."

A search found nothing, but they continued to claim that Juan and Amalia were hiding Leonella and demanded that the Arcoses return her. Tempers rose, and soon there was shouting.

"I do not know where she is, but I will find out," Juan said.

During the days following her disappearance, animosity hung in the air like a dense fog. The friendly conversation disappeared from mealtime. Everyone continually stared at Juan and whispered to each other.

With a sense of mission Juan quietly began to question others in the area and discovered that Leonella had run to her brother who lived in Juawaimi, a two-hour walk through the jungle. She had to pass by the Arcos home, and that was probably when the white girl had seen her. Juan sent a messenger to Juawaimi to discover if it was true.

Another four days passed, and finally Leonella's brother came to the mission and went to Juan. "Leonella is with me," he said. "She does not like it at the school, so came to be with my family." It was a Saturday, and Juan asked him to go to the school with him and to tell his story. The *internos* were playing and Father Aparicio was supervising, but they stopped as Juan and Leonella's brother arrived.

Juan walked over to Aparicio and said, "I would like to speak with you for a moment."

"What do you want, Juan?" he said harshly.

"All of you believe that I am hiding Leonella at my house. This man is her brother, and she is with him."

"What?" he said. "You mean that the girl is not in your house?"

"1 told you she was not."

"Is this true?" Aparicio asked the brother.

"Yes," he said. "She is unhappy here, because the white girls who are in charge of the dormitory abused her and made her feel very small."

More than Aparicio's expression changed. He said, "Juan, I feel so bad about this. I should have trusted you and believed what you said. Now I find that the women who came to help are really to blame. They are vicious, and we will see that they are punished."

Leonella never returned to Yaupi, but Father Aparicio became a good friend to Juan. Even Father Peter was sufficiently embarrassed that he again became fond of Juan. The turning point came one day when Peter talked to Juan at the end of a long day of classes. He said, "Juan, you do the work of two priests. You teach classes, work as the assistant director, teach classes for marriage. You have the key, because you can speak the language, but more important, you love the people. I was wrong to think you could serve God only as a priest."

Several years later, Father Peter was sent back to Cuenca, and another priest came to replace him. Over dinner the first night, the priest mentioned that the Salesians would like to start a new mission at Santiago, about thirty miles farther into the jungle, toward the Peruvian border. They were looking for someone to start it, but the place was wilder even than Yaupi had been, and more dangerous because of its proximity to the disputed border with Peru. The priest continued to eat and didn't see Juan and Amalia as their eyes met. Juan raised his eyebrows questioningly, and Amalia smiled slightly, giving a barely perceptible nod.

SANTIAGO

CHAPTER TWENTY-EIGHT

FIRST MISSION

Santiago was a new frontier in 1960, peopled by *colonos* and Shuar in an uneasy mix. It lay only nine miles from the disputed border with Peru, which added to the tension. But it was a beautiful place, at the southernmost end of the Cutucu Mountains, where the peaks soared to twenty-three hundred feet. Waterfalls in dozens of dozens cascaded from the rounded peaks, and the water drifted downward in lovely curtains that filled the valleys with mist and thunder. Even in the twenty-first century, to travel through these beautiful mountains one must pay a heavy toll in sweat, for the trails are narrow, slippery and almost vertical. To settle in that region was even more difficult. But the Shuar loved this place, although it was filled with spirits, and it was there that the Andes staged their glorious easternmost finale.

The Salesians had identified an approximate location for the mission. It would lie in the lowlands at the feet of the Cutucus, where the little Cushquoco River met the mountain-born Zamora River. Near the rivers, large flatlands were perfect for gardens, but giant floods washed from the Andes, and special care had to be taken to place the mission where the soil was fertile yet above the floods. At less than six hundred feet in elevation, Santiago was hotter than Yaupi, and malaria was endemic. A missionary would have more than a four-day walk to the nearest town. The Salesians tried to find a priest to volunteer, but no one wanted to live in such a wild and remote place.

For more than a week after their talk with the new priest, Juan and Amalia talked quietly together about establishing the new mission, weighing the advantages and challenges. Most important, they could try their plans to help the Shuar maintain their culture yet learn what they needed to survive in an increasingly white world.

Finally, after almost twelve years in Yaupi, they decided they were ready to start their own mission, and Juan volunteered. Behind closed doors, the Monsignor and his council discussed the proposition. After several days of often-angry debate—for some still did not like Juan—the churchmen decided to let the Arcoses take on Santiago.

Early in 1960, Juan organized a small expedition, aided by several priests from Sucua. Their goal was to go to Santiago, identify the site for the new mission and talk with the local Shuar about their plans. Arriving at Santiago, they were welcomed at the little fort that defended twenty miles of frontier. Immediately, Juan began talking with the soldiers who had been on patrols and the Shuar who had lived in the area for a dozen generations. He already knew many of the Shuar headmen, for they had often visited Yaupi. The talks went well, for the Shuar welcomed the mission; they wanted to have their children educated, because the soldiers and *colonos* called them *Jivaro*. An education would prove they were not savages.

Some weeks passed as Juan tramped the dense jungle until finally he identified and marked the location for the mission. When the priests departed, leaving Juan with a prayer and a final word of encouragement, they said, "Juan, you do the work of four or five of us. You could have seventy or eighty boarding students and have no problems while others barely can take care of twenty." It was a nice compliment, but that was all they gave. There was no money to start the mission and no help to build shelters. As a teacher, he received about fifty sucres (sixty dollars) per month from the Ecuadorian government. Still, he had managed to save a little from this meager amount and now he used it to pay the Shuar who gave him assistance. But mostly, he worked alone or with an occasional priest who came for a week or two to help—and to check up on him.

There were, however, encouragements from old friends. One in particular brought tears to his eyes. It was a little bag of money from Father Shutka, whom he had defended as a young boy more than thirty-eight years earlier.

Amalia and the children stayed in Yaupi as Juan built the new mission. At Santiago, Juan and his helpers lived in large *aaks,* for there were no houses yet. Most jungle rains come without wind, so they huddled under the palm roof with a small fire over which they made their simple meals. When the wind blew the rain under the *aak* the men were cold and wet.

But dry season, summer, was approaching. Juan needed to complete the clearing of the four-acre site he had chosen for the Santiago mission. Often working in the rain, they had to first kill the big trees. Some of them were emergents with diameters of more than eight feet, so they were "girdled," the bark cut away in a circle around the trunk, which cut off the flow of sap. In a few weeks the trees weakened, lost their leaves and died. Epiphytes clinging to the branches retained their greenness, but as the trunks died the trees creaked and popped ominously in the wind. Meanwhile, the men cut all the undergrowth from the garden and piled it aside. Not only was it important to remove the undergrowth, but when it was time to cut the trees down, the men wanted plenty of space to run in case a tree failed to fall where planned.

A month later it was time to fell the big trees. Working with axes, they cut each of the huge trees partway through. In the winds that circled about the clearing, the trees swayed in unison, tied together by hundreds of lianas, some as large as a man's thigh. Then the men went from tree to tree, cutting a little more from each trunk. After a week, Juan said to his friends, "I think they will fall today. Be very careful."

Several hours later, as the men sweated in nearly hundred-degree heat, a crack like a pistol shot exploded from the ceiba tree Juan was chopping. It listed slightly, tugging at other trees tied to it. Others joined Juan, chopping in unison as they worked to be sure it fell completely and would not be a "mankiller," falling suddenly and unexpectedly. Gradually it leaned more and more until it began to fall, twisting as the lianas tried to hold it upright. The men dropped their tools and scrambled to safety as the ceiba and four of the other giants crashed about them, startling a family of spider monkeys that had been eating figs in the nearby forest. The men cheered their success as the monkeys scolded and threw leaves and sticks down on them.

A ceiba tree has straight-grained wood and is ideal for making the planks on a roof, or hewing into dugout paddles from the thinner parts of the tapering roots. Not wanting to lose this bounty, the Shuar spent the rest of the day cutting paddle blanks they would use later.

Early the next morning, Juan went to the garden early to pray and to study the ceiba as it lay on the ground. The prostrate tree created a round, straight, eight-foot-high wall, and the first branches began a hundred feet along the wall, toward what had been the top of the tree. Bromeliads and epiphytes, which had been growing in the main crotch and on the branches of the fallen trees, lay scattered over the ground in bright orange-and red-flowered heaps. One epiphyte lay upright on the ground, still collecting rainwater. Juan peered inside. Certain types of frogs lay eggs high in trees, amid the leaves of the water-filled epiphytes. Each day they climb to the nursery and care for their young. Juan found a single baby frog in the plant but, sadly, no sign of an attending parent.

That same week the rains stopped, and the new clearing baked. In days, the drying trees and debris began to smell like smoldering grass. Even so, the forest tried to recover. Little trees already poked upward through the litter, stretching for the sunlight.

One calm morning they set fire to the slashed area. For

two days a thick column of smoke and flame rose into the air, killing the seedlings and devouring the debris. Even the trunks of the fallen giants caught flame and continued to smolder for weeks.

Then it was time to plant. The local Shuar brought gifts—cuttings of yuca and banana, which Juan planted thickly in the ash and among the fallen trunks. Soon after, he eagerly returned to Yaupi, for he missed his family. There were four children now—Pepe (eight), Esther (six), Carlos (four), and Domingo (two)—and they nearly smothered him with their hugs as he walked into the mission after such a long time away from home.

A few months later, in October, Juan returned to Santiago to weed the garden and build a schoolhouse. He used this visit to consider a location for their own house. Wisely, he decided to wait before constructing their home, for Amalia would have her own ideas of what and where it should be. But he did select a site he thought she would like, with a grand view for Amalia, and where the cool wind swept most of the mosquitoes away. He and his helpers built a big schoolhouse twenty-six meters long and ten meters wide, which would serve as both school and a dormitory.

While Juan was preparing the schoolhouse and clearing the gardens, Amalia was planning the move. Amalia's mother, now in her mid seventies, had decided to go with them. She was not at all concerned with the twenty-mile walk, but rather the happy challenge of moving two households. The two women spent their days gathering palm fibers and their nights weaving them into burden baskets. They made extra-large *shigras* for carrying clothing and kitchen supplies. Each day Amalia combed the garden for seeds. She collected them into small leaf packets and tied them with liana vines, then laid them in a little palm box that she wove with two waterproof layers of leaves inside.

Amalia had planned well, and the final preparations were ready a few days after Juan's return. About fifteen people would help with the move, including the four children. Pepe, the oldest, would carry half an adult's load. Esther and Carlos were younger and carried what they could on the two-day walk. No one could carry the children if they tired, not even little Domingo, so the trip would be slow, but Amalia was determined that it would be fun for the children. In her usual good spirits, Amalia kept the little ones amused. Even forty years later they would recall the trip with pleasure.

Half a dozen armed men traveled with the little group to protect the women and children at night. So many people moving through the jungle would make the *tigres* nervous, they hoped, and in fact the big cats did stay away. Even so, the children slept between two adults, and two guards sat by a large fire throughout the night.

As they had no house at Santiago yet, Iticha welcomed them to his. He was known to have been a fierce warrior when he was a young man. But he turned to Christianity, and his natural, friendly personality bubbled to the surface. Iticha was their host for a week while Juan built the home, which Amalia designed following the traditional Shuar style (see appendix, page 366).

On the day following their arrival, twenty Shuar men arrived to help clear the house site, for Amalia had approved it joyfully. "Juan," she said, "This is such a beautiful place; God has given us a wonderful assignment, and I know we will be happy here." As she walked around the thicket that would become an opening, she extolled its view, the wonderful breeze and the soil, which would drain quickly. Juan smiled to know that he understood at least one part of his wife's needs.

As four of the men began swinging their machetes, cutting the undergrowth, others headed to the forest to cut palms that would be the main supports. This time, the house would be in the Shuar style—oval rather than rectangular—for Amalia felt that it would be better for greeting Shuar visitors than a "white style" house. In addition, their Shuar helpers could construct it quickly, for they knew the Shuar methods. They also knew which trees would be strong enough to carry the weight of a large building and durable enough so termites would not destroy it in a few years. They would build a rectangular house later.

The excitement among the Shuar—that there would be teachers and a school for their children—was almost palpable, so they worked with little rest as Amalia and their women brought refreshment in the form of pots full of *chicha*. Cicadas trilled around them with the sound of a distant buzz saw, but the men had only machetes and axes. Occasionally, one of the men would begin to sing a rhythmic three-or four-note cadence, and others would join in, laughing. Some of the men stayed only a day or two, for they had their own farms to tend, but others continually joined in the work, and the simple house was completed in a week.

Once the children were settled and the women began planting the seeds Amalia brought, Juan made plans to go to town. They were short on medical supplies, and they needed several tools to complete the second school building. He also needed to make a report to the Salesian Mission, informing them that he was almost ready to open the school, and requesting certain aid. The success of the mission seemed assured, for already twenty-six Shuar students were enrolled. More were expected.

Classes would begin as soon as he returned, but because of the high enrollment, they didn't wait to build classrooms. Juan found two educated local *colonos*, who came each morning to assist in teaching Juan's classes. Despite the white teachers' presence and Juan's offer, none of the *colonos* in the area enrolled their children.

Classrooms in the 1960s are almost identical to those in 2000. Though Juan's were square, he built his like a Shuar house. To better accommodate the benches, he built floors of springy, split palm. Later, when sawn timber became available, Juan installed that, as it required less maintenance. The walls were split bamboo for the first four feet, with the upper half open to the jungle breezes. Amalia, always attentive to the feelings of the students, suggested they use the split bamboo to make decorative patterns across the opening. Finally, as each classroom was completed, she painted the upper latticework with bright red achiote paste and yellow clay.

Juan:

> I liked the traditional palm thatch roofs on the cabins. We could get them free in the forest. We preferred using the *turuji* palm, which has a Y-shaped leaf with a long stem that is ideal for tying the thatch to the roof. But *toquilla* palm, the same kind used to make straw hats for cowboys in the U.S., works well also. Thatch is picturesque, but the main advantage of palm roofs is the way they absorb sound. When the rainy season begins, it pours, often several inches an hour, for several hours every day. The sound of a tropical rainstorm is awesome. You can hear it coming toward you, moving as fast as a man can run through the jungle. If you turn on a radio and dial it between stations with the volume on low, then gradually turn it up, you have an idea of the sound a thunderstorm makes as it comes toward you.

> Leaves on many forest trees are more than four feet long, and the thundering of billions of raindrops on billions of leaves is deafening. When the rain begins, a class can continue under a traditional roof, because the palm softens the sound. On the other hand, a metal roof is noisy. Once I was in a schoolroom when it began to rain. One of the boys picked up a wooden flute and began to play. He was only fifteen feet away but I could barely hear the flute; it was as if played from a great distance.

> So I liked the traditional thatch, but there was a problem. The thatch over a Shuar house can last for six or seven years, or more; in a classroom, only two or three.

The reason thatch is longer-lived in a house is that the women always keep cooking fires burning. Smoke drifts around the upper parts of the house and gradually seeps through the thatch or out the ends, which are usually left open. In a year or two, a thin layer of dark, shiny, varnish-like material collects on the inner roof, and the smoke kills any insects or insect eggs that might be hidden in the thatch. Even a small roof takes many thousands of *toguilla, turuji* or other palm leaves. To repair the roofs, they had to go farther and farther from the mission for materials. It was very time-consuming, so eventually all of the schoolhouses had noisy metal roofs.

Children sat at wooden benches, three or four to a bench, with a rough table in front of each bench. The two white helpers left, so Juan became the only teacher, instructing fifteen students at a time. After a lesson the first class would go out to play or study, as a second class came in. A class might have children who are age eight to fifteen or older, depending on the knowledge of the child. Many children did not come to school until they were in their middle teens. Today, most mission classrooms have a simple blackboard, but at Santiago in 1960, the children were taught by rote, repeating and drilling continually. Then as now, the textbooks were few, but the children did not move about the classroom and were disciplined to pay attention, so they learned quickly.

CHAPTER TWENTY-NINE

MISSION LIFE

Juan:

The first month of the mission was really an "invasion" of Shuar and soldiers who would visit every day because they were so happy that we were there. For a month there was much help, and we were supported very well. I was happier than anyone and was always working from 6:00 with my machete in hand, working, working. And while this was happening, there were always Shuar women who would bring chicha. It tastes very good when you are working because while in the heat you do not want to eat, but you are very thirsty. So while you are working, the chicha serves as a drink as well as a food. Every hour or two we would sit and drink chicha. By this time Pepe and Esther were big helpers around the mission and with their young brothers.

The mission family, which included all my family and the students, worked very hard to enlarge the gardens to plant yuca, platano and corn. We had to be very careful, especially as the rainy season began, because then the snakes moved around, watching for places to be dry, and they were angry. In the gardens the children were warned to be aware, and to kill any snake they saw.

This was important because, as the rains began, there were many aggressive little *muash* snakes in the area, and Juan always worried about them a little. Despite their size (only about two feet long), they are very poisonous. They are also aggressive and will sometimes even chase a person for short distances. When someone suffers a *muash* bite, within five minutes they begin to bleed from the gums, nose and mouth. Death comes rapidly.

Many of the Shuar wore thin bracelets cut from the skin of an iguana. If a snake bites a Shuar, they cut off the bracelet and begin to chew the iguana skin as an antidote. More than one Shuar claims to have been saved by their iguana jewelry.

The rainy season is particularly dangerous because the cold and wet snakes move about aggressively, seeking warm and dry places. Shuar houses normally sit in a clearing, and each day the woman removes grass and weeds, for the snakes do not like to cross over hot, open ground. But each year the community learned of five or six deaths from the snakes. It is no wonder that the Shuar consider every snake poisonous.

The wife at a nearby farm was weeding her garden one cool morning, and a snake struck her in the face as she leaned over. She called for help as she hacked the snake to pieces with her machete, but by the time her husband arrived she was dead. Believing that other snakes might become emboldened and begin to attack them, the family gathered friends for a "snake dance." It had to be done quickly, to warn the other snakes that the Shuar are a dangerous people and should not be bitten, or the snakes might bite others. The family gathered a large number of land crabs and tied pieces of chicken and other bird meat to their backs. At the end of the ceremony they chanted warnings to the snakes, "See these crabs? They are carrying pieces of snake meat, for the Shuar eat snake. Do not attack us for we are a dangerous people." That year there were no more deaths from snakebite.

By the end of the first year, almost thirty boarding students had come to the school to be educated. The gardens grew rapidly, but still were unable to produce enough to feed everyone. Many children lived on the other side of the Santiago River and were poled across in dugouts—jungle school buses. Juan arranged for several parents to take turns collecting food from the neighborhood. Every few days one of them would pole his dugout up one side of the river, stopping for donations at the various farms, then cross the river and collect more from the farms on the other side. They brought platano, yuca and fish. In return Juan would thank them and would give them gifts, for he had no money. He continued to receive his fifty sucres each month from the government, but still nothing arrived from the Salesian Mission for which he was establishing the school.

Getting enough protein for the mission family remained their most serious problem, so Juan installed palm fence dams at the mouths of the little streams, where they flowed into the rivers. During the rainy season, the Zamora and Cushquoco rivers overflowed their banks, and even the small streams became large. Fish of all kinds and sizes began to explore the flooded areas. Most looked for fruit, either on the submerged trees or fallen from the canopy above. Sometimes Juan and the boys went fishing with lines and hooks, catching piranha, *kanka, boca chica* (bottom-feeding fish with puckered-looking lips), fat-bodied, twenty-five inch *parumit,* huge-finned little *yutui,* or eel-like *wancha,* almost seventy inches long. When the waters dropped, Juan closed the gates on the palm fences. Little fish escaped to the river through the gate bars, but larger fish were trapped to feed the school children later.

In low-flowing streams, or in shrinking pools where fish were trapped, they used the famous *barbasco* fish poison, made from the sap of the *barbasco* bush. Most often they used it in the pools, but it could also be used in the lowering rivers. If on the river, for instance, Juan and the boys would build a little rock dam arching into the stream. To make it more waterproof and hold back more of the river they stuffed openings with leaves until no more water poured through. As they created the dam, others crushed the *barbasco* and laid it into a *shigra.* The shredded branches and roots oozed a pale, milky liquid as the net bag dragged through the water. Rotenone in the milky liquid paralyzed the breathing mechanisms of the fish. In minutes, fish of all sizes floated to the surface, and everyone eagerly waded in to collect them. Most of the fish struggled weakly and were quickly dispatched, either with a head tap on a rock or by a bite on their head. After gathering the floaters, the boys began to feel under rocks and pulled out dozens more. Sometimes a hundred-foot-long stretch of river would yield twenty-five or more pounds of fish in a dozen varieties and in sizes from three inches to more than a foot.

In those days Amalia had few metal cooking utensils, so she often used the old methods. Sheaves of fresh banana leaves were gathered from the garden. Then Amalia and a helper would cut a leaf and lay on it a fish, or cut-up portions of a fish. She would carefully roll the leaf around the meat, fold it in the center and tie the ends together with palm fiber, making a tamale-like package for roasting on the coals of the fire or boiling in a clay pot.

Most of their meat was fish, but sometimes a hunter gave them an *agouti* or a *paca*, the rabbit-sized rodents common in the jungle undergrowth, or perhaps a peccary or a tapir. Nothing was wasted, and the animal was eaten in a specific sequence. The cleaned and roasted intestines generally were eaten first, as they spoil quickly. Then the head was split and boiled, and finally the meat, which Amalia served roasted, boiled, broiled or dried.

Sometimes the boys would return from hunts or walks through the forest with river turtles the size of dinner plates. Tortoises were good to eat, too, and sometimes two or three of them would be carried in from a hunt, trussed in lianas so their head and legs were trapped inside the shell. These Amalia put in little pens, and the children would feed table scraps to them each day until she needed meat for the kitchen. Or when the turtles were mating, the boys followed the turtle tracks on the beach sand and returned with *shigras* full of the round, white leathery-shelled eggs.

On rare occasions, they might find a stone in a fish, agouti, chicken or other animal. This stone, called a *nanda,* was precious and caused great excitement if found by a Shuar woman, who carefully cleaned it and placed it into a little bag she wore around her neck and kept close at all times. The stone guarantees that her gardens will flourish, and it will make her a better and more successful hunter when she goes out with her dogs. The *nanda* are valuable because the woman who possesses one knows there will be food for her family. One day not long after the move to Santiago, as she cleaned a very large catfish, Amalia found a *nanda*. She gave thanks to God and carefully placed it in the little leather bag that hung around her neck, where it nestled beside another she had found as a girl.

Not only was Amalia blessed with fertile gardens and ample meat, but she possessed a distinct knack for reaching out to the children at the mission, no matter whether she bore them.

Carlos Arcos, Juan's son, recalled:

Most missions tried to make the children feel good about being at school, but at some runaways were common. This was true especially of the girls, for the nuns, who were white, didn't understand the Shuar and were very hard on them. From the beginning at Santiago, there were few runaways because my parents tried to enter the hearts of the children and created a Shuar atmosphere in their schools. Like most teens, the older students often suffered from acne, which caused them embarrassment, especially the girls. So mother gathered the goose-egg-sized *huevos de burro* (burro's eggs) fruits. They are orange and have a smooth skin that looks very tasty. Pacas and agoutis love them but they are completely inedible for people. Once she had peeled the fruit, mother showed the girls how to grind the pulp with a little water to make a paste that cured pimples. Mother was very perceptive of the children's needs, and if a problem seemed to be developing, she was usually the one who first noticed. Sometimes it was just boredom, then she and father introduced an exciting activity of some sort—hunting, fishing or food-gathering in the forest. It was fun to grow up in the mission with caring parents and so many other friends.

Like his father, Juan wanted the Shuar to feel at home. This was especially important for the children, who were living away from their families. Juan knew the boarding students would be more comfortable if they could sleep on Shuar rather than "white" beds. So they slept military style, in lines of traditional Shuar *tablas de cama*, beds raised above the ground about two feet, and covered with springy split bamboo for more comfort. On cold nights little smoldering fires burned on the soil at the foot of each bed. When they went on food-gathering trips into the jungle, if they passed by a waterfall they paused to reflect. Many of the older students had gone on vision quests to find an *arutam* spirit and revered the spirits who lived by waterfalls. In Juan's little church, someone had drawn a picture to show Christ ascending. It was a Shuar warrior, his arms outstretched and rising before a large waterfall.

Juan:

> Each day we were busy from morning to night and beyond. We were happy to be living in the forest, helping the Shuar, for education would help protect them from the bad things that the world might try to bring to uneducated people.

After morning classes, they worked in the gardens, planting lemon, *yuca*, *platano*, hot peppers and *pelma* and *papachina*, which produced white, round tubers they could prepare like potatoes. Among the seeds Amalia brought from Yaupi were *cumbia* seeds, which delighted Amalia when they grew. The corn-like plant has red pods that grow at its base. As they ripen, the blackening pods are husked to reveal seedy, yellow innards. Juan, she knew, loved it mixed with meat.

Juan divided the children into three groups, roughly by age. The six-to eight-year-olds were called *Domingo Sabio* and assigned the lighter work with machetes and axes. The next older, perhaps nine to twelve, were *Namancura,* who did the heavier work of weeding and removing debris. The oldest were *San Jose,* who bore the greater responsibilities of hunting and fishing. Sometimes the *Domingo Sabio* boys were distracted when they found a *waampi'a* bush. Its hollow stems made excellent miniature blowguns, and soon they would be shooting spears of grass instead of cutting the weeds. Girls of all ages were distracted by the discovery of little black *yusari* seeds in fruit, for they collected them to make shiny beads for necklaces.

Juan had learned from Father Guinassi the importance of keeping the children busy. Some of them missed their families and didn't want to be at the mission, but their parents thought it was a good place for them and insisted they stay. At Santiago, Juan developed his philosophy about caring for many children. He said, "The minds of children, and adults are like water. If the stream is flowing and busily moving along, the mind is happy. If the stream becomes a swamp and moves very little, it fills with insects and frogs and scum. In the same way, if the mind and body are not kept busy they become like that swamp, and the children look for ways to make mischief."

Juan's schedule for a typical day:

5:00 rise
6:30 Mass
7:00 breakfast
7:30–12:00 classes
12:00 lunch
1:00–4:30 work in the gardens, hunt, etc.
4:30 bathe and play
5:30 dinner
6:30 more play and recreation
7:30–8:30 study
8:30 prayers
9:00 bed

At Yaupi Juan began the practice of setting dormitories next to each other, instead of separated at opposite ends of the mission. Amalia and Juan discouraged shows of affection among the children, even among siblings, to teach the importance of having respect for all of the people at the mission. At other missions, where the boys and girls were split up, the separated groups seemed to have more interest in each other, and the problems that go along with that interest. Several years after the Santiago mission was founded a psychologist arrived to check the Arcos's unorthodox methods. Each day he sat and watched, scribbling notes and asking questions. He was pleasant but seemed to be everywhere—visiting the gardens as the children worked, listening in at the classrooms, going with the parties on hunting trips. After two weeks, he agreed that their method was better than those used at other missions. It created a family-like atmosphere where the children respected each other and relieved tensions. Soon, other missions began to use the same method, and their problems decreased.

Inevitably, older students would fall in love and wish to marry. Juan's message to them was clear and caring: "If you love each other, tell me and I'll help you. Don't sneak and hide." He taught them, "If you are doing something hidden now it will return to you later, and you will not respect each other."

Sunday was a special visiting day. Most of the Shuar were not Christians, yet they often walked long distances to church because, as Juan said, "Missionaries were a new thing, and the Shuar felt these strange people needed a good look." The Shuar visitors always brought food—boiled platanos, yuca, fish and chickens for a community meal. After church the families gathered next to the meeting hall with their children and friends for an afternoon of visiting and drinking *chicha*.

Children and parents often sat together quietly, grooming as they talked. Parents and siblings took turns searching through the partner's hair, seeking lice and mites. When they found one, they crushed it with their teeth and threw the dead insect onto the ground. Some missionaries were offended, but it was an important ritual as old as humanity. As important as the removal of the pest was, the activity itself gave reassurance to the partners and solidified relationships. Juan noticed that among the children, especially when there were strangers nearby, it relieved anxiety, almost like nail biting does for an American child.

On a typical Sunday, as the school filled with people, Juan smiled at their happy socializing, for he could see the sense of community building among the Shuar, which formerly had been difficult because the Shuar never lived together in the traditional human sense. Their continual bickering and wars had kept them from developing villages or group living. By "community," Juan meant the people who lived in the area surrounding the mission, perhaps within a radius of two miles or more, with each farm separated from the others by at least a quarter of a mile.

The school was completely full when the first Christmas arrived in Santiago. Juan and Amalia taught the children about Christmas, its meaning and the celebrations. One of the *colonos*, Mr. Ortiz, was a friend by this time and surprised Juan by arranging for a dozen of the soldiers at the nearby fort to arrive on Christmas morning to share their gifts from home— cookies, candies and highland fruits. They stayed to play soccer with the boys. Then they gathered at the little church and sang praises to God.

Juan:

It was a happy time for the children, but it was hard for me because Amalia was very ill, and we did not know what to do.

In the first days of December she began to vomit and became feverish. The military doctor attended to her, but there was no change. He suggested a warm footbath, followed by a cold one, three times a day. Days went on into weeks, and there was no improvement. Several Shuar women brought medicinal plants from the jungle and prepared them for her in various forms, but she continued without improvement.

Christmas Day was one with two faces. There was happiness with the children, but it was very sad in our house. Amalia was thin and languid and her temperature would not drop. She could not eat anything. I prayed to God, saying that I knew that He was sending us a test and that I understood that it was His will, but I asked Him not to take my wife. If He did I would not be able to work at His mission, because she was my right hand. Outside the children were yelling and playing, organizing games. Inside I was struggling and did not know what I should do next.

Two of the older girls volunteered to help Juan care for Amalia, for she did not want to be left alone. She was afraid that she was dying.

The day after Christmas, Juan sent a message north to Yaupi, where a new priest was now in charge. Father Martin had several *madrecitas,* including Sophie Lomena, a trained nurse. She volunteered to go to Santiago. She immediately put Amalia on a vegetarian diet and cared for her. In a week the vomiting stopped, and the fever began to fall.

Amalia continued to improve, and the night before she returned to Yaupi, Juan and Sophie sat in front of his house, leaning against the warm palm branch wall and talking. "Sophie," Juan said, "I cannot tell you how much we appreciate your loving care. If you had not made the dangerous journey here and worked so hard, I am afraid that my dear wife would not be here now."

Sophie was very humble and said, "This was only one of the tests that God gives us. Like we give tests to the children here, God tests us."

Recalling his own test at Yaupi, Juan wondered when they would be found worthy and when the tests would cease.

CHAPTER THIRTY

MELINIA

While Amalia was mending, a woman came to the mission from Limon. Only saying that her name was Melinia, she declared that she wanted to stay and help with the children. Melinia immediately became part of the mission family and was an excellent, hard-working assistant. Like Amalia she had a happy sense of humor, and as Amalia recuperated they often passed hours talking and laughing.

But she told no one about her former life.

Melinia had been at the mission about a month when a man appeared. He was a Shuar warrior who had five wives. One of them was Melinia, who had run away because she wanted to start over. When she refused to return with him, the warrior went to the local sergeant in charge of the nearby military base and complained, "Juan Arcos has stolen my wife."

The sergeant and the warrior went to the mission to ask for the woman's return. In a few minutes the angry warrior again began to shout that Juan had taken his wife, and he threatened to kill him. The boarding students began gathering around the house curiously and Juan signaled them away with a slight smile before he answered the man calmly, "How could I do this? Melinia came of her own free will and is working in the mission."

Juan sent for Melinia, and when she arrived her husband continued to storm and rave incoherently. The commandant slowly began to smile at the man's behavior. Finally, Melinia stormed out of the house saying, "I won't go back to your horrible house with five wives!"

Taking the husband by the shoulders, the sergeant looked at him earnestly and said, "Go home. If you take her with you now she will only run away again. Besides, you still have four other women who seem happy with the situation. She would only stir things up and make your life miserable." The soldiers led the husband away, and he never returned. So Melinia joined the Santiago community and became a strong supporter of the Arcoses. A few months later she remarried, this time to a local man who loved and appreciated only her. The friendship between her and Amalia continued to grow, and they were close friends for many years, even after Amalia moved to start another mission.

After more than two months of illness, Amalia finally returned to help guide the days of the children as they worked in the gardens and kitchens. This was important because she did so much. Juan described her role: "In other missions there were two or three people to do what she was able to accomplish. Part of her success was in teaching the older girls to help. For instance, when the girl students got older, fourteen or fifteen, they would often be put in charge of the younger children and act as *madrecitas*, another way they learned responsibility for others."

Saturdays, in preparation for Monday laundry, Amalia and Melinia made soap and shampoo from the black flower of the *wabaka*. When this was not available they made *secombe* soap from the yuca roots. It was hard work to make the soap, so whenever they could trade or buy it from town, they did. The humid air kept the laundry damp, often for several days, so Amalia and her helpers used old-fashion irons filled with hot coals. The hot iron pressed the clothes and dried them at the same time.

Juan:

Two years after we started the mission at Santiago, the Shuar Federation formed. This was important as the people are very scattered through the selva of Ecuador, Colombia and Peru. The Federation aimed to unite the people and to have representatives meet each year so they could protect their rights against the white-dominated government in Quito.

Then, I met a new friend. Near Santiago, at Yaapi [a village near Yaupi], there was an evangelist who had started to work with the Shuar. His name was Jan Stuk. As always, there was tension between the evangelists and the Catholics, so we had little communication. One day he was passing by the mission, his head down and ignoring us. I saw him and called out a greeting. At first he seemed not to hear, but when I called again, he looked up and waved. I invited him to come to my house to talk and he accepted hesitantly. I gave him some coffee and tried to have a conversation, but he seemed afraid of us. We were about to eat our noon meal, so I invited him to eat. He accepted. I asked him to offer a blessing, which he did. He gave a blessing without crossing himself and this was the blessing, which I have never forgotten: "Thank you God for this special family that has invited us. I didn't think Catholics had a heart."

After dinner Jan said to me, "Juan, you are a very unusual man. Most evangelists think you are the devil, but I see this is wrong."

"Ah, yes," I said. "But we are both human, aren't we?"

This was the beginning of our friendship. We became like brothers and talked often. A few years later Jan was asked to go to Huangos, to start another evangelical mission. I helped Jan to find a guide as it was two days away. We continued to respect each other's religion, even though we didn't quite understand some of the things the other religion did. Many years later, Amalia and I were in Shell and found Jan and his wife. We attended Jan's church for Sunday service, and were surprised that the preacher was talking about sex and the acts of sex. We were open-mouthed with surprise. But, the man also talked about equality of the sexes, which we whole-heartedly believed. After the service, the preacher asked us what we thought, which led to a lively discussion.

We had, in fact, come to Shell that time to attend a conference between evangelists and Catholics because there had been so much strife. At this point in the discussion with the preacher, I said, "We all believe in Christ and in the same good things. If a man believes in God, he is on a good path to heaven no matter what religion he follows. We both work for the same God."

During this time Amalia was pregnant, and on July 16, 1961, Maria Luisa Arcos was born.

Juan:

The night Maria was born reminded me again of the night Pepe had been born as a *tigrillo* (ocelot) attacked the chickens. On this night Amalia was in labor and Melinia was helping her when, from the chicken yard, a student began to yell that a boa was killing the chickens. I ran to help and found it was small anaconda, about eight feet long and with a body the size of my upper legs. It would kill a chicken, lay it aside, and kill another. Already it had killed four. This time I used a palm lance, stabbing it in the mouth as it attacked me. I pinned it to the ground as it curled its body around the lance, thinking it would crush me. It was very powerful, and my shirt became soaked with sweat as I struggled to keep the lance pressed into the ground. Finally, after ten or fifteen minutes of struggle, it died. But, I couldn't leave the bloody carcass lying in the chicken yard, so I picked it up and threw it away into the bushes. As I had when Pepe was born, I washed my hands and again I knew I would be asked whether I had touched the animal, a snake this time . . . but the baby was in perfect health and stayed that way.

CHAPTER THIRTY-ONE

RIVER TRAVEL

Santiago was in a good location about a half-mile downstream from where the short but strong and clear Cushquoco River flowed into the Zamora River and formed the Santiago River. Whenever possible the Shuar used the rivers for efficient transportation, at least going downstream. Balsa rafts were best to use if the load was heavy, for example with big fronds of orange *chonta* fruit. After floating the load downstream they sold the cargo and the raft then walked home. Balsa trees grow very quickly, sometimes reaching forty feet high in only a few years. With simple tools—a machete and a mallet—one man can construct a balsa raft in a little more than a day. Balsas float well, but they are infamously clumsy, and passengers' feet are always wet.

Even so, a downstream trip on a balsa is generally relaxing, and Juan and his friends enjoyed their time, talking as they watched the noisy jungle sliding by. Sometimes, five-foot-long iguanas lay sunning atop a bare branch of a tree a hundred feet up. As the saying goes, they taste like chicken, so the Shuar often tried to shoot them. If they missed, the iguana would dive into the water. It is impressive to see such a big lizard flying downward. When it hit the water it would usually disappear; they can hold their breath an incredibly long time and are superb underwater swimmers.

When a maneuverable boat is needed, or cargo must be kept as dry as possible, the Shuar use dugouts, called *canoas*, most about three feet across, thirty feet long and made from a single tree. They are much harder to make but last longer—up to fifteen years if they are properly constructed and cared for. Their disadvantage is that they are tippy.

One day Juan and two Shuar friends, Efrain Chacon and Savio Kajeca, responded to a medical emergency. They were in a smaller dugout about twenty-five feet long and with a draft of two feet. Each of the men perched on a narrow cedar thwart wedged into the three-foot opening of the hold. In the bottom of the dugout nestled three canvas-wrapped packs filled with medicines and gifts for friends a day's journey downstream. They carried a rifle as protection against the *tigres* and in case they happened on some game animal or saw an iguana.

The air was gray in the mistiness of morning, and flowers shined brightly in the low light. As they drifted toward the main river Juan noticed a yellow and orange heliconia flower dangling over the water. Its two-foot-long blossoms oozed a clear liquid. At its tip several big wasps had gathered for a morning drink. A bala ant, an inch-and-a-half long, silently crept toward the feeding wasps, but the dugout drifted on, and Juan never saw the end of the hunt. Birds were active in the cool air, and one of them, an Amazon kingfisher, flew low over the water with its crackling call. Four white-throated swallows flew even lower, occasionally dipping their beaks into the water to drink or feed. Juan said a little prayer of thanks, for he loved the mornings.

The men ran three long stretches of rapids. They became suddenly alert, however, when they entered a stretch of water so calm it reflected every detail of the forest canopy. Something was slowing the river. Perhaps a tree had fallen from the bank and was creating a giant snag with whirlpools to tip and trap a dugout. The dangerous snags occur even on the deep and winding rivers. Most of them are at the inside edges of curves, and since a river snakes every few hundred feet, often turning back onto itself, there are many places for snags.

Juan tracked the curving of the river by watching the sun's

location. On this day the sun started in front of them, then was at their right, then behind them, then back in front again. At one of the bends a branch extended into the river, and seven dinner-plate-size turtles (which could grow to the size of hula hoops) lay sunning. When the dugout paddled into view the turtles plopped into the river and disappeared. Efrain and Savio grinned at each other and mentally marked where they had seen them for a later return. Turtle soup is delicious and a nice change from fish.

In the Santiago River now, they settled into a routine. Efrain acted as the *puntador*. His job was to watch for rocks and snags. As they traveled downstream, he dipped a long straight pole of *cana brava* into the water, probing for the deepest channel of the river. To show Savio, the sternsman, the depth of the water, when he dipped he put his hand on the pole to show how far it had gone into the river. Savio paddled or poled from the rear while the Juan sat amidship, using his weight to maintain the dugout's balance. After several hours, they had traveled many miles and were drifting down the middle of the river, where the current is fastest. A black hawk settled onto a bare branch near a single green Amazon parrot, which ignored it. Only the heads of the two birds moved as they silently watched the dugout racing downstream.

When it is low, the Santiago is a braided stream, and little rain had fallen for a week. Efrain kept alert, guiding Savio from one side of the river to the other as he searched for a channel deep enough to float the dugout. Sometimes, where an island split the river, the channel was so shallow that the three men leaped into the water to pull and push the dugout over the rounded rocks until they reached deep water again.

They noticed a storm cloud over the jungle to one side of the river. Heavy rain poured as it drifted away from them, but the runoff began clouding the Santiago with dark water from the side streams. They rode in sunlight atop the surge, half a dozen feet higher than the flow a mile before. They no longer needed to watch for rocks or push the boat, but the danger from snags increased. As the storm continued, muddy water poured over the riverbanks and into the forest, then out again. All along the river's edge, as the powerful current pushed against the shore, the soft clay of the steep banks gave way, calving off into the river with huge splashes, like soil glaciers. They rounded a broad curve, and Efrain suddenly shouted, pointing downstream only 150 yards.

They watched in horror as a 180-foot ceiba began to sag dangerously as the overflowing river washed the soil from around its roots. The ceiba's topmost branches were three and four feet in diameter, each laden with lianas and epiphytes, which made it even more top-heavy. When the soil finally collapsed from around the roots, the tree dropped straight down for eight feet then slowly began to lean toward where the dugout was about to pass in the river. If it hit them, they would be crushed or drowned. Each man grasped a paddle and back-paddled frantically. The dugout slowed, but the current drove them toward the tree. Gradually, the ceiba leaned further, gained speed and fell into the river with a splash like a wave crashing on a beach. Its branches brushed the dugout, which rocked dangerously yet didn't tip.

The twelve-foot-thick tree trunk now extended almost to the center of the river, creating a dam and whirlpool that swept to the other bank. There was no escape. The dugout swirled among the leafy branches as the men dodged one, then another of the huge limbs. Efrain bravely grasped an arm-sized branch and was pulling the dugout under control when he suddenly yelped in pain, stung by something on the tree. When he let go, the dugout spun out of control and crashed at an angle against another giant branch. The current wedged the prow downward, and water swirled into the boat. Juan and his friends were thrown into the river as the rifle and packs washed from the dugout.

Juan was being pulled from the *canoa* but he was a strong swimmer and stroked back to it quickly. Grasping the gunwale of the boat, he looked around for the others desperately, for he knew that neither of them could swim. He saw them near the other end of the dugout, struggling to stay afloat. He pulled himself hand-over-hand along the gunwale, then reached out for Savio, who grasped Juan's outstretched hand firmly. Juan then reached out and grabbed Efrain by his long hair just as he was going under. The three clung to the dugout in silent fear as it spun round and round the whirlpool, stuck in the center of the swirling water like a leaf in an eddy.

"Kick!" Juan shouted. "Kick hard with your legs the next time you see the shore." Each time they saw the shore ahead of them, they kicked as hard as they could, and gradually the shore came closer. On the sixth circle, the whirlpool spat them out and they drifted to land.

In their struggle they hadn't noticed a Shuar house near the river, but the people had seen them and helplessly watched the drama from the shore. Once out of the whirlpool, the three exhausted men clung to the dugout until one of the men from the house leaped into the river and pulled them to shore where they sprawled on the rocky beach, thanking God and these people for deliverance.

The mother of the house gave them hot *chicha* and dried their clothes over the fire. She boiled some yuca and cooked crispy, sliced twice-fried plantains called *patacones* and laid them on a banana leaf for the travelers to eat. Several hours later the men were warm again and the river began to subside. The rifle was gone but the children of the house found the packs and one paddle swirling in an eddy downstream.

Juan and his partners had medicines for people in need, so the travelers thanked their new friends and continued on their way.

CHAPTER THIRTY-TWO

JUNGLE DOGS

At Yaupi they had been so busy that Amalia did not have any dogs, and she missed them. So at Santiago where, there were "only" thirty-five students for the two of them, plus their own five children, she felt it was time to get a dog or two. Like most Shuar women, she wanted the dogs for protection, but mainly so she could take them hunting.

The dogs were typical-brown or brindle-colored, with long tails and large ears, about two feet tall and rangy to the point of emaciation. Amalia cooked plantains and yuca then pre-chewed them to make a special dish for the dogs called *ma'miki*. Sometimes she stirred in the blood from the animal they killed that day and some of its meat so the dogs would learn about their prey. Older dogs seldom get meat except from scraps. However, she gave lactating females with pups meat so they could produce milk. Dogs are important to the life of the people. If a female dog's milk were insufficient for her litter, Amalia would often see women suckle the pups from their own breasts.

From her mother, Amalia had learned to housebreak her dogs, even training them to urinate and defecate in a specific place away from the house. In the process, if the puppy messed in the house she threw cold water on it then carried it outside to the place where it was supposed to "do its duty." Generally the puppies learned very quickly and went to the same spot each day.

The children loved to play with the dogs, and it was

common to see Carlos, Esther or little Maria wrestling with one in the yard. At night, the dogs stayed tied by the door on the women's side of the house or snuggled on a bed with the children.

In the days when war was common, the dogs had been valuable as early-warning systems, barking when intruders came near, even attacking with their masters if warriors entered their territory. They might still be needed for this at Santiago, Amalia thought, and indeed they would be. But she kept them mostly because she loved dogs and hunting with them. It gave her a chance to break her routine, and it was a thrill when her dogs were chasing an animal to feed her family. She named each of the five dogs and knew them by their howls and barks. Even half a mile away she could tell what each was doing and the kind of animal they were pursuing. If one dog was silent, she knew there might be a problem.

Amalia's mother always had a little area of the garden where she grew special dog plants. Slightly hallucinogenic, *mikiut* or *yawa* (dog) *maikiua* eaten by the dogs before a hunt would sharpen their power and make them better hunters.

When the first litter of pups was are about six months old, Amalia began taking them on the hunts so they could learn from the older dogs. It was a difficult time, for the pups returned from their first hunt filled with blood lust and needed training to calm them down. If uncontrolled they would turn against the household animals—chickens, tinamous (a large chicken-like bird of the jungle they often kept with the chickens) and even the pigs.

Early one morning, Amalia called the dogs, "Ta-ta-ta-ta-ta." They began to squirm and wriggle, excited because they knew that call meant they were going hunting. Just before dawn, Amalia started out with four dogs, all tied by palm fiber leashes. She carried a few matches, a spear, a three-inch fishhook and line and her machete. The morning sounds had begun an hour or more before, and Amalia and her pack were surrounded by birdsong as they walked into the cool predawn. Each dog eagerly trotted along with her slowly, sniffing the dank morning air and listening for the sound of retreating animals.

About three miles from the mission, Amalia began to hunt in earnest. She needed meat but wanted to protect the dogs. As her mother had taught her, Amalia always sang a silent song while she hunted, asking the jungle spirits and God, to protect the dogs. Most of the dogs had white spots on their eyes from ant bites, but they didn't seem bothered. Sometimes, the animal they were hunting fought hard and injured the dogs, and she sang the song to avoid a problem. When a dog was injured, Amalia would give it as much care as a child, bathing the wound in warm water and using antiseptic plants from her garden.

About three miles from home now, Amalia smelled the rank, acidic scent of a collared peccary. Peccaries are dangerous at any time for they are fast and very agile. The collared type is particularly intelligent and often runs in a circle, even turning back slightly on its trail to confuse the dogs. If it hides in a hollow tree or cave its razor sharp teeth can rip even experienced older dogs. On this morning she had two pups along on their first hunt, so decided against chasing the wild pig this time. Would this day be successful, or would one of the dogs be hurt? Silently, she sang the protection song again and said a little prayer.

Though a peccary was dangerous, Amalia's main fear for the dogs was snakes hiding in the undergrowth. Pausing to reach down and stroke her favorite, Negra (which means "black female"), Amalia recalled the day Negra limped back to her, holding up one leg. She had two puncture wounds on her paw from the bite of some snake. Judging from the distance between the wounds, it had been a large snake, and the wound was already swelling. Amalia had carried Negra home and washed the wound in very hot water, then made a poultice of hot peppers and *yuca* leaf, which she changed several times a day. Amalia and Juan followed the Catholic principles, but the snake bite to Negra caused her mother, who still lived in much of the traditional way, to recommend that they put on a snake festival and invite the neighbors. If she had used a shaman, the shaman would have followed the same taboos as if he were healing a human. Amalia's treatment worked though, and Negra lived to hunt with Amalia again on this day.

A typical jungle dog of the type that Amalia often bred.

The dogs became nervous and broke her reverie. A mile from where she had smelled the peccary, she loosed the dogs, which began to circle, sniffing the ground as she continued slowly down the dim forest trail.

Suddenly, Brim, the oldest male, began to call and ran off through the undergrowth. The others followed, and Amalia encouraged them by calling, "sik-sik-sik-sik." She could tell by their barks that they were onto an armadillo (*shushui*), and she knew it had gone into its den for the dogs called, "how-howhown." The hollow of the den echoed as the dogs took turns barking and howling into the hole. She found them digging around an eighteen-inch hole in the ground. As usual the armadillo was smart and had placed its hidden home well, among the roots of a large tree. A human often walks right past a den, but the dogs weren't fooled. One by one, starting with the pups, she caught and tied the dogs to nearby trees near each of the armadillos's escape holes then returned to the main den entrance.

There are several ways to get at the armadillo, all of which require patience. Amalia knew that digging was no option. Although the den was only about a foot-and-a-half deep, the soil above was crisscrossed by an impenetrable roof of roots. Sometimes a hunter can start a fire over the den, asphyxiating the armadillo. Planning on just such an operation, Amalia had brought her supplies. She pulled a thumb-sized, fourteen-inch-long giant earthworm from a pouch and used it to bait the hook and nylon line she carried. Tying this to a short pole, she gently thrust it into the entry of the hole and went armadillo fishing. Several times she pushed the bait into the den then pulled it out. When she felt the armadillo take the bait, she gave a yank to set the hook and began to pull. In the hole, the armadillo braced its sharp-clawed feet against the den walls and held fast. Patiently, Amalia kept pressure on the hook. Minutes later the animal shifted and she pulled it a few inches closer to her. Each time the animal weakened, she pulled a little more until she saw its head appear at the entrance. One quick stroke with the machete killed it. There would be rich armadillo soup for dinner.

"Thank you," Amalia said to the dogs, and then whispered a little prayer of gratitude.

CHAPTER THIRTY-THREE

THE DANGEROUS
OLD WAYS RETURN

By 1964 tensions were rising again. Father Juan Shutka and other Salesians had finally been successful in helping the Shuar to establish the Federation of Shuar Centers (better known as the Shuar Federation). The main goal of the Federation was to provide economic stability for the Shuar people while protecting their cultural integrity.

But an incident that occurred eight years earlier and two hundred miles to the north continued to fester.

Back then a North American, Howard Stephen Strouth, had discovered after years of searching a profitable oilfield in the northeast. It seemed a boon to Ecuador, one of the poorest countries in South America. As North American petroleum companies began to move into the selva to build roads and drill wells, Huaorani Indians plagued the workers, killing many. The Huaorani were a small tribe, probably fewer than six hundred in all, but they were uninterested in having any part of white culture. They wore gigantic earplugs and were naked except for the men, who tied their penises up by the foreskin to a soft ceiba fiber belt.

Whites called them *Auca*, a name that in the Huao language meant "savage," and the Huaorani hated it as much as the Shuar hated being called *Jivaro*. They were, indeed, a violent tribe, but until the oil workers began their invasion, the violence had mainly stayed within the Huao group. Among the whites there were rumors that the Huaorani killed unwanted children and even buried dying people before their final breath, which enhanced their image as savages. Whenever a white settler caught a Huaorani child it was enslaved and quickly became almost a zoo specimen, but certainly a slave to the captors. Then a little group of evangelist missionaries took on the mission to make peaceful contact and to save the Huaorani. They over-flew the jungle and identified a broad river where they could land a plane. But first they began dropping gifts—metal pots, machetes, beads and other trinkets. One day a group of missionaries landed and made brief contact, giving more little gifts to the naked and hesitant people. After several such visits the five missionaries thought they were making progress. Then, suddenly, they were attacked and speared. Rescuers found the men's bodies and buried them where they had died.

But the missionaries were not yet finished with the Huaorani. A Huaorani woman named Dayuma had been discovered at a nearby hacienda, and the missionaries bought then freed her. Speaking both Spanish and Huao, she became a convert and interpreter. This was important because Rachel Saint, the sister of one of the murdered missionaries, planned to go back to the Huaorani to live with them. Elisabeth Elliot, the widow of another of the dead missionaries, had much the same plan.

In the United States, the deaths created a huge interest in the work of missionaries, and within a short time hundreds volunteered to the cause of Christianizing, especially among the *Auca*. In addition, there were many more believers who provided gifts of cash—the missionary organization had hit upon a public relations bonanza that produced especially great rewards when Dayuma visited and toured the United States.

By the early sixties both Rachel Saint and Elisabeth Elliot were living with the Huaorani, apparently making considerable progress. Even some of the murderers became Christians. The Huaorani culture, however, began to fragment. Soon, clothing and enlarged earlobes without earplugs in them became the mark of a Christianized Huaorani, a notice to white settlers that the person was a Christian and should not be shot on sight.

The Shuar watched the changes carefully. Certainly, the Huaorani had more trade goods, but they had learned some unhealthy habits. They began to play the Catholic and evangelist groups against each other. The evangelist groups within themselves began a sort of competition for the prize of an uncontacted tribe. But what appalled the Shuar—and caused them fear—were the changes in the once-proud people. Originally, the Huaorani had no concept of prayer or asking for divine help. Now they made up chants and magic songs to attract more of the gifts the white people brought. They referred to Rachel Saint in words that meant "star" and "queen." The Huaorani were gradually acquiring shotguns. With the more powerful weapons, they killed more animals, which they sold to the oilfield workers, depleting their own supply of meat but giving them more money to buy metal pots, clothing and flashlights. The Huaorani learned to use dynamite and DDT to blast or poison fish from the rivers, and the environment that had supported them now began to fall apart. Emaciated Huaorani even appeared in cities.

The Shuar Federation was a great step of progress for the Shuar, but as they came together—and as they saw the changes in their enemies the once-powerful Huaorani—the Shuar began to rethink their relationship with both evangelical and Catholic missionaries. At Santiago the community split into two almost equal groups: One group for and one against the missions and white education.

As usual now when there was a community concern, the people gathered at the mission. This time, however, they were not coming together for happy socializing but to decide the particular fate of Amalia and Juan.

When it was his turn to speak, Juan rose and addressed the people humbly and gently, seeking to ease their fears that the mission was working against the Shuar. He asked them to look carefully at the mission. Were the children not living as Shuar even at the mission? Did they not eat the same food as in their homes? The goal of the education that Juan and Amalia provided was to give the children the special tools of arithmetic, the Spanish language and ability to write. With these tools they could protect themselves against whites—or any people who might want to take their land or cheat them. By speaking the Spanish language they could be considered citizens of Ecuador. Without it they were not truly citizens.

Although the men seemed to understand and the meeting broke up quietly, the mission was still in danger.

A few nights later, Juan worked late at their cane press, which had been given to them by a friend in Sucua. They raised a little sugar cane and used the press to make molasses, which Juan sold to raise cash for the mission. Exhausted from working the manual press for hours, he returned to his house at about ten o'clock in the evening where Amalia had already put the children to bed.

Suddenly Negra began barking nervously and was joined by Brim, then the whining pups. Juan and Amalia gazed into the *selva*, but saw nothing. The dogs continued to bark. In the darkness toward the storage room with the cane press, a little spark of light glowed in the blackness. It grew quickly and Juan heard men running, laughing into the forest.

"Amalia," Juan shouted, "get the children out of the house and the students from their beds, in case that fire blows to the dormitory." He ran toward the growing flames and dashed into the building and dragged the cane press out. Others arrived to help and they pulled out bags of rice and the jugs of molasses Juan had made that evening. Melinia noticed that the pan used to boil the syrup was still in the fire. It would melt, and along with it their one source of income. Without a word and before Juan could stop her, she covered her head with a blanket and leaped into the flames by the door. Wrapping the big pan in the blanket, she ducked from the flames and out an opening in the wall. Juan used a wet blanket to put out the coals in her hair and on her clothes, scolding her in his fear.

What would come next? In the morning, as the distraught couple combed the remains of the building, they realized how much they had lost and how little food remained. "We must make sure that things appear as normal as possible, or we will appear to be weak and they will attack again," Juan said.

"You are right, but I will go to the women to be sure they know of our need," Amalia said over her shoulder. She started toward the house of their nearest neighbor, one whose husband may have been among the arsonists. An hour later she returned with a *shigra* full of rice and fruit. Several other women arrived the next morning with food and promises to bring more.

Strangely, the violence abated immediately, as if the people had vented their frustrations and realized that the mission did help them. As Juan recalled later, "The anger burned away with the thatch and blew away with the ashes."

CHAPTER THIRTY-FOUR

STUDENT SOLDIERS

The Shuar seemed happy again, and the Arcoses settled into their work with a new enthusiasm. But another challenge was rising, this one from the soldiers who were stationed nearby at the border with Peru. The commander of the base changed every few months, and when the new one, a captain Alvan, arrived, it was obvious that he was nervous about his new responsibility. Despite the fact that there was no evidence the Peruvians were on the march toward them, he believed they were going to attack at any moment.

One day, captain Alvan called on Juan and firmly announced, "Mr. Arcos, your mission is in a very dangerous place. It is in a military zone. Because my soldiers must patrol through here, and because they cannot march through your mission, you must move immediately.

"But captain," Juan tried to reason, "look at all those students and buildings. We have almost eighty children who live here and many buildings. It was the work of almost a year to establish the mission here, and with so many it will take much longer to rebuild it."

"I am sorry but you are in the way and must go."

Frustrated, Juan said, "Before that happens we need another person to look at it with us. I will go to Pastaza and talk with the commander there. If he says we must move, we will move."

Alvan agreed and returned to his fort.

At Pastaza, Juan was taken to the commander and was

surprised to find it was an old friend, William Amaroso. They knew each other from Amaroso's tour of duty at Yaapi shortly after Juan joined Guinassi. Amaroso had been a guest of Father Guinassi's on many occasions and Juan and Amaroso became friends. The new commander had been married only a week before learning he was to be sent to the remote jungle post. and missed his wife, Yoli; Juan was considering marriage, and the two men spent many hours talking of love and companionship.

When Juan arrived at Pastaza, Amaroso greeted him enthusiastically and listened to the story. He agreed and told Juan to return to Santiago. "I'll be there in a week, and we can look at alternatives," he said. Unfortunately, his alternative would be almost as difficult as Alvan's.

A week later, commander Amaroso flew from Pastaza to Yaapi, where he loaded his team into a large motorized dugout and continued upriver. A thorough man, he spent much of the time with his orderly, dictating notes about the countryside and its defensibility. Although the river was high, the powerful but noisy motor carried them upriver quickly.

When Juan heard the boat coming, he knew a little public-relations welcome would be good, so he gathered all of the students near the boat landing and gave them instructions. As Commander Amaroso arrived, the children stood at attention around a large breadfruit tree and sang the national anthem. Although the commander was a hardened soldier, Juan noted that he quickly wiped away a tear as the song ended.

"Mr. Arcos," he said formally, "this is wonderful patriotism, to hear our national anthem so deep in the jungle. These children have moved me. Tomorrow I would like to visit your mission to see what should be done."

He returned to the army post with Alvan, who also had arrived to greet him. Juan thanked the children for their nice singing and praised them for their poise in meeting a stranger. Then they returned to work. As Commander Amaroso and

Captain Alvan walked toward the army post, Juan looked at Amalia and asked, "What do you think is in their thoughts?"

"Both of those men are very good at hiding their true feelings," she said. "I'm not sure whether that tear really was any indication of softness or sympathy toward the mission."

"I agree."

About ten the next morning, Commander Amaroso and Captain Alvan arrived. They greeted Juan politely but told him they wanted to see the mission without his accompaniment. They said that they "knew he was busy" and promised to get him when they needed his counsel. As they strolled around the mission, Amaroso continually spoke to his orderly, who scribbled more notes. From a distance, Juan watched as the men occasionally paused to look at something in greater detail. They would gaze together into the distant hills, gesticulating as one or the other explained his thoughts.

Then, without calling for Juan, they walked back to the post. When they returned at mid-afternoon, they boarded the motor dugout and continued upriver past the mission a mile or more. When they returned and passed by on their return to the post, they waved to Juan in a friendly manner but continued without talking with him. Amaroso was obviously considering something very carefully.

With the morning prayers finished and the students in school, Juan looked out of his classroom and saw the two officers approaching. This time they marched directly to his classroom, and Amaroso said, "It is time for us to talk."

Juan asked one of the older students to continue drilling the others in the use of the preterite (past) tense of Spanish, then he went out with the soldiers. The three men talked of little things—the weather that day, the children's enthusiasm for learning, the happy atmosphere at the school. "Please, let us sit here," Juan suggested as he indicated three small benches overlooking the play yard.

"Captain Alvan makes a good point for moving the school away from here. If it were two hours more toward the mountains, there would be greater safety for the children," Amaroso began. "But, I do not believe there is a true threat, so the school may stay for now. Besides, some of the soldiers would like to bring their families to be with them, and their children can then attend your school."

Juan breathed deeply, relieved. But Amaroso was not finished.

"Both captain Alvan and I agree, however, that the older boys are an excellent resource and we will begin immediately to make use of them."

"What do you mean?" Juan asked suspiciously. "They are students, and even the oldest are only fifteen years of age."

"It is simple. We will train them to be soldiers. Each afternoon Captain Alvan will bring a few of his men to the mission, and the children will be drilled."

Juan was grateful that the mission did not have to move, but aghast that the young boys would be forced to train as soldiers. At least a shot had not been fired in the "war" for several years, so the likelihood of danger was small.

"It is either this, or the mission will move," Amaroso announced as he looked intensely at Juan. Behind the commandant, Alvan smiled triumphantly at Juan.

"When will you begin?" Juan asked.

"Tomorrow," Alvan answered. "Have the boys who are aged fourteen and older ready at this place just after you have finished your noon meal."

"Of course," Juan answered heavily.

"Now, we must find another site for the army post, for it will be moved a little upriver," Amoroso announced. Juan noticed that Alvan's smile had less of a sneer now.

The three of them boarded the motorized dugout and traveled upstream. The mission of Santiago perched on a small plain, barely above the level of most floods. Juan hoped the school would grow, and as it did he had planned to gradually move it to a second plain a few hundred yards downstream and on higher ground, for greater security. To Juan's relief,

Amoroso ordered the dugout beached more than a mile and a half from the mission, at the third plain.

"Juan," Amoroso asked in a more friendly tone, "do you think this site would be secure against floods?"

Juan studied the flow of the river, which gently curved away from a broad beach. The river narrowed slightly below them and created a fast current that would be more difficult for attacking Peruvians to cross. Juan noticed a slight rise and suggested they look at it. When they stood on the top and looked down, he said, "See how the cliff below us is very steep? There is no debris at the bottom, which means the river often rises to there and carries the soil away. From here, as you can see, we have an excellent view both up and down the river. You could put your fort here, but be sure the buildings are well away from the edge of this cliff, for it is gradually falling into the river. That open plain below should give you excellent protection too. Did you notice that there are not even small seedlings growing on the beach? It looks like the floods cover it often, so the trees never have a chance to grow. That clear space should also make it difficult for anyone to sneak up on your men."

Amoroso smiled broadly. "I had thought to put the men on that hill over there," he said, indicating a lower hill devoid of trees and closer to the river. "But you are right. I can see the mud marks on the trees now. The buildings would be unsafe there. Captain Alvan. Build your new fort here."

Within a few days Amoroso left, and Alvan's soldiers broke into two teams. One started to build the new fort, and the other began to drill the young boys. Each afternoon they marched up and down the soccer field, learned about military discipline and were shouted at by the soldiers. When they boys complained to Juan, he smiled and said, "Yes, it is hard work, but you are doing an important job. Of course you are learning to defend your country, but you are also distracting the soldiers, so they do not have time to worry about the rest of us at the mission, and we can get back to our schoolwork."

Classes resumed, and Juan slowly began to move the mission to the second plain. As a building fell into disrepair, he replaced it with another a few dozen feet higher, and within two years the mission would sit a few hundred feet away from its original location and several dozen feet above the river floods.

In a few months, as usual, Alvan left and another officer replaced him. By this time, however, Juan realized the importance of good relations with the soldiers. He and Amalia thought carefully about how they could demonstrate to each new post commander just how well run the mission was. They always invited the new commander to eat and have coffee with them, and to tour the mission. The new officer usually responded with offers of assistance and promises that there would be no problems between the soldiers and the young girls under the Arcos's care. Of course, the daily drills continued, although Peru never attacked. As tensions relaxed, the soldiers came to the mission to help with various projects and to play soccer with the boys. Each Sunday after church, the soldiers mingled with the visiting Shuar parents and stood at attention as the children raised the Ecuadorian flag then sang the national anthem.

CHAPTER THIRTY-FIVE

SHAMANS AND SOLDIERS, BOTH GOOD AND BAD

By 1967 two more babies, Patricia and Mariana, had joined the Arcos family, and the Salesian Missions had sent several extra helpers for the school. The mission was well established and respected among the Shuar, but there was trouble in the surrounding community.

Juan Nestor was a shaman, but he used his powers as black magic—to harm instead of help. More than once he was accused of sending spirit arrows to injure his enemies. Soon, evil-minded people began to visit Nestor, paying him to send the arrows against their own enemies.

Whether the results were imagined or real, many people were injured in various ways, from sickness to accidents, and the Shuar became more nervous each week. Nestor was about forty years of age when several Shuar asked Juan to talk to him and see if he could change the evil shaman's ways. Juan went to the shaman's house and, as they sat drinking *chicha* in the sunlight, Juan asked him, "Why is it that you do these bad things against your neighbors?"

"Mr. Juan," he replied, "I am not an evil shaman. Unfortunately, these bad darts are powers that were forced on me by another shaman. Years ago, I was asleep by a little river, for I had been hunting and it was too dark to return to my house. As I slept, I saw a *tigre* approaching. It came to me and said it was giving me special powers to right wrongs and to take vengeance on people who have done bad things to other people."

"How do you determine who is telling the truth? Perhaps you are doing bad things to people who are actually good, and the one who comes to you is the evil person? Your neighbors think you are the only evil person here. My friend, that could be dangerous for you."

Nestor thought for a long time then said, "I appreciate that you have talked to me about this. But I also think that the *tigre*-shaman who is in me is too powerful to resist. I must do as he has instructed me."

The conversation ended, and Juan left, unaware that this would be the last time he would see Nestor.

A few weeks later, a neighboring Shuar family's eleven-year-old son died suddenly. Only a few days before, the father of the house had argued with Nestor about some trivial thing. In their anger and despair, the family blamed the shaman for the death. The dead boy's older brother was in the military and stationed at the nearby army post. When the news reached him, he became angry beyond reason and passed by the mission on his way to avenge his brother. Juan tried to calm him saying, "The shaman, Nestor, did not do this to the child. Usually it is the old ones who die, but sometimes the young ones do, too. You know that."

Seeming to calm down, the brother agreed and returned to the military base. But over the next week he brooded more deeply and began talking with his fellow soldiers, who also became unreasonably angry. Then the news came that a second child in the same family, this time a little sister, had died.

The young soldier went to his superior, a sergeant, and accused the shaman of sending spirit arrows. As he listened, the sergeant felt compassion for his soldier and agreed that the shaman must have been responsible. He gave the young man permission to go and arrest Nestor.

The next morning at five o'clock, a little platoon led by the aggrieved brother arrived at Nestor's house. They charged in with guns at the ready and began to accuse Nestor, who seemed not to understand the reason for such anger. Nestor's family escaped out the door of the women's side of the house and ran for help.

Several soldiers dragged Nestor outside, and one shot him in the head. But he was still alive and begged them not to shoot him again, pleading that he was innocent. They shot him again, and he died. He had barely finished twitching when they dragged him to the Zamora River, where they cut off his arms and legs then cast the body parts into the dark water. Returning to the military base, they reported that Nestor had tried to escape, and they had killed him.

Father Raul, an old friend of Juan's, had arrived at the mission only the day before to perform various holy ceremonies, such as baptism, that Juan could not. At six o'clock on the morning of Nestor's death, he and Juan were in church with half a dozen Shuar. Just as he completed his sermon, *tuntui* drums began beating throughout the valley.

Juan and Raul knew there was a problem and asked a Shuar man what the drums meant. The man said, "The drums are saying that people should go to the house of Juan Nestor, for there has been trouble." White robes flying, Raul and Juan led the congregation on the path.

When they arrived, there was already a large crowd gathered around Nestor's wife and children. Sobbing uncontrollably, his wife described what had happened. The blood spattered on the house, the trail of blood from the house to the river and finally the blood pooled at the riverbank confirmed the story. But the body was nowhere to be seen—the caimans and fish had done their work.

"It was the soldiers," Nestor's wife sobbed.

When Raul and Juan went to the sergeant at the military

base he received them angrily. "This is none of our business," he said forcefully. He seemed to support his men, but Juan sensed that he was afraid.

Raul started for Sucua the next day, pausing at several military posts along the way, as was his custom. At each, he saw the soldiers were very tense. Rumors were traveling that the Shuar were preparing to attack all the little forts.

Finally, the soldiers at one fort arrested Father Raul and put him into a room where their sergeant began to question him. "Why are you encouraging the Shuar to fight us?"

"That is a ridiculous idea," Raul said calmly. "The missions are here to teach the Shuar to be peaceful. Why would we go against our own teachings?"

Finally, the sergeant said, "Get out of here and tell the Shuar that they should not fight."

A few miles from the fort, he encountered a war party that was on its way to the fort he had just left. Surrounded by armed warriors in feather *coronas* (crown-like headgear) with red achiote—and black genipape-painted bodies, they held a council on the narrow trail.

"What happened to Juan Nestor was wrong," Raul began, "but we cannot blame all the soldiers for what was done by a few. Please give me a little time to see what happened and who did it. I just left the soldiers, and they are very nervous. Their guns are pointed at the jungle, and they will kill many of you before you can kill even one of them." The men agreed to return home but only for a few days.

Meanwhile, armed soldiers gathered at the mission, ready to kill any Shuar who sought vengeance. Juan tried unsuccessfully to persuade the sergeant to let him get the children out of harm's way. He sent runners to the community around the mission, asking the Shuar to be patient, for if shooting started, their children would be in the middle of the fight.

The women from several miles around gathered at the mission, moving in to protect their children as a sort of living shield. Although they smiled and quietly went about their work, the soldiers knew the women would resist any attempt to hurt the children. They respected that, and over the next two months, the tension between the two groups gradually relaxed. Finally, orders came from Quito to replace all the soldiers, especially the ones the Shuar knew were responsible.

As the transfers began, the murder was avenged, however not in the way everyone expected. The sergeant who had approved the raid crashed in a plane headed for his new assignment in Limon. When the plane's crash site was finally discovered two weeks later, the bodies were badly decomposed. It was ironic that, just as Juan Nestor had been quartered, so was the sergeant, in order that his body could be carried from the jungle.

This left the avenging brother of the dead children alive and seemingly unpunished. But about five months after the murder, he and two other men were traveling upstream on the Zamora River when their motorboat hit a snag in a strong current. The young man drowned, and his body spun away underwater. It finally surfaced miles downstream, where it came to rest at the very place that he had dumped Nestor's body into the water.

But progress had been made, for the Shuar did not seek vengeance. Everyone was amazed to see the way the drama played out and that the guilty were, indeed, punished. Now when the priests said, "Vengeance is the Lord's," the people listened carefully.

CHAPTER THIRTY-SIX

LEAVING SANTIAGO

In early February 1970 Monsignor Jose Feliz Pintado visited the mission. He came apparently just for a pleasant visit, but he had something on his mind. After several days, he walked with Juan in the schoolyard and said, "You have done a wonderful job with this mission, Juan. Perhaps it is time for another to take over and for you to help other people."

"What do you mean?" Juan asked.

"Have you heard of a place called Miasal?"

"Yes," Juan said. "I was there several years ago with Father Peter when he went on a mission downstream to Porto Morona. It was a difficult place and the soldiers near the frontier made slaves of the Shuar women nearby."

"The place is still very remote," the monsignor continued. "The name means 'my salt' and is named for a nearby salt spring. There are no missions for dozens of miles, and its remoteness makes Santiago look civilized. For some months now I have been studying a map of old airstrips. There is one near Miasal, on the eastern side of the Cutucu Mountains. It is a little farther from the border with Peru than Santiago, but the military would like to see the airstrip reopened. They might be willing to help us to establish the mission if we clear the airstrip. It is about a five-or six-day walk from Santiago, and the country is much wilder than here. From the maps I have seen, Miasal appears to be at an elevation of almost thirteen hundred feet, so the climate will be cooler, and I understand there are few mosquitoes or malaria."

Juan listened to the monsignor's explanation quietly. He agreed to think about the offer, but in his heart the adventure of a new place sounded exciting. He was now almost forty-eight years of age and Amalia was pregnant with Juanito, their eighth and final child. But he was not certain whether she would go with him—or let him take his family.

Juan:

I have always liked to work very hard, but my wife said that I was crazy to think about starting another mission. She was settled well into Santiago and happy there. To start a mission is very hard work, and she wasn't sure whether she wanted to go through the startup again. Finally, in 1970, after ten mostly happy years at Santiago, I told the Monsignor that I would like to found a mission at Miasal.

Amalia continued to be unhappy about the move, although it was many months away. She had about decided to stay in Santiago and to let me go alone when something happened. All day she had been praying what to do and that night she was exhausted. She fell into a deep sleep and had a dream. In the dream she was in the church at Santiago and praying to the Virgin. As she looked at the statue it smiled at her and asked, "Why are you not going to go with your husband to do this great work? Go to Miasal and help your spouse in his work as a missionary." When she woke the next morning, Amalia told me she had decided that she wanted to help start the new mission, but she did not tell me about the dream until much later.

MIASAL

CHAPTER THIRTY-SEVEN

WHERE THE TSUIRIM
MEETS
THE MANGOSIZA

Juan:

The walk was long, five to six days each time I went from Santiago to Miasal, as always traveling with several Shuar friends who volunteered to help. The first trip, near where we thought the mission should be, we met an old friend from my earlier visit, the balsa-raft builder, Domingo Chumpi, who became a big help to us. Domingo was a little man with a powerful body and happy spirit. He was always joking about one thing or another. To be with him was a joy. He wasn't a Christian but was eager to help us as we started the mission. He always insisted that my friends and I stay with him at his house, and when he could he joined us in the labor.

The old military airstrip was reported to be at a curve along the edge of the Mangosiza River, a clear-water river, which would be an advantage. When we went to fish I could look into the water and see my canoe paddle almost two feet down, and we could see the shadows of big fish way below. Domingo reported that, with some hard work, the airstrip could be reopened and would give us another connection to the rest of the world. We found the airstrip and began to look for a good site for the mission. I wanted it a little away from the airstrip, for a greater sense of privacy and so there would be less distraction for the children.

Along the Mangosiza River, the jungle was so thick that it was virtually impassable. It was especially difficult to envision what the place would look like after the forest had been cleared for the mission. The mission had to be close to water but on high ground that would not flood. Rivers often rose twenty feet overnight, and Juan wanted to be certain that the children and buildings would be safe. For several days he and his friends cut their way through the forest with machetes, wandering haphazardly, almost feeling their way through the tangle of trees. Finally, Juan decided on a somewhat level site overlooking the Mangosiza River as the first site of the mission. (In 1973, the mission was moved uphill and several hundred yards away, next to the river *Tsuirim*, which means "hot water" in Shuar. It was named for two thermal waterfalls about five miles upstream.) No Shuar had settled into that part of the jungle, and its condition as an old, primary jungle was evidence that none had ever had a farm on the site, eliminating any potential for land disputes.

Over the next month Juan and his Shuar friends began to clear the site with their machetes. They girdled the big trees to kill them and cut down the smaller ones with machetes. In a few weeks they had created a littered but open clearing about two hundred feet square. By this time the big trees had begun to die and were dropping their leaves, letting in the sunlight and drying the soil.

Domingo Chumpi now joined them, and together he and Juan built the first house for the mission using mostly split palm for the walls, straight and stiff *winchipo* trees for the roof supports and *tocilla* palm thatch for the roof. Juan knew from past experience that the mission would need three houses for the children—a dormitory each for the boys, the girls and a third for a combination dining and classroom. As the mission took shape, other Shuar from the neighborhood of Miasal enthusiastically joined in the work of building the mission. This time the Salesians gave Juan money to start the mission, ten thousand sucres (about one hundred dollars). From this

Juan paid the Shuar, for he wanted the mission to help their economic as well as their spiritual and educational status.

But the prospect that their children would receive an education was enough to excite the people, and many came to volunteer their help in the building and clearing gardens to feed the school children, many of whom would be *internos*. Indigenous people of the rain forest normally practice slash-and-burn agriculture, and the Shuar are no exception. They cut down the plants, let them dry then burned the garden. Most of the time, the Shuar merely let the plants rot, either in place or by stacking them in low walls that wound around the edge of the garden. They planted corn (which gave two crops a year) and yuca stock Juan bought from Shuar in the area. In about two months they were ready to start the mission, although the gardens would not give their first produce for another four months.

Juan still needed bananas and plantains, which do not grow from seed. He and Domingo bought huge and heavy rootstock from neighbors then lugged it to the school garden to transplant. Juan knew that the original plant would take two years to grow a stalk of fruit that they could eat, but then all they would have to do is to cut down the twenty-foot stalk and remove the bananas. A new stalk shoot would have already begun to sprout and would grow with phenomenal speed to twenty feet in about two years. Normally, bananas and plantains are the last plants put in a garden before it is abandoned because it grows in even poor soil, but Juan needed to start a grove, so planted them right away.

Juan:

I returned to Santiago and finished the school year. Then I had to figure out how I would bring my wife and family to Miasal from Santiago. At the end of the school year, I left for Miasal with an *interna* to cook for us, and two *internos* who were brothers. We arrived at the house of Domingo again and the next day began to clear the airstrip near the

Mangosiza River so that supplies could be brought in. Over the years the airstrip had overgrown with trees of all sizes, mostly balsa and cecropia. The only tools we had were our machetes. Even once the strip was cleared, we would have to return to it each month and, using the machetes, cut the new growth of grass and little trees. It was hard work but necessary for the success of the mission. So we were looking for economic help for the foundation of our mission in Miasal. In addition to the money that the Salesians had given me several scientist friends gave us a little cash to build the houses at the mission.

Every week we had a day that was dedicated to the clearing of the airstrip. We used paid as well as unpaid mingas. A minga is a form of cooperative labor in which the community comes together to get a project completed quickly. In the past they were forced. Now the people are either paid or volunteer their time and effort, as in this case. The workers were always given all the food and chicha they wanted. In one month we prepared the airstrip so that small airplanes could land at Miasal.

Years before, Juan's family, including the children, had walked from Yaupi to Santiago when he started that mission, but this was a six-day walk for men. It would be ten days or more with children, and still very dangerous. The Salesians could offer no help, but Juan got it from an unexpected source. One of his friends, an evangelist from the Summer Institute of Linguistics, offered to use their planes to transport his family and their few belongings. Amalia and her mother, Masuink, were ecstatic. Besides the length of the walk, Amalia was seven months pregnant. Amalia once said, "Even a Shuar woman wants to take it easier during the last part of her pregnancy." Instead of ten days, the flights took one long morning and two flights to set the Arcos family on the airstrip near Miasal.

A week later Juan and a few Shuar left for Macas. He continued to Quito to report to the Salesians and to buy necessities and school supplies for the mission. When he returned to Miasal, they were ready to open the school so he called a meeting, inviting about three hundred of the Shuar who lived in the region of the Rivers Macuma, Mangosiza and Tsuirim.

Juan:

> As the people gathered to hear us, I told them we were there to work with them and to see things improve, to be sure the children learned the things that would guarantee they would be treated as good citizens. There were some in the crowd who knew me from Yaupi and from Santiago, and they were very happy to see me at Miasal. There were others at the meeting who were suspicious about my having internos who were both boys and girls because I did not have adult madrecitas like the other missions. They were concerned about problems that could arise between the boys and the girls in the mission if there were no madrecitas. I smiled and said, "Brothers, let us test the system to see if it will work." I told them that I worked with my wife. The ones who knew me were less reluctant to leave their daughters with us, and so on 11 October 1970, we opened the mission and started the school with twenty internos and almost thirty students. We promised to hold a meeting in a year, at which time the community would decide whether we could continue. Since the gardens were not yet producing, the families who had canoas took turns bringing food for us every two days. The food was not a gift. At first they were unwilling to take the money, but I knew that if they were to provide us free food they would soon become tired and the food would stop. So I used part of the money from the Salesians and paid the people in sucres. This gave the local people income as well as the incentive to continue providing food to the mission.

Every day Amalia would make *chicha* so that the *internos* would feel more at home. And each day they followed the same schedule as at Santiago and Yaupi, working in the gardens in the afternoon so they could become self-sufficient as soon as possible, for the little money Juan had was dwindling and his requests for further help were refused.

Amalia was her usual energetic self, but Juan noticed a difference. While at Santiago, when she originally said she did not want to go to Miasal, she had seemed somewhat dissatisfied. As they settled into their new home at Miasal she became happy again.

Juan:

> When a Shuar woman works in the garden, she sings traditional songs called anent (which speak to the souls of the plants and the animals of the garden) and other songs that she has created just for joy. She sings these with great feeling, honoring certain animals and other things from nature. The songs are as much a part of her life as a Shuar woman as the making of chicha. I had heard those songs less and less at Santiago; now, as they worked in the gardens, Amalia and her mother sang every day.

Much of white society has rediscovered the fact that shamans and women of the various tribes have uses for many kinds of plants, for medicine, food, etc. Ethnobotanists today often come to the forest to work with the shamans and women to learn from them. But there is an important difference. Scientists collect the samples then try to take them apart to discover the compounds that do the healing. They take the dry plants to laboratories to dissolve or dissect them, then study bits of the "cadavers" under microscopes where they have no dignity as plants and are only collections of the elements from which they were formed. In the forest, however, the people treasure every plant as it is. Each shaman or woman appreciates the unique combination that makes it what it is, whether beautiful or ugly, covered with flowers or thorns, growing in the soil, in the air or on another plant, whether vine or leaf or fruit or seed. They appreciate the spirit that lives in the plant, and they often tell it so, never taking its gift for granted. So the women were happy again, and they sang to their gardens.

CHAPTER THIRTY-EIGHT

MIASAL,
THE BEAUTIFUL SITE

Miasal was and still is a typical, larger mission. The open clearing was about fifty yards wide by a hundred yards long. The middle offers a courtyard for games and ceremonies. Of course barefoot soccer was very popular with the boys, and most days there were two or three games going on whenever the children had free time. Even when the ball was old and deflated, they had a good time playing.

The buildings, which Amalia again painted in bright red, yellow and blue, with decorations on the upper parts of the bamboo walls, sat around the perimeter of the courtyard. The kitchen and dining room was at one end of the courtyard, about thirty feet above the Tsuirim River. Next to it were two houses for the teachers, and in one of them was the shortwave radio for contacting the Shuar Federation in case of an emergency, or to gather weather information in case a plane needed to come to the airstrip. Continuing clockwise were the two dormitories, one for boys and the other for girls followed by a community house with an open-sided thatch-covered gathering area beside it, for neighbors and families of the *internos* to have picnics after Mass each Sunday, or to stay if they came to visit. Trails led to other teachers' houses, the school gardens and the little cemetery. The end of the courtyard opposite the dining room house opened to the jungle, and the remaining side was comprised of classrooms and the church, or *Casa de Medicaciones*. The central plaza provided an area for games and special events. At its center stood a little altar that reminded them daily why they were there in the jungle: in the wet cement, which he used to create the altar, Juan thought about Father Darde back in Gualaquiza as he wrote, in the wet cement, "Suffer the little children to come unto me." Matthew 19:14.

Exterior of a typical classroom. Note that the quiet thatch roof has been replaced by the more durable but noisy metal roof.

Interior of a typical classroom, now with a chalkboard to aid learning.

Juan:

Things continued in Miasal. We were working, always working. We cultivated plants and caught fish. In the Mangosiza large fish that are about a meter long can weigh eighty to one hundred pounds. Sometimes the fish could be speared from a dugout canoe, and other times we used traps like the ones we used at Santiago, where the fish could go in but not out, or we used the barbasco poison to paralyze them.

The biggest change was the airstrip and its communication with the outside world. Now a radio transmitter, with its howling whistling, became a part of the mission. There was no electricity so one person turned a crank rapidly to generate the power while a second person talked. By this time the Shuar Federation had two airplanes and several pilots being trained to fly them. If there was an emergency, I could call for assistance, and unless the weather was too bad, which was often, a plane would arrive with that help. In greater emergencies the military pilots often came to our aid because they had better navigation equipment and often flew in bad weather, where the smaller four-passenger planes of the Federation or Aero Misional could not even have found Miasal.

CHAPTER THIRTY-NINE

THE MISSION GROWS AND THE FIRST CHALLENGE ARRIVES

Amalia was getting larger with the baby yet still working as hard as ever. As the time neared for the birth, Juan built his eighth and final birthing house for Amalia. As required, it was new and clean, about sixty yards from the central house. After only two months in Miasal, Amalia went into labor. On Juan's forty-eighth birthday, December 16, 1970, Amalia delivered another son; they named him Juan Raphael Arcos.

Even through Amalia's pregnancy they both worked without rest to build the school. In that first year, from time to time, the Shuar were still a little nervous that Juan and Amalia were the only staff and that white visitors often came to see how things were going. The people knew that at other missions there were always problems with *internos* running away or fighting among each other. As one would expect, small problems arose, but Juan and Amalia were patient people and focused on their mission to educate the children. When Juan walked across the schoolyard the children eagerly followed him, jabbering and asking questions as children do. The mission started to grow, slowly at first as the local families sent their children. Then, as the children began to learn to read and do math, impressing their families with their new skills, families from farther away began to send their children as well. By the end of the first school year, seventy students lived at the mission school.

At the end of the first year, as he had promised, Juan called a meeting of the local community—families from four or five miles around—to ask if they were happy with the mission and with the work at the mission, and whether it could continue. The people were delighted yet could not believe that so much could be accomplished by only two people. In other missions like Taisha, there were always problems between the students, but at Miasal the children were happy. The Shuar enthusiastically gave their permission for the mission to continue.

Juan becomes a deacon.

Juan:

Then help came. My old friend from Yaupi, Padre Raul, joined us, and together we made a good partnership. He was the priest and could perform all the religious functions. I began working to become a deacon so I could assist, and even perform marriage ceremonies, but had little time for the proper studies. Raul made long walks through the forest to visit the Christians who needed him. Each circuit for marriages, baptisms and religious instruction took fifteen days, and he did it every three months. So while he was gone it was just the two of us again. But I loved this tall and skinny man with his long hair and beard, and those wonderful bright blue eyes that sparkled with love for the world.

One day Juan and Raul sat on a bench at one end of the Miasal plaza. Each held a little girl on his lap, caressing the children's foreheads, talking quietly together about the week's work. From time to time a visitor or one of the other students stopped to visit and express concern for the girls. Both girls stared with dark eyes sunken into their pretty, sallow faces, moving only to go to the nearby latrine for another bout of diarrhea, for they had taken on the habit of earth-eating. They had become infested with worms and other parasites that lurked unseen in the soil. Someone had to be with the girls all the time to help them when they became ill, give them *manzanillo* (lemon grass) tea with sugar to keep them hydrated, and to prevent them from eating more dirt. Amalia also gave them daily doses of *aceituno* bark to kill the amoebas lurking in their young intestines. Earth-eating can be a problem with some children in the jungle, especially those who are under stress. In this case both girls had been abandoned at the school. Their mothers had been raped by *colonos*, and although their mother's family would have adopted them, the memory was too strong and vile. They wanted no reminder of it. It was good for Juan to have Raul to help even in such a mundane but important task as protecting the little girls.

Juan Arcos and Padre Raul entertain two girls sick from eating earth and who have many parasites yet still want to eat the soil.

The school became very successful and other teachers came to help, but even so, or perhaps because of that success, there were those who resisted them. Over the first thirty years of the mission's life, three meetings were held against them, and official letters sometimes arrived at the headquarters for the Shuar Federation denouncing the mission's work.

During the mission's fourth year one of the most dangerous of these meetings occurred, for the people believed that the Shuar children were not being respected as Shuar but being made dark versions of white children.

Because he loved and respected the Shuar way of life, Juan had been very careful to make sure that did not happen. He disputed the charge. On the appointed day, more than two hundred people gathered at the Miasal community center. The women passed *chicha* as the men discussed the situation. As the afternoon wore on, the meeting became increasingly noisy, and soon there were shouts against Juan and Raul. Five or six men in particular had decided that Juan must go.

Juan:

One man, the parent of one of our students, seemed to be the leader. Among the Shuar, if a leader is a good speaker he can change the way a meeting goes, toward the good or toward the bad, and this man wanted to burn the mission and all the planes.

"Why would you do this?" I asked him. "The mission and the planes are here only to help the Shuar. What riches have we gained here? We live as you do." They could not name any.

Gradually, the people began to quiet down, but the father was still angry. He was from Chiahuasa, a two-day walk, and his daughter had been boarding and learning with us only a month. She seemed to be happy and was doing well, so her father's anger was all the more strange.

"Well, we will talk more tomorrow," the father promised, as the meeting broke up for the day.

Later that night, a bushmaster snake bit the little girl and she went into a coma. Her father came to me now with a different attitude. "Compadre," he said," please help my daughter." Of course we were already doing what we could and had radioed for a plane to evacuate her, one of the very planes he had wanted to burn only a few hours earlier. I rode in the plane with her and the father, to help in any way I could and to talk with the doctors. She was taken to the hospital at Shell, where she stayed in the coma for two weeks.

After two weeks, the doctors shook their heads and told us, "It is better to take her home so she can die there. We cannot help her." I said I would return for her the next day and flew to Miasal to prepare for her arrival. Raul and I gathered the children in the church and began to pray. We prayed and sang hymns for her all night.

When I returned to Shell the doctor said, "She's a little better. I believe she will live." She continued to improve and is now living near Miasal with her own family.

After this the people again supported us, even the little girl's father who had spoken against the whites.

Even after three decades of work, there was always a little danger that the families would turn against the teachers.

In any small community tiny slights and imagined insults can erupt out of proportion, turning into serious issues that threaten the peace of the community. Hidden tensions are always at play—capricious, fluctuating in intensity, and every one potentially explosive. As the new century approached, one man began to see the job of president of Miasal as a source of personal power. He began to speak against Juan and the church, and to press his case for the job. Shuar men are very jealous to protect their image in front of others, so Juan tried to speak with him alone and gently, not criticizing his abilities. "My friend," Juan said, "if you want the job of president to help the people, this is right for you. If you are seeking it because you want to be more powerful, then you must let someone else be the president."

This angered him so much that he raged against Juan and the others, even threatening to kill them. This went on for days, and each night the situation became increasingly tense. Then suddenly, the man's anger melted when he suffered a stroke that paralyzed his right side. The opposition crumbled again as Juan and Raul tended to his needs.

CHAPTER FORTY

ARMY ANTS ATTACK, TO AMALIA'S DELIGHT

Huge families of wandering ants live in the jungle. These army ants, which are entirely carnivorous, are the stuff of legend, for they build no permanent home and as they continually move through the forest they eat alive anything in their path. The army is blind and affected by sunlight, so it often travels by night. When they rest, they build a bivouac camp, usually in a huge ball of living ants with the queen in the center. Some nests are as much as a cubic yard in size and contain passageways, doors and openings of living ants, as if it were a nest built in the ground. In their search for food, the ants fan out through the forest in an irregular, amoeba-like pattern; larger ants run alongside as if they were officers giving instructions to their troops. In advance of the horde, antbirds begin to twitter excitedly and gather, not to eat the ants, but the spiders, mice and other creatures hurrying away or stirred from the leaf litter by the advancing line of hungry ants.

One day such an army approached the Arcos's house. Amalia became very excited, not out of fear but from delight, for the house had become infested with insects, and at night the palm thatch rustled with the sound of jungle rats. First she opened boxes and storage containers to give the ants full access to them. Then she gathered the children, caught the chickens, dogs, parrots and other pets and moved across the Tsuirim to camp for a day or two. She knew the ants could cross over a smaller stream, but the Tsuirim was fast and about thirty feet wide, not a likely path for them to take.

In a few hours, as night fell, the silent army moved into the house. Within a few minutes the entire house shimmered with their pulsing black bodies as they searched. The ants ignored the kettles full of *chicha* and the baskets of fruit but attacked every living thing they found. Giant brown cockroaches tried to escape but the ants tore them apart. As the ants moved onto the roof squealing little palm rats struggled to escape. In their panic they fell into the mass below and were quickly killed then eaten. A large spider, stretched itself to fit the shape of its X-shaped web and waited in one corner of the house. But the army ants poured onto the web. In seconds the spider was the prey. Another, smaller spider sensed the danger and dangled safely from a single strand of web as the war raged about it.

The next day the ants were gone and Amalia moved back into her immaculate house.

CHAPTER FORTY-ONE

THE RADIO SCHOOL

In 1972, the Shuar Federation began to broadcast lessons to the tribe, who were spread for perhaps thirty thousand square miles throughout the jungle. Each day the *Radioescuela Telefonica* broadcast lessons in the morning. Different channels offered lessons for the early grades up through the eighth grade.

First, a lesson was broadcast in Jivaroan, the primary language of the people. Following the lesson, Shuar music or even European classical music filled the pause. Next the lesson was repeated in Spanish. In the afternoons and evenings, news items, traditional music, information and bulletin board-type of notices were broadcast to the Shuar and Achuar tribes The *Radioescuela Telefonica* began to educate; but more important, it created the sense that the Shuar and the Achuar were a unified people.

More teachers came to Miasal to help as *teleauxillaires* (teacher's aides). The radio instructors did the actual teaching, but the aides made sure the students understood the lesson, and of course encouraged them to listen carefully. Their pay, however, was low—about twenty dollars per month—and it was difficult to keep them at the school for any length of time.

Next, the Shuar Federation built a high school at Sucua, where promising students could further their education. Soon, many students went on to study at the Salesian's indigenous university in Quito and the indigenous university in Puyo. But unlike many students in similar situations, they returned to the jungle. They were equipped with two languages and could move easily between the white world and the Shuar. Always a proud people, the Shuar became even more so because of the self-confidence education gave them. In the city, if you were to see a Shuar from a block away, you could recognize him as Shuar by his manner of confident bearing.

Before the *Radioescuela Telefonica,* five percent of the Shuar were literate. After the school had broadcasted for ten years, most of the Shuar—some say ninety percent—were educated.

CHAPTER FORTY-TWO

HIKING WITH CHILDREN TO AGUAS TERMALES

In the valleys above Miasal, flowed two small thermal waterfalls that affected the entire Tsuirim. People seeking them had to climb steep trails, ever alert for snakes, and take care not to touch the red and black poison-arrow frogs. The hike up the river itself was four miles long, clambering over rocks and swimming through little lagoons, a beautiful two-hour trip the children loved. One day the children at Miasal completed their radio school quarterly exams in advance of a two-week vacation. As a reward Juan had promised that the four best students would go with him to the falls. So about noon, the five of them set out. Juan and the two boys wore rubber boots, but the two girls were barefoot and politely refused Juan's offer to give them boots. The girls wanted to be able to use their toes, which would give them a better grip in the slippery soil and over the rocks.

Within a few minutes of the mission, they waded into the clear Tsuirim. The children paused to move rocks and chase flashes of silvery fish in the shallows, then they started up the faint jungle trail, barely visible as it meandered through the thick forest. When a piping guan, a chicken-sized black bird, whistled high in a tree, one of the boys imitated it perfectly and the bird peered from a branch to have a look at its rival.

Juan paused to show them the clear wings on a turquoise-colored cicada as it clung to a tree trunk, shrilling. Moss and vines mantled the big trees, and the little leaves of young philodendron vines plastered themselves on tree trunks as they began the climb upward. In a few years their huge leaves would wave in the sunlight a hundred feet up. The boys found a cluster of *boca chica* and teased the girls about their pouty-lip-shaped flowers, red-orange like the painted "mouth of the little girl."

Wading across a narrow channel, the little group began hiking up the river and discovered the clam-like fossils of brachiopods and snail-like ammonites. Some were embedded in huge gray boulders that edged the river while others were fist-sized rocks lying in the streambed. Always the teacher, Juan told them how the animals had been turned to stone. One of the girls said, "I wonder if they were good to eat, before they became stone that is."

The four continued upstream, ascending the edges of little waterfalls, walking easily across trees that had fallen over the stream (creating bridges from one side to the next), and swimming across clear green lagoons. The gorge of the Tsuirim was steep-sided, and its slopes wore blankets of green, from moss-like plants with eighth-inch-wide flowers to giant elephant-ear-shaped plants four feet across. In the sunny places, orange and yellow heliconia flowers hung in zigzags two feet long, oozing clear, sticky sap that attracted bright-colored hummingbirds. Dozens of butterflies flitted through the air like scattering confetti, a few with transparent wings that added glitter to the mix. But the most delightful butterflies of all were the four-inch-wide, iridescent-blue morphos. To the Shuar they were devils, the spirits of ancestors, but to Juan they looked like shards of fallen sky. The morphos flew singly up—or downstream, just above the water. Meeting other morphos, they would circle each other two or three times then continue on their way. When one landed on a branch to rest or feed, the butterfly folded its wings and disappeared, for while the tops of the wings were brilliant blue, their undersides were the color of dead leaves on tree trunks.

Around one more bend, the children became very excited to see clouds of steam rising into the air. *"Las cascadas,"* they shrieked eagerly and splashed ahead. By the time Juan arrived they were already spread-eagled on the red rock of the hottest waterfall, which was almost 106 degrees. The boys climbed to its top and leaped ten feet into the pool below. The girls, still wearing their thin cotton dresses, giggled behind their hands and let the hot water flow over their backs and heads. Then, as if by signal, the four dashed to the second waterfall, at the bottom of a long rock chute worn smooth by hundreds or thousands of years of water and grit pouring down it. That waterfall was cool, but beside it, from a little hole in the rock, hot water spouted as if from a faucet, warming the cauldron. Since Juan's previous visit a tree had fallen from above and lay upside down in the water like a branch-filled spear. The children used it for a climbing pole, cannonballing into the water to splash each other as their laughter echoed through the canyon.

Juan splashed with them for a while then went to fix a snack—a can of fat Ecuadorian sardines in olive oil laid atop soda crackers. As he sat by the stream and opened the can, he noticed a silvery-brown flash in a clear pool and the sharp dorsal fin of a little poison catfish. He'd show it to the children then teach them about nature's ways of protecting her children. The little fish were usually not deadly but would cause various parts of the body to swell. He'd seen a man stung on the left heel when he stepped on the spine of a five-inch-long catfish. In minutes the man's right eye swelled to the size of a golf ball and stayed that way for more than twenty-four hours.

Then out of the corner of his eye Juan saw a snake. It wasn't like the golden yellow five-foot-long boa his Shuar friends had smashed to a pulp nearby on the last trip. This one was dusky gray-black and barely visible against the rock on which it had been basking. The foot-long creature began to slither away. Juan knew it was not a poisonous variety but the Shuar consider any snake dangerous and kill any they see, like they had the yellow tree boa. Over the years, Juan had tried to teach them about snakes but got nowhere, so he let this one go its way, knowing he wouldn't tell the children it had even been there; it would only spoil their day.

The hike to the hot waterfalls had taken three hours. The trip home was even more fun and took about half the time, as they floated and swam through a series of lagoons, leaped from one waterfall pool into the next, slid down mossy slopes, clambered over boulders then through the dusky green jungle and back into the schoolyard. It had been a good day.

CHAPTER FORTY-THREE

TUKUP,
THE BIG MAN

The next day the children returned to their homes for their two-week vacations. Some parents came for their children but most of the students knew the way home; even the seven— and eight-year-olds went off on their own, often traveling two or three miles through the jungle. It was quiet at the mission, and Amalia wanted Juan to go away for a while. If he stayed home they'd think of work that needed to be done, and after two years without rest, they needed a break. If he left she could spend time relaxing and visiting with friends.

So she said. "Juan, you enjoyed your hike with the children so much. You should do that more often. In fact, I have some things that need to go to my friends who are the wives of Tukup. Why don't you take a break, too? You can deliver the gifts and go visit Tukup." For more than six months, except for the walk up the Tsuirim with the children, Juan had not even left the area of the mission. Tukup, the Great Man, most respected warrior of the Shuar and the Achuar, was always interesting to visit; plus, Juan could spend time with his adult friends in the jungle he loved. He thought about asking Amalia to go, too, but realized she had her plans. So he decided to see if he could find any of the local Shuar who might like to go on a visiting and hunting trip. It didn't take long to find companions.

At the community hall, several young men lounged on

benches or played barefoot soccer. Juan sauntered over to them and visited awhile. Several of them were good hunters and knew the forest well. One in particular, Bolivar, had a great sense of humor, and Juan hoped he would be interested. "I'm thinking of going down the Mangosiza to visit Tukup. Would any of you be interested in going along?" he asked. The men paused in their soccer game and looked at the ground and each other, considering. "It will be a trip of about ten days," Juan added. At this, several of them became excited, including Bolivar, who leaned back on his bench and made a little joke that made the others smile. At six feet, he was four to six inches taller than most of the Shuar, and a leader in a positive way. His mother had been raped by a miner and when she became pregnant the Shuar family adopted him as if he were born in the "correct way." Juan needed only two companions, for his *canoa* was large enough to carry but three people. "Would you join me, Bolivar?" Juan asked.

"Of course," he answered.

"Can you be ready to go in the morning?"

Bolivar grinned even more broadly. "I could be ready in an hour," he said. Because he had relatives downriver and often made trips there for the mission, he would be the main guide and *puntador,* riding in the bow of the *canoa* and leading them through the river's narrows and shallows.

Juan then chose Luis, a promising student about sixteen years of age, who was about to graduate. Luis and Juan would take turns as paddlers. Going downstream they would not be overworked, for the current was fast even in the low river. On the upstream push they would all have to work hard.

Almost jogging, Juan returned to his house, his own excitement mounting. He hadn't seen Tukup in several years, and each time they met they charmed each other. It was as if they had been childhood friends, although the difference in their ages was more than twenty years.

About seventy years of age at the time, Tukup was one of the last of the "big men," a once-dangerous warrior. Despite his age and the fact that he had been a Christian for many years, he continued to inspire awe and fear. As a warrior he had taken the *arutam* spirits and made *tsantsas* of more than thirty-five men, but always in war, never through sneak attacks.

Now most of his days were spent hunting, visiting friends, or playing with his many grandchildren. He had three wives. Because they were not sisters, which created some friction among them, each had a house and a little farm plot—a *chacra*—of her own. They were only half a mile apart, making it easy for him to spend a night or two with one then move to the next.

At his age, most men were content to settle back and let their sons take care of them. Tukup, however, remained in charge. He enjoyed hunting and did it almost every day. Tukup encouraged the Shuar to believe that he was Shuar and the Achuar to believe he was one of them. Politically and otherwise, this was a very helpful deception, for neither group would move against him.

As a leader among both groups, he felt he needed to know what was going on around him, so he often took long walking trips through the jungle, visiting friends and former enemies. Bolivar told Juan that he had been more than thirty miles from Tukup's house one time, visiting some Achuar friends, when Tukup strolled into the village. He stayed for the night. At dawn he shouldered his rifle and jogged off again, headed away from his homes and further into the forest.

Although they would often eat with families along the way, Amalia had prepared food for the travelers—part of her plan to get her husband out of her hair. In fact, she had been preparing it for several days before she asked him, knowing he would be eager to go. So the next morning she poured the concentrated travel *chicha* into calabash gourds and filled palm-net *shigra* bags with cooked *yuca* and plantains wrapped in banana leaves. Juan set the provisions atop more banana leaves in the bottom of the *canoa* along with their little gear. Juan carried his muzzle-loading rifle, and each man carried his machete.

As they were about to leave, Amalia gave Juan another *shigra* filled with packages carefully wrapped in banana leaves and tied with liana vines. These were the gifts for Tukup and his three wives. The travelers planned to stop along the way, visiting friends. They would stay in their friends' houses whenever possible, or they would build an *aak* along the shore if needed. If it rained during the day, they would simply get wet or just land and wait under trees until it passed.

The men weren't concerned about the rainstorms, however, as they set out. For weeks there had been little rain, and the Mangosiza River was quite low. Besides, it was early March, when it seldom rained in the Cutucus. Sometimes, within a few hundred yards, the river would change from deep to shallow as it braided its way from one rocky channel to the next, and Bolivar kept busy in his position at the bow. They drifted past half a dozen *chacras* in the first few miles, a very crowded area that had grown up around the school. Children ran to the shore and waved noisily, calling, *"Hola,"* *"Buenos dias,"* to practice their Spanish as the *canoa* floated past. Eventually, the greeters dwindled as the river widened and there were no more farms.

For hours the jungle drifted by, and the three men relaxed and talked. Bolivar was the man who usually led trips downriver and knew both the people and the river well. He was a good storyteller, and it seemed he had one to tell about every person along this stretch of river or who had lived at that abandoned farm. He knew the various bends and enjoyed telling about the animals he had seen there: "See that steep riverbank that ends in fast water over there? Last time we came here I watched three river otters playing on the bank. All of them were adults or nearly so because they were almost as long as Luis is tall. They wrestled in the mud, then slid down the bank and splashed into the fast water. They kept playing in the rapids, dunking each other and splashing as they were carried downstream. Then they swam back upstream, climbed the bank and did it again. My friends and I watched them for about half an hour before they got nervous about us and swam away."

Luis, though, was a good observer and, Juan suspected, a good hunter. About half a mile away, a pair of macaws flew toward them with their distinctive, fast wingbeats. "Blue and yellow macaws," he stated firmly.

Juan and Bolivar laughed and said, "Luis, those are only two dots. How can you tell what kind of macaws they are?" They thought he was just having fun with them. But the birds continued upriver, and as they neared the *canoa,* there was the flash of bright yellow breasts below blue bodies. Luis smiled at the other two and shrugged good-naturedly.

The Shuar continually surprised Juan with their seemingly wonderful eyesight. But this observation seemed unusually keen. Was there something in the way they flew? Or, was it their height above the ground? Maybe it was the sounds they made as they talked to each other. Luis couldn't explain. He just knew.

On the second day the men approached the edge of the mountains, and the water began to rise. Although they had seen only distant clouds, it was obvious that, on this stretch of river, rain had been falling for several days. The Mangosiza's curves began to sweep more grandly, carving deeply into the outer edges of its banks and depositing rocky beaches, often a hundred yards across, on the inner curves.

On one of the rocky beaches two children tended a smoky fire and waved excitedly. Then the men saw a Shuar man running toward them, also waving for them to pull in. Since their journey was unhurried, and guessing there could be trouble, they poled across the current to the shore. The man waded into the river and helped pull the *canoa* onto the rocks, so it wouldn't float away.

He shook hands with everyone and said with a huge grin, "I have something you might want to buy." Over the smoky fire the children were tending he had stretched a big jaguar skin. The children, a boy of about nine and a girl about eight, were drying and smoking it as a quick preservative. They, too, shook hands with the three visitors. Bolivar and Luis were interested, but Juan didn't want to buy the skin. If he did, it would encourage the man to go shoot more, and his old enemy the *tigre* was becoming very scarce, endangered even here.

The men sat on the beach in the sunlight as the mother arrived with a pot of *chicha* to refresh them. "Tell us about the *tigre,*" Juan said. The man, whose name was Santiago, puffed up a little and told this story.

The day before had been clear, and for most of it the sky gleamed an unblemished blue. After several days and nights of rain, the children and their puppy, a typical brindle-brown hound, were glad to be released from rain bondage and ran to the cobbly beach. While the girl stacked rocks to make a model house and farm, the boy and dog wrestled and tugged with a heavy stick. The family canoa with two paddles lying in its bottom balanced lightly on the shore in the already falling river. At the house and garden, on a rise overlooking the river and two hundred yards away, Santiago and his wife Juana watched and smiled, enjoying the rumpus on the beach almost as much as the children were.

Then a movement caught Santiago's eye, and instinctively he shouted, "Run!" A female *tigre* almost eight feet long leaped from a twelve-foot-high thicket of cane and charged toward the children so fast that her belly almost touched the ground. The alert jungle children heard the shout, saw the *tigre* and ran to the *canoa.* As the girl perched in the stern pushing hard with a paddle, the boy shoved the boat into the river and they thrashed away from shore. When the dog ran into the river, so did the *tigre,* for that was its real quarry—for the moment.

The panicked dog swam after the *canoa* and tried to get in. Already the *tigre* was half a *canoa* length away. Bravely, the girl grabbed the dog's neck skin and pulled it into the boat where it turned and bit at the cat, which had reached the *canoa* and was trying to claw its way over the gunwale. The children used their leaf-shaped *canoa* paddles, beating and jabbing at the snarling, slashing thing. For a moment the cat caught the girl's paddle and held on but the boy jabbed the sharpened end of his paddle at the cat's jaws. One of the tigre's teeth broke and fell into the boat. The addled cat let go of the girl's splintered paddle just as the boy jabbed it again. As the *canoa* spun into deeper water, the beast fell back into the current and shook, trying to clear its head so it could refocus on its new prey, the children.

Meanwhile, Santiago and Juana ran screaming to the battle. Santiago carried his rifle in one hand and a *chonta* lance in the other; Juana brandished her machete. By the time they reached the shore, the *canoa* battleground had drifted into the main current and was rushing downstream. They ran down the shore and finally got ahead of the screaming, snarling, splashing fight. Santiago cocked his rifle and waited, hoping for a clear shot, where he wouldn't hit the children. Then, just as the boy's paddle splintered with a loud, cracking, pop across the *tigre's* head, sending it back into the water. Santiago held his breath and pulled the trigger. The hot roar of heat and fear burst from the barrel and rolled, echoing around the little opening in the somber jungle, scattering a flock of green Amazon parrots and a toucanet. But the jaguar never heard it. The bullet popped into its skull, creating a pencil-size hole below her left ear, instantly scrambling her brain, then tore a two-inch hole on the right side as it exited. The jaguar's head spurted blood and she went limp in the water.

The children and their parents cheered in relief as the lifeless body drifted downstream amid a widening pool of red staining the dun-colored water.

Then things became practical. The children paddled themselves to shore where their mother swept them into a hug, the type she could give only when relieved of the fear they would never be able to hug again. Santiago, meanwhile, set his gun down and went to retrieve the jaguar's body. He swam and waded as he chased it downstream for a quarter mile before he could grasp its long tail and pull the heavy beast into an eddy where he rested for a while. Then the whole family pulled the cat, which weighed about two hundred pounds, onto the shore. Its skin if sold could feed them for more than a month. And, of course, Santiago now hoped that Juan and his friends would like to buy it.

The travelers were impressed with the story and convinced of its truth when the little girl showed them the claw marks on the gunwale of the *canoa* and the tooth they had broken out with the paddle. But when they left, the skin still smoked over the fire. It was mid-afternoon by this time and the birds were moving again. On the shore, a sun bittern fluttered and displayed its beautiful yellow tail markings shaped and colored like the rising sun. Cicadas droned in the hot, humid air, which carried with it the pleasant scent of moist and moldering leaves. They left Shuar territory and entered a countryside different from their Cutucu home. The rapids flattened out, and the river meandered more broadly. The mountains finally disappeared into the distance. The houses in this lowland area were perched atop twenty-foot-high riverbanks, built yet higher atop four—and five-foot-high piers because the floodwaters reached even to there.

A family of Siona Indians had recently moved to the area, bringing with them the bitter *yuca* they prefer. This kind of root crop had to be grated then squeezed to remove the poisonous juices from its pulp. Then the mash was cooked on a thin metal griddle into tortilla-like flatbreads about fifteen inches across. Juan bought some from a woman who draped her bread over liana ropes to dry, creating a scallop-edged effect. Although Juan had heard of manioc bread, this was the first he'd ever seen. It was hard, and it rattled like cardboard-dry Mexican tortillas in a *shigra* on the bottom of the boat. Its texture reminded him of blotter paper. At dinner they broke it into chunks and floated it in *chicha* to soften it, which helped it to taste a little better, but the men missed their usual boiled *yuca*.

The next day they began to notice more *colonos* than Shuar. They had come to the area in response to the government's offer of free land, even if it was remote and a week from any church. In some places, Shuar lived almost next door to *colonos* from the city. Still, some things hadn't changed much since Juan was a boy. The Shuar had lived in the jungle for hundreds, perhaps thousands, of years. They knew its secrets. But the *colonos* did not believe the *Jivaros* could know anything that would be of help to them and ignored their advice.

The *colonos* planted their gardens in rows, filling them with one or two crops packed together. Insects readily crawled from one plant to the next, slowly devouring the gardens. The diet of the Shuar was quite varied, so they had a good mixture of vitamins and minerals; their children were healthy. What's more, the Shuar limited their children, often nursing a child until it was two years of age. *Colono* children often shared their parents with ten siblings, many yellow-skinned and malnourished.

As with the Shuar children, the *colono* children gathered on the shore to wave, eager for anything new. The men approached a section of river that they could see was not good for a farm. The land along the bank was very flat. It would flood often, and the water would stay long enough to rot even *yuca*, which should be the main crop of the farm. Most *colonos* had avoided it, and no farms had been built. Then the men saw a group of six children, the eldest carrying a small baby of perhaps a year old balanced on her hip. Unlike others they had seen, these children stood without movement, solemnly watching a woman below them. The woman, their mother, was leaning over the gunwale of her canoe, wailing uncontrollably and washing out a long white object in the river. When she saw Juan and his companions, she leaped up and frantically waved with her palm down and fingers pushed from them to her. Please come help, she was pleading.

"It's Eva," Bolivar said to Juan. "I remember when her husband brought her here ten years ago. She was the most beautiful woman I have ever seen. Now look at her. She is no more than 29, and look how old she is." He was right. The wailing woman with sallow skin and filthy, graying hair looked more than 50. As they again poled out of the current and swung toward shore, they saw that the white object she had been washing was a cow's intestine. She was cleaning it out to use later for stuffing with meat.

She threw the intestine into her *canoa* and ran to help the men with theirs. As she sobbed, she ignored Bolivar and Luis, speaking directly to Juan to ask for his help.

Her husband had gone on a hunting trip two days before. Alone with the children, she had gone to milk their one cow a few hours before Juan and his friends arrived. She caught it and looped a rope around its neck, then realized that she'd forgotten the pail, so she tied the cow to a tree and ran to the house. Although she was only gone for a moment, it was too long. By the time she started back she could hear the cow thrashing in agony. Something had panicked the poor beast, and she pulled back against the rope. As it squeezed off her breath, the panic increased, and she fell to the ground. Eva tried to untie the rope, but it had pulled too tight. She ran to the house for the machete, but by the time she got back and cut the tight rope from the cow's neck, it was dead.

And when the cow died so did Eva's little hope.

Among her children, the youngest was a set of twins. One lay in the house, sick and weak, and the other was the one Juan had seen perched on his sister's hip. Either one or both would die without the extra nutrition from the milk. The *colono* diet lacked calcium, so rickets often curved the children's legs into bows. Several of the watching children already showed the symptoms. In Shuar, Bolivar spoke to Juan. "I know the Shuar who live just downstream. They told me that many times they have tried to help and offer advice, but Eva's husband always laughs at them. He planted rice instead of yuca and never planted plantains. He planted his garden in rows instead of separated patches, which would have kept insects from traveling from one plant to another." From where they stood, Juan could see that Bolivar was right. The garden was sickly yellow, and the leaves were full of holes. Where there should have been grain, there were only ravaged, dead heads.

Shaking his head sadly, Juan asked Eva, "What can we do to help?"

"Padre Raul has told me that you also are a man of God. Can you baptize my babies?"

"No. I am not a priest. I would be glad to offer them a blessing, but I cannot baptize."

"Then I would ask this. When you return this way please take the meat from the cow. The children and I have cut it up and now will smoke and dry it. Then you can take the dried meat, sell it for what you can and buy two christening dresses. When Padre Raul comes next time, and I hope it is soon, he can baptize them. Then if they die . . ." Unable to speak more, she bowed her head and her shoulders shook as she wept quietly.

Back in midstream the men paddled quickly with the current. The dugout sliced its way along through the water, which was now the color of coffee with cream. The men sat in silence, thinking of the family, as white foam drifted from the bow and spun gently away until the bubbles popped. High in the treetops, iguanas sunned on branches a hundred feet above the water, but Luis didn't even think of shooting them. Black silhouettes of anhingas and cormorants perched in the sunlight, atop leafless snags near to the water, holding their wings out like wet laundry to dry in the sun, but they reminded Bolivar of no stories. Little brown bats flitted from the undersides of snags jutting from the river, then returned to their perches after the *canoa* passed. The jungle may have looked like a·

paradise of plenty, but the reality was that one must learn to live with it, not to fight it. In this case it may have been a fatal mistake for the *colonos* to think that the indigenous people had nothing to teach them. Juan quietly prayed for the safety of the family, and made the decision to study harder to become a deacon so he could baptize properly.

The mountain river Mangosiza joined the flatter Morona, one of the major sources of the Amazon itself, and they knew they were almost at the end of their journey. The river was now several hundred yards across and dozens of feet deep, so Bolivar dozed in the bow. Every half an hour or so he would awaken then, without glancing at the river, wave his hand in a "continue forward" motion and return to dozing.

A large stream flowed into the main river, and Juan suggested, "Let's pull into an eddy and see if we can catch some fish for dinner." As if to confirm that the fishing was good, two pink river dolphins rolled across the surface with a gasping, breath-spurting sound. Many of the Indians of the Amazon believed that the dolphin was a magical being, that it could change form at will. A man alone in the jungle might see one that has changed to a beautiful woman coming to seduce him. Many a woman claimed that the baby in her womb was the fruit of a dolphin that came ashore as a handsome man and bewitched her. Because of the awe they inspired, and because the people feared magical retaliation, the Indians almost never hunted the dolphins. But, man, woman or beast, these dolphins were barely curious about the men in the dugout. They circled once, gave another little gasping spout, and dove to return to the confluence where fish gathered.

It was early March and the *chuwis* (oropendolas)—both Montezumas and chestnut-sided—were nesting. Flights of the big birds passed overhead, their wing-beats sounding like the rotors of distant helicopters. They made typical oriole-style nests, bags woven of fibers and grass, but theirs were three feet long. The males perched on nearby branches, making their territorial calls. Flexing their wings to show golden yellow markings, they dipped forward, shook their wings and gave a deep "glunk-glum" call that sounded like dripping water.

Several cuckoos also perched in nearby trees, watching the oropendola colony with cunning eyes. When a pair of oropendolas flew away from the nest, Juan knew that a cuckoo would fly into the hole at the top. A moment later, one oropendola egg would drop from the nest and the cuckoo would lay her own in its place. Juan knew she was busy hurrying to lay her own in place of the other. In less than a minute she would flash away before the owners returned. Most of the time, however, the oropendolas would recognize the foreign egg and give it a proper shove to the forest floor. But the birds in this colony seemed to be tolerating the cuckoos, as there were no signs of broken eggs on the ground. Clouds of botflies, which would parasitize baby birds in their nests, told Juan what was happening.

Botflies would buzz into a nest and lay their eggs. When the eggs hatched, the botfly larvae would begin to eat their host, slowly killing it. But if a cuckoo were in the nest, its egg would hatch first and quickly become active and aggressive, attacking any insect movement in the nest, keeping it and their oropendola nestmates botfly free. So when there were many botflies, the oropendola allowed the eggs to remain in their nests.

As they were near the Peruvian border they came to the army post Juan had visited years before, where the soldiers had kept Shuar women as slaves. There was a different attitude this time as soldiers bearing machine guns waved them to shore. They gave the boat a desultory check, and when they were finished, the soldiers and travelers visited. Every Ecuadorian male had to serve in the army for a year when they turned eighteen. Most of the young men at the post were Blacks from Esmeraldas, by the ocean. They were bored and glad of the company. Each day their daily patrols lasted a few hours then they oiled their guns in readiness for a Peruvian invasion. But mostly they played barefoot soccer on the airfield, which they kept trimmed short with their machetes. William Sanchez, the lieutenant in charge, was a career officer. About thirty years of age, he was clean and pressed, even in the jungle. His dark moustache was neatly trimmed, his bearing erect. Several times each day he went to the radio and, while a private cranked the radio to provide the power to run it, William reported that all was well. It was supposed to be a secret transmission, but he had to shout to be heard, so everyone in the compound was aware, including the three visitors.

At Miasal a rumor had circulated that the government was creating a new road so more *colonos* could come to the area northeast of the Mangosiza. William reported that the story was true and asked Juan and his friends if they wanted to join the squad on their afternoon patrol. They did and climbed into the armored powerboat for the three-mile trip downstream.

Juan appreciated the speed but disliked the vibration and the disconnection that he felt from the forest. Of course the jungle slid by faster than when they paddled through even the biggest rapids, but the motor's roar overpowered the reassuring sounds of the forest. Plus, they were going so fast there was no time to observe what was occurring on the banks.

Then there it was, a two-track path through the jungle with the trees cut down for about fifty feet on each side. Roads such as this one usually brought more trouble than opportunity. While the soldiers continued downriver, Juan, Bolivar and Luis walked up the deserted road for a few miles. They'd walked for a mile when Luis asked, "Have you noticed how sad the birds are? None of them are singing. Every trail in the forest has tracks and signs of animals crossing it. Since we left the river I have seen nothing."

For the time being, the road ended at the Morona River but Juan and the others knew that soon two or three poor houses would stand on each side of the river and that the road would continue the same way on the other side. A ferry most likely would go back and forth, carrying settlers and miners who did not respect the forest, and who would abuse the Shuar. Juan shook his head sadly, remembering the same scenario from his boyhood days, which seemed destined to be repeated.

Author's note: I visited the place in 1997 with Carlos Arcos and saw that Juan's fears had been realized. Two nasty border-type houses (one of which was probably a whorehouse and the other a little cafe with pigs and chickens scurrying about under the tables) hug the riverbank and are known as "Porto Morona," Port of Morona. A ferry travels back and forth across the river as needed, following a cable that keeps it from drifting in the current. On the other side of the river, a similar house crouches by the road, which continues into the jungle about seven more miles. It ends at a little settlement of colonos who came there because they heard the rumors that the government believed there was oil under the jungle in that area. In some of these kinds of places the people have denuded the forest, but here the settlers have not. There is little impetus to cut down trees, for it is an 18-hour bus trip to the nearest city, and that is just too far to haul trees when one forest giant would fill two trucks. Because Porto Morona is so close to the disputed border with Peru, floating logs down river is no option either. Meanwhile, the colonos farm and scratch out a miserable existence.

There were two white prostitutes at the cabin, when I visited, and each had several children. One woman was very fragile and fearful. Her companion was rather pretty in a rough way. She seemed the more independent and showed definite distaste when their—yes their—husband appeared on the ferry one morning, strutting and demanding. My son Justin, a friend and I were stuck at Porto Morona for the night, when the boat we'd arranged failed to arrive. Carlos rented a little two-room space from the women, so we wouldn't have to sleep on the bare ground. He climbed into a canoe with some other fellows and went to search for a boat and boatman. Our room had no beds. It was merely a six-by-six foot space, large enough to lay out sleeping bags. As we opened the door, four-inch-long brown cockroaches scurried into the darkness. Our traveling companion decided to sleep on a small table on the porch rather than on the floor. The boatman never did arrive, and we had to wait two days before Carlos returned with another boat for us to use. As we sat, waiting and sipping warm Cokes, an explosion echoed across the river and in seconds the ground around us splattered with spent shot pellets. A man at the house on the other side had, perhaps, shot at a bird in a tree and peppered us.

Presidents of Ecuador come and go like thunderstorms in the night. A president's term is supposed to be six years long but in ten years, five different presidents had been forced out of office. The president at the time of our visit was Abdala. As we waited for a boat, a delegation of soldiers arrived from the frontier. They were bringing schoolbooks to give to the local children, a gift from President Abdala, who wanted all the children of Ecuador to read—a good idea but also self-serving, for the back cover of each book bore the smiling image of El Presidente. Abdala raised money for various funds by producing CDs on which he sang rather poorly but lustily. He liked publicity and insisted that all milk cartons carry both his picture and name. It was called Abdalaleche, Abdala milk. Most of the people of Ecuador thought he was crazy, and in a few months he was forced out of office. But it turned out he was crazy like a fox. His son had been made some sort of minister and in that six months cleared several million dollars, which ended up in his pocket. Abdala himself left the country, allegedly with his "retirement fund" of several million

American dollars, which he somehow had allegedly stolen from the treasury.

As the second day ended, we still had no boat, and there was no sign of Carlos. In the middle of that second night a truck horn blared in front of the little cabin. When we looked out we saw a large truck honking for the ferryman to come and take it across the river. Behind the big truck a smaller one held an unusual load. One side had a skinny brown horse; the other held a twenty-foot-long dugout tipped against the cab and almost touching the ground behind. Morning came too early, and by seven o'clock we were famished. As we breakfasted on hard-boiled eggs and drank more warm Coca-Cola, a long dugout nosed into shore near us. It was powered by an ancient, rusted outboard motor and captained by two young men. We went to talk with them and were surprised at their cargo. Lying in the bottom of the boat were three huge catfish, each more than four feet long, with whiskers that swept across the width of the boat and overhung the gunwales. We were admiring them when Carlos also returned with a boat. We bought about ten pounds of catfish to cook for later and left as quickly as we could.[a]

Juan:

We hiked back to the river just as the patrol returned, and William picked us up then returned us to the army post. By noon we continued on our way to see Tukup. On the way downriver, we rode in midstream. Now we poled slowly along the shore, where the current was slowest. It took several hours to cover the two or three miles we had gone downstream to the army post. The next morning we continued another four miles to where a little unnamed river flowed into the Morona. This little stream, which led to Tukup's house, was clear and dark, almost black. Although it looked very small, the flow of the nameless stream was huge for its size. A distinct line formed, one side dark and clear, the other tan and thick. Separated in an undulating line, the two ran side by side for a quarter mile before mixing.

We put down our poles and began to paddle again, for although the river was no more than thirty feet across, it was twenty feet deep. Trees draped over the river, creating an archway covered with moss and epiphytes growing on the branches. In the forest it was cooler but very humid, and soon we were soaked in sweat. The call of little birds named screaming pia echoed through the forest and gave us assurance that there were hills and dry land not too far off into the forest for the birds only live where there is land. The Shuar call them pueepweeo birds for the sound of their call, which is so powerful it seems it must come from a bird many times the size of the little pia. Then from trees by the water came the growling-huffing, prehistoric sounding call of hoatzin birds. We laughed as five or six adults flew and crashed from one branch to another and several babies dove into the water. They swam using their wings like arms, then once under cover, they used claws on their wings to climb the roots and hide. Hoatzins are pheasant-sized birds that look almost as prehistoric as their call sounds. We needed meat but no one raised the gun or a blowgun, for we all knew that hoatzins taste awful—their common name among the Shuar means "stinky turkey."

Although the water looked calm, it was moving very fast. They paddled hard, following the shoreline as it meandered its way through the forest. By this time it was late afternoon, and they needed to find a camp. Juan watched the lowering sun. First it was directly ahead of them, then it slid to their right, then behind them, and finally ahead of them again as they followed the meanders of the river.

Finally they found a little sandbar with a grove of *guarumbo* (cecropia) trees. The undergrowth would be thick there, but smaller and easier to clear for a campsite. The fast-growing, white-barked *guarumbo* arched upward for about thirty feet to where the parasol-shape tops spread their three-foot-wide leaves. Juan watched for sloths in the branches, for this was one of the sloth's favorite foods, but there were none. Exhausted, they beached the dugout and set up camp.

Juan:

I was taken back in memory more than forty years as we built an aak and began to heat our simple meal.

About half a mile away a black howler monkey began its loud, challenging call. Luis and Bolivar discussed where the troupe would be sleeping. If they could find them very early, we could have meat next morning.

Then a jaguar coughed. We looked at each other and realized the night would not be restful. I thought to myself, "Nothing has changed. There are still *Tigres of the Night*, and we must protect ourselves."

Our campsite was at the inside edge of a curve of the river, with a magnificent view up and downstream for several hundred yards. As the stream disappeared toward the west and the setting sun, a single ceiba tree rose above the jungle, its broad gray trunk shining in the light like a two-hundred-foot-high wall. Huge lianas hung from it as if tethering it to the ground and grew onto the smaller trees below. We watched in awe as the sun began to slip more quickly downward and the tree turned to silhouette. The air began to cool and cicadas slowed their trilling, screeching calls as tree frogs began theirs, a passing of the torch from the animals of the light to those of darkness. Then we heard the macaws coming. From every direction pairs of macaws were returning to roost. As they flew with their characteristic fast wingbeats, they continually garble-talked about their day. Squawks and screeches, low moans and flashing iridescent colors filled the air around the tree. I tried to count the birds and, within twenty minutes, estimated there were more than two hundred. Even after everyone was home for the night, fluttering and rustling—and of course that strange parrot talk—continued throughout the crown. Then at the final darkness, the tree fell silent except for a few screeching arguments over some choice perch, and the silhouette of the tree gradually dissolved into the jungle and the night sky.

The three slept nervously that night, one man always on guard, but the *tigre* never came near. Well before dawn Bolivar and Luis left with their blowguns to find the howlers. Macaws had delicious meat, and they considered shooting some of them, but they decided that one monkey would feed the hungry men better than three or four of the birds, which were probably too high in the tree anyhow. An hour later, they returned with a young male howler monkey tied on Luis like a backpack. They'd had a good shot at the alpha male when it stood on a branch challenging them but chose the young one instead. The Shuar try never to shoot the alpha since it has much of the wisdom of the monkey troupe and to kill him would be to deprive the family of knowledge that would ensure its survival, and thus the survival of the Shuar.

Luis built up the fire, and Bolivar laid the carcass on it, rotating it often as he singed off the hair and killed the ticks. Bolivar then skinned it and cut it up. While the meat boiled in a pot with *yuca* and plantain, Juan spread *guarumbo* leaves on the ground and set out a little gourd with a salt-and-hot-pepper mixture. Luis stirred the clear river water into another gourd with the concentrated *chicha*, and they sipped as they waited for the food to cook. As dawn broke, the macaws began to stir and talk. Wings battered lightly as they stretched then began to fly away, a few pairs at a time. When a small group passed overhead in the sunlight the earthbound men noticed there were several types—blue and yellow, scarlet, and even the lovely and rare hyacinth macaw.

They finally arrived at Tukup, the airstrip village the "big man" or *kakaram* (warrior) had named for himself. Children dove into the tannin-darkened water from a broken tree trunk, laughing and waving as the men approached. They swam to the *canoa* and chattered excitedly as they held to the gunwales of the boat then helped pull it onto the shore. About eight to ten years of age, they were the children and grandchildren of Tukup. One ran to tell his father that Juan had arrived for a visit as the travelers gathered their gear and started toward the settlement.

Settlement was actually not quite the word, for it consisted of a metal-roofed school building made from sawn timbers and a single house for Tukup's second of three wives, Mercedes Hirarit, an Achuar. Because school was not in session, Juan suggested they put their equipment in the schoolhouse. It had been closed up quickly as the children and their teacher dashed for freedom, so the benched tables were jumbled around the dusty room. While Bolivar and Luis moved them to the edges, Juan used a broom he found in one corner and began to sweep the floor. When they were finished, they had cleared just enough space for the three of them to lie down.

Suddenly, they heard a shrieking scream. Mercedes ran from the garden calling that a snake was chasing her. A ten-foot-long pole used for knocking papayas from a tree leaned against the schoolhouse, and Juan grabbed it as he, Bolivar and Luis ran to help. When Mercedes saw them she ran toward them just as a dusty brown snake not quite two feet long slithered from the garden and followed her. Juan recognized it as a type that is very aggressive. Indeed, it appeared to be chasing her. With the long pole he pinned it to the ground and was considering how to get it safely away when Bolivar solved the problem. With his machete he cut off its head then pulverized the creature with the flat of the blade until even the twitching muscles stopped. Using the machete they dug a little hole and buried the head then threw the rest of the carcass into the forest.

The children, too, came running and gathered around Mercedes, now calm, who thanked the three. "I was busy weeding the garden and singing one of the songs to the garden spirits when I heard a rustle behind me. I looked just in time to see the snake coming toward me. That was when I screamed and ran." She laughed and said, "You must be hungry and thirsty. Wait here, and I will bring you *chicha* to refresh yourselves."

They sat on the ground, in the shade of a large breadfruit tree, talking about the snake. In a few minutes Mercedes returned with a pot of fresh *chicha*, which she served to them one at a time. As they drank, the boy who had gone to notify Tukup returned. "My father says please come to see him later this afternoon. He has just returned from a hunting trip and is busy preparing the peccary he has killed. He says please come to eat with him tonight."

Back in the schoolhouse Bolivar and Luis immediately went to sleep. Juan sat on the little porch, leaning against the schoolhouse wall as he watched the children at play. He prayed, thanking his God for their safe arrival, for their arrival just in time to help and for the opportunity God had given him to live in such a wonderful part of the world. Then he, too, dozed.

He woke about half past three and stood to stretch. His movements woke Bolivar and Luis who asked eagerly, "Is it time to see Tukup?"

"Yes," Juan said. "It is about a mile to his house, and perhaps we should start."

With a warrior's mentality, Tukup had built his house atop the only hill in the area. The trail was steep, and because Tukup was impatient with winding trails that took too long to climb, it went straight up for almost four hundred feet. Roots, which Tukup had used for steps, grew across the trail, but he and his sons also cut steps in the clay soil with their machetes. When the men reached the top, none of the three paused, for they were all jungle-hardened and barely panted with the exertion of the climb. It was another three quarters of a mile by a trail through the forest before they heard the dogs barking.

The dogs belonged to Tukup's first wife, another Achuar named Tsenia Kashijint, but since he wanted everything about him to appear big and dangerous, he bought her the largest he could find. Normal jungle dogs weighed fifty pounds. Tsenia's were at least sixty-five. Juan called, "Tuuhey!" in the traditional greeting that says, "I am here and come in peace." Tukup's sons had built a covered platform for the dogs. From this raised porch four brown dogs barked, snarled and strained at their tie ropes as the travelers sidled past. Juan had seen Tukup's dogs before, but Bolivar and Luis were wide-eyed at their size and aggressiveness.

Then they saw the "great house." It was built like most others, but half again the size of a typical Shuar home. Tukup knew how to keep his visitors slightly on edge, part of the reason he was still alive.

Juan stopped at the door. He heard no sound inside the house to indicate anyone was home, but he knew that everyone, including Tukup's wives and all his family, would be waiting. When he called a greeting, the voice of Tukup himself answered from the darkness, "Friend Juan. Come into my house and be welcomed."

Bolivar opened the plank door, and the three stepped in, walking to the right and immediately sitting on the bench along the wall. Tukup sat on a boa-shaped *chimbi* stool by the *pau*, the support pole at the center of the room. Wearing only running shorts, he was weaving a fish trap from palm fibers and did not rise but smiled at the three men when they stepped in. As was customary, the room went silent so the visitors could rest. Tukup liked big things, but he himself was small, no more than five feet six inches. As Tukup worked in the light of a candle, Juan noticed the notch at the bridge of his nose where a bullet creased him in a battle some forty years earlier. He was almost eighty now, a little round in the stomach but muscled and healthy-looking and certainly not fat.

After a respectfully silent time, Tukup spoke quietly, and Tsenia brought in her pot of *chicha.* Juan was surprised at the change in her appearance, for she was not well. The last time he had seen her, Tsenia was an energetic seventy-five-year-old woman with a round face and quick step. In the semi-darkness, her face was skull-like with thinly stretched skin over bone. She carried the heavy *chicha* pot with difficulty but neither expected nor received any help with it.

She gave Juan a broad smile as she filtered the creamy *chicha* into an achiote-red ceramic bowl of the Achuar type, wiping the edge and licking the residue in the traditional way, to show it was not poisoned. Then she handed it to Juan, who drained the bowl and returned it to Tsenia. After the men had drunk their first bowlful, Tukup opened the conversation, and his happy but reserved personality came out.

Juan gave him a pack of cigarettes he'd brought as a gift. As Tukup contentedly smoked Juan brought out the gifts for his wives from Amalia. Soon the adult sons came into the room, also barefoot and wearing only shorts. They shook hands with the visitors then sat on an opposite bench. As they sipped bowls of *chicha,* the evening began. Laughter filled the room, and from the family side of the house occasional giggles spilled from the women and children.

Tsenia and Mercedes laid banana leaves on the floor and poured out little piles of a salt-and-hot-pepper mixture for dipping. Then pots full of boiled plantain and *yuca* were poured onto the fresh banana leaves. As the men ate the vegetables, Tukup's wife, Nunkui, the only Shuar wife, brought another cooking pot filled with gray ropes of boiled, steaming peccary intestine. With her machete she cut the rubbery meat into two-foot-long strips and laid some before each man. Talking ceased as everyone settled in to eat. Juan and his friends were famished. They'd eaten nothing all day except *chicha*. Tsenia smiled broadly as they continued to compliment her cooking, saying, "*Rico, muy rico*" (delicious, very rich and delicious).

When they had finished eating, Nunkui brought in a pot of water. Each of the Shuar took a mouthful and sprayed it onto their hands, wiping them on their shorts. Juan poured a little over his hands instead.

The room was almost dark now, so one of the women brought in two candles, which she set on the floor. Almost two inches across and eight inches high, the flames guttered in the light breeze that slipped through the walls of the house and stirred the smoke from the cooking fire, which drifted just over their heads and out the open tops of the walls. White moths flew around the candle flames until they singed their wings and fell into the hot wax at the candle base to be entombed when it hardened.

As the men laughed together, enjoying food and gossip, a jungle storm approached. Rain frogs, which looked like giant bullfrogs, began to whoop. The Cofan Indians to the north believed that the rain frogs actually called for it to rain, and conversation stopped as they listened to first one then another joining in the chorus until rain frogs *whoop-whooped* from the forest all around the house. If a needed rain does not come, the Cofan would copy the sound of the frogs and try to call it in, the jungle equivalent of a rain dance. Laughing, Tukup and one son made frog calls and in minutes lightning began to flash strobe-like, casting shadows through the vertical palm walls and filling the room with the scent of ozone. Then the curtain of rain swept over them with a rush and roar that lasted for an hour.

Tsenia spoke quietly to Tukup, who turned to Juan. "My friend. One of the children is sick. Would you see if you can help?"

"Of course," Juan said.

Tsenia and her daughter-in-law led Juan into the family room, which was lit only by the cooking fire. In the rafters over the fire, a puma skin, stretched with sharpened palm branches, dangled in the smoke-filled rafters, slowly rough-curing beside drying meat. Two new clay pots almost four feet high stood curing atop little wood platforms; an old darkened pot was still half filled with *chicha* if more should be needed that night.

Juan smiled and greeted the children sitting in the room. The littlest ones snuggled against their older siblings and watched the stranger with wide-eyed, fearless interest. Traditional Shuar beds raised above the ground circled the room's perimeter. One had a little palm fiber hammock hung over it so the baby's mother could be nearby yet sleep well herself. The sick child was napping securely in it, and when Juan lifted the little girl, he was glad to see that whatever was wrong did not seem serious. He gave her half an aspirin in a little cup of *chicha* and told the mother to give her the second half if she woke in the night.

Returning to the room of the men, he found Tukup talking about the difficulties of feeding his large family. "We had a good hunt this morning," Tukup began. Juan urged him to tell the story of the hunt.

Tukup recalled the day.

"When I woke this morning I could smell the peccaries. The wild pigs had passed by in the night and went through our garden. We knew because of that rank, almost sour smell they have. It seemed to be everywhere, so I knew there must be many of them. Two of my sons and I took our spears and rifles, and we ran after them. They were easy to follow, because

they were eating their way through the forest, and we could
see where the mud on their bodies had rubbed off on the
leaves.

"We found them in a place where the forest was very thick.
I could not see them, but they were clacking their teeth
together to warn us to stay away. It sounded like pieces of
wood being hit together. I've seen as many as thirty in a herd,
but this one had only ten. Still, they were very dangerous."
He smiled as he continued. "Once I was hunting alone and
shot a young peccary from a herd. The others turned on me,
and I dropped my gun to climb a tree. They circled the tree,
squealing and beating their teeth together for a long time then
laid down around the tree. It was many hours before they
got hungry and left so I could climb down.

"Today we had better luck. I shot a half-grown female,
and the others did not chase us. They turned and ran, so we
chased them, but they were too fast. The three of us were
separated, and it took us almost an hour to get together again,
calling and calling then walking toward the sound. By the
time we got back to the dead pig it was covered with ants. It
had many ticks too, but they were beginning to drop off since
the heart had stopped beating. As we were sweeping the ants
away I heard a piping guan. It's one of my favorite birds to
eat. Have you ever eaten one? Their feathers are shiny, what
you call iridescent, black. They are about the size of a chicken,
but they taste much better. So while my sons prepared to carry
the peccary home I found and shot the guan. Now we have
food for everyone for almost a week."

Juan could picture the return, Tukup in the lead followed
by one son who carried the pig slung over his shoulders. As
the men entered the clearing by the house the women eagerly
gathered around. Then the women laid banana leaves on the
ground and the pig atop the leaves. As the men relaxed with
bowls of *chicha*, the women poured pots of boiling water over

the carcass to clean the pig and loosen the hair, which would scrape off easily with a machete. After a final rinse they moved the cleaned animal to fresh banana leaves, where it was cut up. The rinsed intestines, which would spoil quickly, were cleaned then went right into a pot and had been served for their dinner. The other parts were cut into smaller portions and hung in the smoke over the cooking fire to preserve them.

Now that there was plenty of food, Tukup and his sons were planning a hunting trip, this one for tapir. Did Juan and his friends want to come along? "It's a very remote place," Tukup said as if his home somehow were not.

To hunt with Tukup would be a great honor. Juan eagerly accepted for the three of them. And it was agreed they would leave early in the morning.

At first light the six men—Tukup and two of his sons, Bolivar, Luis and Juan—climbed into Tukup's dugout with their gear. This *canoa* was made from *moral*, a grayish wood that contains bits of silica and which is so hard it dulls iron tools. Almost thirty feet long, the *canoa* itself was quite heavy but was well balanced and easily sliced through the water as they poled and paddled up Tukup's river for two hours.

"There it is," Tukup announced. "The Zabalo River." All Juan could see was a sandbar with several inches of water flowing over it and into the river. "There was a flood a year ago, and when it had passed, the mouth of the Zabalo was filled with sand," Tukup explained. The men would have to push the heavy dugout upstream for a quarter of a mile. Without wasting time, the men climbed from the boat into the eighty-degree water. They took positions along the side of the dugout and began to count and push. In ten sweating minutes they had pushed it a hundred feet.

Then Juan noticed a cecropia grove with a sloth high in its branches. When they were clearing the airstrip at Miasal they had cut down hundreds of such trees. He remembered the slippery underbark and had an idea. As the others rested, he and Bolivar cut down one of the trees and cut the trunk into four-foot-long poles, which they carried to the dugout. Bark chips fell onto the water-covered sand as the men stripped the poles to reveal the slimy under-lining. Juan laid these under the dugout as rollers and the boat slid forward almost easily. As each pole rolled to the end of the boat, one man would move it to the front again. About half an hour later they arrived at the lagoon where the river continued.

"A very useful trick," Tukup mused to Juan as the men climbed into the boat and continued upstream.

The Zabalo was a little smaller than Tukup's river, only thirty-five or forty feet across, so the archway of trees was complete, creating a green, trilling and buzzing canopy over the men. The clear water flowed quickly toward the sandbar, carrying bits of fluff from the ceiba tree, which the men gathered to dry and use later for their blowgun darts. Basilisks, "Jesus Christ lizards, "scurried over the shallow water near shore with light splashing sounds, then up the damp shores. Barely a breath of wind passed over the hunters below, but far above in the canopy, the branches swayed silently. River turtles the size of hubcaps sunned on logs midstream plopped into the water as the *canoa* approached. The damp air was heavy with the scent of mold and the perfume of flowering trees. Thousands of tiny pink and blue flowers drifted down from high in the canopy, settling on the water to join the thousands of others already swirling on the surface.

Flights of noisy macaws flew overhead, settled into a *kaningacho* tree and began to attack the fruit. *Kaningacho* nuts are thick-shelled, but soon the tree was filled with the sound of parrots cracking them with their huge beaks. They wanted the brain-like custardy layer inside, which they loved to eat, after which they'd drop the shells and nuts. Occasionally one dropped a whole, heavy nut, and it fell with a loud cracking sound like a pistol shot as it bounced from branch to branch, scattering fruit from other trees and lianas, until it finally settled on the forest litter or splashed in the water. The surface of the stream rippled as fish rose for their share of the fruit, and that night pacas and agoutis would claim their portion from the forest floor. If the men hadn't been after bigger game, this would have been a good place to hunt in the evening.

When they heard a loud warning call, the men watched in delighted awe as a hundred-foot-tall tree began to shake as if a giant had it by the throat. It was filled with dozens of squirrel monkeys, all making their escape. Males stood on branches, bouncing up and down and hooting warnings and defiance. Lianas draped the tree and connected it to others. These became highways with silhouettes of long-tailed monkeys dashing away. Then as quickly as it began, the shaking of the tree ceased, and the monkeys were gone.

By the time the hunting party had gone a mile, the river's character began to change. Instead of an open canopy of trees over a clear river, it suddenly became choked with trees and lianas just at or below river level. Sometimes when a dugout would just barely fit under the trees, the men laid low so the boat could slide under as they watched for snakes and bala ants that might drop on them. Then they might paddle a hundred feet or less to climb out of the boat onto a log that spanned the river. Standing on the log, they would pull the dugout onto it, balance the boat for a moment like a see-saw, then get in and push on to the next. Sometimes a tree was over the river, and they couldn't go under or over it until they cut out a section in the middle. One fallen tree in particular was strange to Juan. When the axe bit into the wood, the chips were bright red and so heavy that, instead of floating, they sank.

By late afternoon they had traveled almost ten tortuous miles. Somehow, in a forest that all looked the same, Tukup suddenly pointed into the jungle and announced, "The salt lick is over there. When we find a sandbar we will camp." A few hundred yards later, a sandbar appeared across the inside of a curve in the river, and they beached the *canoa*.

Bolivar began searching the forest for a certain plant he needed. When the dugout had passed under one of the overhanging trees, he had brushed against a stinging caterpillar. Its poisonous hairs penetrated his skin, raising welts in a line across his arm; several dozen white bumps were already swelling together. He said it felt like a burning branch laid on his arm, but he had remained quiet for some hours. Amalia had shown Juan this medicine, so he knew the plant too, and together he and Bolivar found it quickly. When they found the plant Juan crushed several of its leaves and mixed with a little clay to make a moist paste, which he smeared across the welt. Then he used a whole leaf of the same plant as a bandage and a liana-bark string to hold it in place. In half an hour the pain ceased.

Their campsite was surrounded on all sides by animal sounds—from the softening chirrings of the turquoise-colored cicadas to the increasing pippings of tree frogs and the rustlings of little animals eating their way through the forest litter. In the early dusk it was dark on the forest floor, but the sky was light, almost white. An occasional lightning bug trailed a line of light as it shot upward through the foliage, shining like a miniature shooting star.

Juan had brought a flashlight, and after eating, the men decided to see if there were any caiman nearby. Relatives of crocodiles, they lay along the edges of streams and waited for food to come to them. Usually they were no problem, preferring to eat fish or unwary capybara, the giant guinea-pig-like animals, but some caiman grew to be fifteen feet of more long. If the hunters had one for a neighbor, it would be a good thing to know.

Walking quietly along the tangled shoreline, Juan put the flashlight against his forehead and shined it over the edges of the water. Suddenly, little bright ruby lights appeared, the eyes of a caiman. The others couldn't see the eyes until they, too, held the light against their forehead and shined the light outward. While most of the red eyes were only an inch or two apart, they did find one set with almost six inches between the eyes, a truly large fellow.

Mosquitoes began to buzz around them, and Luis cut a little tree with an ant nest in it. The others gathered more nests, and when they returned to camp the nests were put into the edge of the fire until they began to burn. They would smolder most of the night, the smoke chasing away most of the mosquitoes. But just to be sure, they also gathered little citrus-scented fruits of *limoncillo*, which they crushed then rubbed against their arms and necks.

Before dawn, the men were awakened by the sound of birds, hundreds or thousands of them calling in the distance. Carrying their weapons, they jogged in the direction of the birds, exactly where Tukup had pointed the night before. About half a mile into the jungle, following a little side stream, they came to a strange landscape. At the edge of the stream was a tunnel, perfectly round and five feet wide, as if a culvert had been pushed into the bank and pulled out, cookie-cutter fashion. The peccaries had visited there often, eating the mineral-rich soil.

Overhead, green amazon parrots and bright blue and yellow macaws gathered on a cliffside of the same mineral. They squabbled and flapped as they gnawed at the pale tan clay soil, their beaks cutting little grooves as they nibbled away at the hill. Because parrots often ate green fruit, the clay helped them digest what was indigestible, or at least it provided an antacid affect. In the treetops 150 feet above, untold numbers and varieties of birds squawked, squealed, trilled, hooted and whistled as they impatiently waited their turns at the cliffside.

Then, at the edge of a putrid, urine-filled pool, Tukup spotted a tapir footprint. Its strange, three-toe print with little horse-hoofed shapes at the ends of the toes was unmistakable and very fresh. Tukup led as they jogged after it. Within a few hundred yards they found the tapir swimming in a muddy pool by a flowing stream. Its nose, like a short elephant trunk, swiveled above the water. The tapir churned the water to froth with its powerful body. Climbing from the pool it shook its pig-like body as it reached to nibble a leaf. Tukup, meanwhile, had drawn a bead just below its left ear. The shot rang out, and startled birds flew into the air by the thousands. The tapir never heard a thing; it collapsed where it stood, twitched once or twice, then lay still.

The tapir weighed about four hundred pounds. There would be food for a long time. But they had to move quickly, for the meat would spoil. Dragging it to the edge of the flowing water, the men began to pour water over it, rinsing away the mud. On this day they could take only the meat so, as they removed the innards, they cast them into the stream. But it was not piranha that came to the feast. Instead, as the pieces floated away, hundreds of neon tetra-like tropical fish gathered to nibble at the bounty.

When each man had a portion of the meat to carry, they hurried back to the campsite and laid leafy branches in the *canoa*. They put the tapir meat on that layer and covered it with more branches. In a few minutes more they pushed away and started downstream. The trip back was faster than it had been to go upstream. The current pushed them along rapidly, and they easily followed the path they cut the day before. At the sandbar at the mouth of the Zabalo the cecopia poles lay in the sand of the shallow water, so the men pushed the boat along easily as Tukup mused again, "A very useful trick." By early afternoon they were at the house where the women took over.

The next day, Juan and his friends laid their belongings into their *canoa* and prepared to leave. Tsenia gave them drying tapir meat, already somewhat smoked and impaled on a dozen palm stems. It would continue to dry in the sun as they went upriver, and if they got hungry they could simply pull off a piece of the tasty jerky.

Juan offered a blessing to all, then he and his friends paddled out into the river. Even Tukup had come to wave farewell. At the main river, the Morona, they floated midstream to where the Mangosiza flowed in from the mountains. They pulled into the slower currents at the edge of the river and began the arduous work of poling, paddling and pushing the *canoa* upstream. Four days later, tired yet exhilarated, they paddled into the Tsuirim River and tied up near Juan's house. Children would be returning to school the next day, and Juan knew it would be a long time before he would have another "vacation."

CHAPTER FORTY-FOUR

AMALIA IS HEALED BY A SHAMAN-LIKE DOCTOR

Juan:

There were often problems, but when they came, it made me closer to God because He was the only one who could really help. Life was a little difficult sometimes because I had two distinct and separate responsibilities. The first was my family. The other was caring for the internos, which was like having fifty children that keep you busy from four in the morning until nine in the night. For the missionary there are no vacations, and every minute of every day is occupied with work.

The first years of the 1980s were peaceful, and the school grew. By 1982 there were forty *internos* and fifty day students, making Miasal the largest of the bilingual (Shuar and Spanish) schools. Five other teachers worked with them, each instructing two grades per classroom. The teachers received their room and board plus a salary from the Ecuadorian government, about twenty dollars per month.

Juan:

So, we were in Miasal for quite some time, and after a while, my children Pepe and Esther became my right hands with Amalia. Pepe returned from his school in Cuenca, and soon thereafter Esther returned from her school in Quito. As they had been educated in the city, they had a little difficulty readjusting to the life in the forest, but because they were Shuar, they could speak the language. Because they had lived in the forest all their lives, they were quick to adjust and were soon teaching classes in Miasal. They worked and taught school with much enthusiasm.

But the stress of years of work without end had begun to show on Amalia, and she became seriously ill. Each morning she awoke with a sharp pain in her uterus followed in the afternoon with vaginal bleeding. Trying to medicate herself, she drank *baco* sap tonic. The *baco* is an emergent tree with white sap that pours out of cuts in the bark, easily filling a cup. That sap is a great cure for headaches and fatigue. The cut on the tree congeals quickly and seals the gash for later use. She drank four and five cupfuls each day for a week, but while *baco* normally helps women's bleeding, it did nothing for Amalia. She tried several other plant medicines she knew and asked friends for their advice. Days passed into weeks. Nothing helped, and as the bleeding continued Amalia became weaker.

Amalia had refused to go to the city for help, but became afraid that it was cancer. Juan left Pepe and Esther in charge of the mission and hurried with Amalia to Cuenca for help. The doctors could offer no remedy, and Juan and Amalia were again hurtfully shunned by several of the Salesians. With little money, they slept in a dirty, cheap hotel then continued to Quito with their little savings. The thirty-passenger bus cost pennies but was a nightmare. It was packed with at least fifty people and their gear including several clucking chickens and a squealing pig. As they ground over the Andes Juan prayed that God would help him find a doctor who could heal Amalia.

Two doctors met with them and for small fees checked her condition. One finally tested her for cancer, and the couple was relieved when the test was negative. But the doctor could not tell what was wrong with her. He prescribed several medications and told them to return in a few weeks.

Back at Miasal Amalia continued to work, but the disease had an awful rhythm that slowed her. The mornings would bring the pain in the uterus; late afternoon would bring the vaginal bleeding. Amalia ate seldom and poorly, gradually becoming as thin as a young girl. Her skin texture changed and became gray.

When it was time to return to Quito, she was so weak that Pepe accompanied them. They stopped at Cuenca and went again to the Salesian mission to request a place to spend the night, for they had almost exhausted their little money, even with the contributions from their friends at Miasal. When the priest in charge of the mission refused to help, Pepe's patience broke.

"You have known my father for years, and you know how much he has sacrificed for the Salesians and for God," he raged. "Why do you refuse to help? You must give them a bed so my mother can rest."

As the priest cowered before Pepe's rage, Pepe continued to demand to know why he did not have a room for Juan and Amalia. One of Pepe's former teachers heard the noise and ran in, talking quietly to calm Pepe and ease his frustration.

"Pepe," he said, "you must be calm. The mission cannot be of help, but I have found a man who may be able to help you find a cure for your mother. A German was here recently. He knows of your parents and has even been to Miasal. When I told him about your mother's illness, he said he would be glad to help if he could. You cannot stay here at the mission but if you go to Quito he will find you a place to stay."

At Quito the German, Herr Schneider, met the couple and took them to his own home. They were led to a room like neither of them had seen before, and Herr Schneider told them it was theirs to use.

Juan was almost in tears as he said, "I appreciate your offer my friend, but I have no money to pay for this wonderful room or our food."

"Don Juan," Herr Schneider said with great respect, "I

appreciate the hardships you and your wife have suffered and the good you are doing for those children. You may stay here in this room without charge for as long as needed."

"Now," Herr Schneider continued, "I have been talking with several people and have a list of clinics that might be able to help." He gave Juan the list and told them to relax while he went to see about something for them to eat.

"Thank you Father," Juan prayed as he helped Amalia to bed.

Herr Schneider offered his car and driver to take them to the clinics, and they began to make daily trips. Each doctor checked Amalia carefully, then shook his head and said he could not help. At the end of a week they still had found no relief, and Amalia was dangerously weak.

One afternoon as they returned home, Amalia slept in the back seat, and Juan sat in the front with the driver.

Juan:

I must have looked very depressed. The driver and I began to talk, at first little pleasantries, then I could see that he had something on his mind and he asked, "How is your wife doing?"

I felt the world's weight on me when I had to say, "Not well. The doctors probe and test but they cannot seem to figure out the problem."

The driver then said, "No, no, no, no. You should not go to those doctors because they can do nothing. There is a doctor who is very well known and will be able to help you. If you like, I can take you there tomorrow, but we must go very early for the doctor is very popular, and the line will be long."

Next morning, at four, he drove Amalia, Pepe, Carlos (who had just joined us to help) and me to this doctor's office. But, as early as we were, others were already lined up. There were about twenty people, many who had slept on the sidewalk as they waited. One of the men in line said he had been waiting to see the doctor for three days. They said that each person had to take a turn. The doctor was so good that people thought of him as if he were a shaman. Even the high-ranking police were always going to him. I did not know what to do, for I felt that Amalia could die at any moment. Then I had the idea to write a note to one of the policemen who were coming into the office. The note said, "Mr. Officer, my wife and I are missionaries from the oriente and have no money. She is very sick, almost to death. Please help me to get into the doctor to have him see my wife." I gave the note to the officers who gave it to the doctor.

It was not five minutes after the doctor got the card that a woman came into the lobby and called us in. Why, I thought the other people in the office were going to hit me. They exclaimed, "He has only been here for half an hour!"

The policeman said, "Excuse us, but this man is a friend of the doctor," and the people calmed down.

We were led into the first floor and up a flight of dusty stairs to a door that opened into a small room. As we opened it and came into a darkened little anteroom, a very excited lady was gathering her belongings because the doctor had just helped her. We greeted her and she smiled eagerly, then looked at us and asked a strange question, "Do you have your eggs and cigarettes?" When I looked puzzled, she gave me three eggs from a little bag she carried, and three cigarettes.

When the doctor saw us, he reassured us with words and his kindly approach, saying that we should not worry. Things will be better soon. I was beginning to worry that he was a charlatan but the room had a crucifix on the wall and other things to indicate that he was a Christian. I began to relax. Then I noticed something strange on a table in the middle of the room, a human skull.

"Good friends, I am glad you are here," he said quietly. "Tell me what is the matter."

After we had told him he continued with the treatment. I'll tell you exactly what my wife and I and our two sons saw, but even for those of us who were there it is hard to believe.

He picked up the eggs and laid them in a line on Amalia's stomach. Then he spoke in a loud voice, calling on God to help him to "cure this sick woman." Other than his loud prayers, and my silent ones, the room was still and expectant. Next, he shook the tobacco out of the cigarettes and onto a piece of newspaper, making one large cigarette, which he lit and he blew the smoke over Amalia's body. When the cigarette was finished, he said another speech that was similar to the first one.

Next he lowered his head and put his ear to Amalia's stomach, where the eggs still lay. He began to make a noise as if he were calling something. It sounded like a noise a child would make as they pushed the air out of their lips in short, loud bursts. Things had been rather normal so far, a combination of shamanistic rituals and Christian prayers. But now we were about to see something we could never have imagined.

The doctor spread a piece of newspaper on the table beside Amalia and picked up one of the eggs. When he broke it we were all astounded to see what came out—not the yolk of a chicken but a beautiful snake-like creature with legs. It fell onto the table and began to walk around like a drunk. Our mouths were open in astonishment, for this was truly a powerful shaman-doctor. I have lived many years with the Shuar where there are many Shamans, but I had never seen anything like this. When he took out the second egg, Pepe, Carlos, and I leaned forward eagerly to see what would be in it. Cracking it on the edge of the table, he pulled open the shells and blood poured out onto the newspaper.

The third was a normal chicken's egg.

I could stand it no more. "Doctor, what does this mean? Explain it to me!" He smiled gently and said "You, sir, are a great man. You are a man who works for the people, but there are some people who do not support you, and the ones who do not like you do not want to have you around. They have sent this curse to your wife so you will become depressed and leave the mission. They have tried to put a spell on you but it is not possible to do that because you have a very strong soul and they cannot harm you. So they put the spell on your wife. You should continue working, but very careful."

Then he put his hand on my arm and looked deep into my eyes. His voice lowered almost to a whisper as he leaned toward me and said, "If you would like me to, I can send the bad things back to the person who sent them. It would then be bad for him." I recoiled almost as if I had been hit. The thought of returning evil for evil was against all my teachings and personal morals. I said, "Thank you, but no. Let's leave it up to God. He knows, and He has allowed this man to do these things to my wife. He knows what the evil one is doing and will see that they receive what is due to them." The doctor smiled broadly, breathing deeply as he leaned back again and said, "Sir, you are a very special man. I am happy that you do not want to seek vengeance."

As we helped her from the table, Amalia smiled and said that she thought she was feeling better already.

"How much do I owe you?" Juan asked tentatively, for he had little money left and expected that the doctor would charge more than he had.

"Two hundred sucres," he answered, the equivalent of two dollars.

Juan was amazed. If this doctor was a charlatan, he certainly wasn't making any money at it.

"Will she be okay?" Juan asked.

Yes, the doctor said. Amalia would improve almost immediately. Then he gave Juan a list of things at the market that would help to strengthen her—carnation flower and other medicinal plants—and instructed Juan to make them into a tea for her to drink each morning for nine days.

As he thought back on the experience fifteen years later, Juan said, "I felt a numb excitement as I said my thank-yous and left. I must say that I was outside of myself because it was the strangest thing that I have ever seen in my life. We returned to Herr Schneider's house where my wife began to improve very rapidly. In a few days Amalia was totally well, and we returned to Miasal to continue with our work. The problem never returned."

CHAPTER FORTY-FIVE

BRINGING THE WORLD TO MIASAL

Juan and Amalia had been at Miasal for about ten years when the Salesians asked him to consider starting another mission. Although he told them he would think and pray about it, he realized that Miasal would be his last mission. Neither he nor Amalia wanted to begin again, and both loved their home along the beautiful Tsuirim River. Juan was almost sixty years of age and energetic. But now it was more than just he and Amalia. Most of his children were grown, had settled nearby and were helping with the mission. Besides, Amalia's mother, Masuink, was in her early nineties, and the thought of moving her deeper into the jungle was unthinkable.

The next day he sent a message that he thanked them for the offer but that he preferred to stay at Miasal to continue work with the Shuar. He would teach and help as much as ever, but that Miasal was their permanent home. "Of course this gave them another reason to be unhappy with me," Juan said later.

The Ecuadorian government, by that time, had set aside areas that were considered exclusively for the Shuar (although, because oil had been discovered in much of the *oriente,* the government kept all mineral rights). Now that they had decided to stay at Miasal, Juan asked his sons Pepe and Carlos to look for a piece of property near the school. After a few months they found a Shuar who owned about twenty acres across the Tsuirim from the school and they bought it, putting the title in Amalia's name because she was a Shuar and only they could own land in the reserve. They began planning a house, the first one they had ever truly owned, for all their others had been part of the missions.

Juan:

> Since it was to be our permanent home, we decided to build it as we might in the city, with a foundation of concrete blocks. In Sucua I made arrangements for the blocks to be made for me, and they were stacked up near the airfield in Macas. Aero Misionario now had a two-engine Dornier, and they agreed to fly a few of them to the field at Miasal whenever they had space. Over a four-month period, dozens of forty-pound blocks and bags of cement were carried into the Cutucus. Then we loaded each shipment into a canoa and floated them downstream two miles to Miasal.
>
> Even the metal roofing came on the little planes, laid on the floor of the cabin under the passengers' feet.

Carlos was beginning to work with another man to bring tourists to Miasal, so they planned and built a two-story house with guest bedrooms on the top floor. Storage rooms and the Arcos's bedroom were on the ground floor. A separate building housed a small store and the kitchen, complete with a propane refrigerator that needed no electricity. A metal roof attached the two buildings and created a little library and dining area where visitors could gather even if it was pouring rain.

Beside the gringo-style house, Juan built a Shuar house for Amalia. She preferred to cook over a fire instead of on the propane stove. Shuar visitors who came had their choice of houses in which to meet, but generally preferred the traditional one. Around the compound there was always a sense of relaxed busyness—everyone did their assigned work with little instruction, but Amalia was very much in charge.

To wash laundry was difficult in the humidity of the jungle

for it could take days to dry. Juan eventually added a separate laundry building with open sides and ends and even an open top so air could move through it as much as possible. To this day, Amalia uses two old-style irons. The tops lift off and she fills them with coals from the fire to make them hot. By pressing the clothes, they dry faster as well as look more presentable.

To provide the Shuar with some of the necessities from the city, Juan built a little room with three shelves that he could use as a store. The shelves were stocked with matches, candles, cans of big Ecuadorian sardines, a little cloth, thread and needles. People were glad to get them at first but there was a problem. Juan sent lists of items he needed to friends in Macas or Sucua. They bought the items and Juan paid them back plus a little for their shopping time. Then he added a little for his profit, mainly to pay for building the store. So a can of sardines cost one hundred sucres plus fifteen sucres for the person picking it up, plus ten sucres to recover the cost of building the store and for Juan's profit. Soon the Shuar began to complain: *Why, I can buy those sardines in Macas for 100 sucres. You are trying to rob us and get rich.* Although Juan tried to explain the costs to them, they did not understand. What he had begun as a way to help the local Shuar had become seen as a way he was taking advantage of them. He tried to keep the store going but finally, after several years of continual explanations and struggle, Juan closed its doors.

CHAPTER FORTY-SIX

THE
VALIANT DEATH
OF MERCEDES
MASUINK ENTSAKUA

By the mid-1990s, Amalia's mother, Mercedes Masuink Entsakua, was in her late nineties and perhaps even older. Her mind was sharp, and her grandchildren and great-grandchildren loved to be with her, for it was from her that Amalia had inherited her humor. Masuink moved slowly and could no longer walk without help even from her house to Amalia's, only two hundred feet. Juan had built a little house for her near theirs, because she wanted to be independent as possible yet still she needed daily assistance, which Amalia was glad to give. Masuink continued to work hard in her house. Each day at dawn, Amalia took her *yuca* from the garden, and several times during the day Amalia would return with various handworks they could do together. They spent many hours together, working and talking, usually laughing about one thing or another.

The rainy season was a very dangerous time for snakes because they continually moved about, searching for mates and trying to find a warm and dry spot. Juan would often find them under benches and even in hammocks, so everyone became careful when the rains began. One night in April, as day followed day of rain and the rivers flooded back into the forest, a venomous *miconcha* snake slithered unseen into Masuink's house late one afternoon. When the early evening rain began, the snake curled up by a cooking pot near the warmth of the fire, and when Masuink reached for the pot the snake struck her. Angry, she hit the *miconcha* with an aluminum pot, and it struck her again. Her machete lay nearby. She grasped it firmly and struck back at the snake, cutting it into several pieces. The dying snake writhed by the fire, singeing its scaly body in the hot coals as Masuink called out for Amalia. But the rainstorm roared so loudly that no one heard her. Masuink knew her time was near. Without fear, she settled back onto a bench, leaned comfortably against the wall and quietly watched the fire as she had done thousands of times before. She must have smiled as she thought back over her life, for when Amalia found her next morning her face showed great peace.

CHAPTER FORTY-SEVEN

AN OLD GOOD
DEED SAVES TODAY

Not long after Masuink's death, the local Shuar became nervous about the mission school and began to gossip about Juan. Soon unfounded suspicions grew as believable fact.

Juan:

> By this time many Shuar near Miasal were particularly well educated, having been through the school and gone on to others in the city, some even to the university. Like most of the Shuar, however, they chose to return to the jungle instead of staying in the noisy and smelly city. Back in the forest, they began to look for ways to use their intellect. As former students, many now had ideas of how to run the mission better. I was glad, of course, to listen to their ideas, but sometimes we could not agree on what to do. Because I continually urged people to come to the school and warned them against the dangers they would face if they had no education, some began to see me as a negative thinker, a quality the Shuar particularly dislike.

Letters began to flow into the offices of the Shuar Federation, accusing Juan of working more for the Whites than for the Shuar. As usual, the federation was particularly concerned about any kind of accusation in which the proud Shuar might be considered less than first-class citizens. So they sent a man named Timaias to investigate. As it turned out he was a relative of the main accuser at Miasal, and because of that relationship he went first to the Centro Numbue, about an hour and a half from the Miasal, downriver toward the little *colono* town of Morona.

While at Numbue, Timaias invited people who had words to say against the mission to come and speak, but his mind was already made up, and he would not listen to any speaker who had good things to say about the mission. After several days of Shuar-style discussion in which the gossip continued, he returned to Sucua where he told the Shuar Federation officials that, indeed, the allegations against Juan were true.

But the president of the Shuar Federation at that time was Miguel Tangamash. He and Juan had been friends for a very long time, having worked together for three years when Juan lived in Sucua, and Miguel knew that Juan was a good person, more Shuar than White. Miguel addressed a council meeting, saying, "I do not believe that the findings of our friend Timaias are true. He never went to Miasal or talked with the people there. It is very difficult to get an honest picture of a place if you are an hour and a half away, so I propose that we go to Miasal and have a meeting with the people of that neighborhood."

The next week they arrived at Miasal and called for a community meeting. At the appointed time the community hall was filled. Soon shouts echoed across the soccer field as both sides drank *chicha* and defended or accused Juan and Amalia. Then, Miguel began to ask questions about Juan and about the mission. Everyone involved in the mission was a very strong supporter of the Arcoses, saying the children were very well cared for. Juan, they continued, is not just interested in the children; he is very helpful to all of the people.

"Give us an example of this man's caring," someone challenged.

One man, a stranger to the community who had heard about the strife and had come to listen, rose uncertainly and came to the front of the room. "My name is Sebastian, and I think I can help," he said. This was the story he told:

It happened more than twenty years ago, when Juan and I were young. At Totanangosa, two families were so angry at each other that they were ready to go to war. Tomas Junto, a leader of one of the families, went to Juan and asked for help. He and Juan arranged for two police officers from the area to go with them to the other centro, for it was very dangerous. Juan and Tomas Junto went with the policemen and Tomas later told me what happened as they traveled to Totanangosa.

As they paddled along in their canoa, they talked about what to do. The policemen were afraid, and Tomas was very concerned, so Juan asked that he be allowed to do all of the talking. Of course, because of their fear, they agreed. They were a peace party but were prepared for anything, because the two communities might turn their anger on them instead of each other.

They knew that both of the Shuar communities would be at the meeting place and would be heavily armed.

Along the way to the houses where the problems were growing, they encountered many Shuar. Juan was careful to explain that the three men were coming with Tomas and that two of them were armed policemen. When they arrived at the community, the only one there was a very old woman. Juan told her that they had come to talk with the people about the problems that had arisen in the region. She said nothing but invited them to sit and take chicha. In about half an hour, twenty Shuar arrived, one group from upriver and the other from downriver, prepared for war and painted with achiote, their dugouts bristling with rifles, machetes and spears.

Tomas and the policemen were very nervous now. They had expected that there might be armed and angry men but not so many. But Juan Arcos did not appear afraid. The Shuar were very surprised to see how young Juan was but gave him the respect he deserved. By now the two policemen were ready to panic. Tomas was afraid the policemen might begin shooting. Juan surprised everyone when he smiled at the crowd and told them all would be well. Without showing any fear, Juan said a little prayer—I think he was asking his God to speak through him—as the two groups of warriors gathered in an angry circle around them. Then, Chirapa, the leader of one centro, began.

"Welcome," he said cautiously. Then, unable to control himself, he became angry and asked why the "peace" party was armed.

Juan remained calm and said, "I am not armed, as you can see. Neither is Tomas Junto. Besides, I have only brought two officers with me." Suddenly, Juan surprised the men when he growled fiercely, "Let us speak without the guns and machetes. Everyone. Put your weapons on the ground. This includes you too," he said to the policemen.

Then, like old people, they put their weapons at his feet. After this was done he said that they must talk. So Chirapa began to talk and talk and talk. Then it was time for Catana, the leader from the other side to talk, and he talked for about an hour. Finally, Juan seemed to understand and he began to smile broadly.

As I have said, when they arrived there was an old woman who greeted them. As it turned out, she was seeking revenge against a young boy who had supposedly been mean to her. "Well," Juan asked, "Is this is what you are fighting for? Because of an old woman who is mad because a young boy did not do what she asked?" The image struck everyone as very funny, and scowls turned to smiles and smiles into laughter. Then someone ordered the old woman to bring chicha and food. It was a very happy hour, especially for me, for I was the boy the old woman had accused. Juan Arcos protected me without knowing this.

"As you can see," Sebastian ended, "Juan Arcos is not new to the federation, and he understands the Shuar people very well. I thank God that there is a man like this, who wants to help the Shuar, who understands us so well and who can guide us. I cannot understand where this slander came from." The crisis ended with a fiesta and more *chicha*.

Juan thanked Sebastian, whom he finally recognized as the young boy from years before. Then he quietly left the meeting to return home with the news. "When one does a good deed they never know what will be its result," Juan mused..The next day Miguel Tangamash stopped to thank Juan and to say farewell, then he and his commission returned to Sucua. Things at the school returned to normal, and the slander stopped—for a while.

CHAPTER FORTY-EIGHT

CATTLE
IN THE SELVA

Juan experimented with cattle in the 1980s and early 1990s. But jungle life was hard on cattle, which were often covered with ticks and other parasites. Juan and his friends followed instructions from the Ecuadorian ministry, cutting large areas of jungle and planting three types of African *grama lote* grasses—*elefante, blanco* and *severado*—for grazing. The grasses grew quickly at first and formed thick pastures six feet tall. But *grama lote* is watery and low in protein, so it takes about two and a half acres to feed one cow. The moist grass did have an advantage though. Because it contained so much water the cattle could be staked out to graze instead of building fences. Each day the owner simply moved the stake. But the forest kept growing back, and each week Juan and the students worked to cut out the trees that tried to grow in the light gap. A single young calf cost thirty or forty thousand sucres (seventy-five to eighty-five dollars), and many died before they matured. One at a time the animals were brought to Miasal, trussed and lying in the back of one of the little airplanes. Despite the work and risks, Juan and others thought raising cattle could be profitable, and if it provided money and food for the school it might be worth the effort. As the herd grew they cut more and more of the forest around the school.

When it was time for an animal to go to market it would

be led to the airstrip for a return to Macas or Sucua. Staked at one end of the strip it was tended until the message came that a plane was ready to depart for Miasal. Then two men ran to the airstrip where they killed the animal and cut it into five or six pieces, which they laid atop its own hide in the back of the plane before it departed. Within two hours the meat would be hanging in a butcher shop in Macas. Occasionally the cattle would go wild and became dangerous. Once, two students walked from the Mangosiza to the mission and found the trail blocked by a young bull. The animal was black and shining with health except for an oozing sore on its left side near the backbone. The festering, wormy mass was a gunshot wound, probably from when it had threatened a man on a hunt. At first the bull turned and walked away from the boys, then seemed to feel threatened and turned to challenge them. They stepped off the trail, looking for some kind of pole to use as a spear but were unsuccessful. The bull followed them, and for some minutes they ducked from one banana plant to the next until the bull finally snorted and bucked off into the forest.

The poor jungle soil under the trees supported the *grama lote* for a while, but gradually the grass became worthless as food, and even the jungle ceased growing into the light gaps. The cattle grew very slowly, and Juan was concerned that they always looked thin and hungry. After a dozen years he gave up and sold the last of the cattle.

Today the pastures are gradually returning to forest. Still, the trees are fewer and are not growing as fast as they would in a normal forest. One can still see the pasture edges ten years later, while in places where the trees fell and created natural light gaps, the openings disappeared in five years.

CHAPTER FORTY-NINE

PEPE THE PILOT

Pepe was in his mid twenties, and Juan could see he was becoming restless. He loved teaching the classes and working with the children, but every time a plane flew overhead his eyes fixated on it until it was out of sight.

One morning Juan and Pepe lingered over coffee before walking to their classrooms. Juan could see that Pepe wanted to talk and he waited patiently. Finally, Pepe cleared his throat, took a sip of his hot, sweet coffee and said, "Father, I have dreamed of being a pilot and have a chance to learn. Will you help me?"

Juan had flown many times in the little planes but was always nervous. At first he thought that Pepe was joking, so he said, "Leave the flying for the birds. Flying over the jungle is very dangerous. Haven't we, in fact, had twelve planes crash in the past twenty years? You know the stories and how there are seldom survivors."

Pepe seemed to agree, but Juan could tell there would be more. A few days later Pepe tried another tack. "The real reason I want to fly, Father, is so I can carry you in an airplane, and you won't have to make those awful, long jungle walks anymore. I have been saving my money for two years and have enough to take a class."

Juan smiled at this, realizing Pepe had already made up his mind and that he should respect his son as the man he was. So Juan agreed, and shortly after the school year ended, Pepe left Miasal and went to Quito, where he began to take flying lessons. It was hard work, but like his father he was very focused on his goals. Within three months he completed the requirements and was given his pilot's license. Not only did Pepe receive the license but also the praise of his instructors, who reported that he had an aptitude for flying. Out of money for the moment, he returned to Miasal and continued to teach school.

At that time the Salesians began to have problems with their flights into the jungle. They did not own any airplanes but rented them from a local evangelist group. One day the evangelists decided that the Catholics could no longer use their planes, and from necessity the Salesians began to put together their own little fleet. As before, they would carry missionaries into and out of the jungle, evacuate sick Shuar and carry supplies to the people. In a few months they had raised enough money to buy two airplanes and found an experienced pilot who was also a flight instructor. Miguel Aptos began to fly to the various airfields throughout Shuar and Achuar territory. He was a natural flyer, fearless yet careful and with a little confident swagger in his walk. But energetic as he was, everyone soon realized the job was too much for one man.

Whenever he was at Sucua, Pepe hung around the airfield, and the two flyers became friends. One day Miguel landed in Miasal when the rain was too hard to fly. He walked to Miasal, and over coffee he and Pepe talked with Juan about the future.

"I am looking for another pilot to assist me," Miguel said. "Pepe already has received his pilot's license but needs to fly more hours under the supervision of an instructor. I would be glad to help him if you give your permission. You would need to pay for his food and a place to live for about six months. Are you willing to do this?"

"Of course I will," said Juan without hesitation. "This is what Pepe loves, and we know it will make him very happy."

Pepe began almost immediately and within six months completed his first solo flight. Aero Misionario's head, Juan's old friend Father Barale, hired Pepe as the second pilot. Soon, Pepe was living in Macas and flying missions throughout the Cutucu Mountains. Juan often thought of the strangeness of the situation. Only two decades before he had struggled through the jungle on days-long walks, threatened by dangerous snakes and jaguars. Now his son was soaring over the forest traveling in an hour the distances that Juan had taken days to walk.

Juan:

> I was very happy for Pepe, but it was a great loss for me because he had been my right-hand man at the mission. I understood, however, that he needed to find his own path, even if it was in the sky instead of with me at Miasal.

But Pepe's love of flying was about to take a new twist. The forty-year war between Peru and Ecuador began to heat up again. Miasal was only about fifty miles from the disputed area, so when fighting began over some trivial dispute, the government moved more soldiers into the Miasal area. They first set up a military camp by the airstrip then moved to the mission. In a few weeks they had transformed Miasal into a military base. Pepe and other pilots throughout the nation were called to fly for the military and to take instruction in case they were needed by the army.

Juan suspended classes and sent the *internos* home. The captain in charge, however, refused to let the older boys leave. He intended to make them into soldiers. A month passed as the soldiers prepared and the barefoot teenagers and regular soldiers drilled. When nothing happened, tension began to relax. Soon the soldiers and students were playing soccer in the courtyard. Then very early one morning the military radio crackled, and the camp commander was ordered to return to their home base. As quickly as they came, they went.

Within another day or two every soldier was gone from the mission. Juan waited a few more days then sent word to the parents that school would begin again. The civilian pilots were released and returned to flying supplies and sick people again. The military had been such a presence for five or six weeks then were gone almost without a trace. Pepe, however, was delighted with the outcome, for he had received more flight training, and it had been free. Now he flew over the jungles with even more care and understanding, which increased his ability to do it safely. Juan and Amalia watched with pride but now breathed more easily.

CHAPTER FIFTY

Shamans and
the Little People

The next two years were busy but tranquil. Almost seventy *internos* lived together at the school, attending class in the morning and working in the gardens or fishing in the afternoon. It was common for two or three visiting families to stay at the community house for a few days as they proudly visited their children and saw what they were learning. Amalia enjoyed their visits, for the women brought food to share, often gathering to help her in the kitchen, laughing and gossiping as they prepared the meals. After a day or two of loafing and talking, the men avoided boredom by gathering toquilla leaves and repairing the thatch on the various school buildings or helping to clear new gardens, a continual process, since the soil wore out after only three years.

Other visitors came as Carlos's ethnotour business grew. At first when the white Europeans or North Americans came, the students were silent. But as more arrived, the children relaxed and soon were practicing their Spanish and even learning a little English and German as they talked with the visitors or helped on the hikes near Miasal. As in a typical family, the older students felt responsibility for the younger and helped with their education and care. When they worked in the gardens they all worked hard, but the air was filled with laughter and the constant chatter of conversation.

Juan:

Yes, we were very happy as one big family. But the devil must have seen us and been unhappy because of our success. One day, as was our custom, we had traveled to one of the chacras (garden plots) about half an hour from the mission and were working in a yuca garden. The children were chopping weeds and piling them to rot in a low wall around the garden. It was a sunny day but not too warm, and the red stems of the yuca leaves shined brightly against the bright green of the garden. Children laughed and joked as they worked, pausing occasionally to sip the chicha the younger girls brought to anyone who was thirsty. There would be a good crop for making boiled yuca and for more chicha. About four in the afternoon, when they were called in from the fields, the children gathered as usual, but there was one missing. It was Achanaki, a boy of about thirteen years of age who had recently joined the mission from Cashpim, near the border.

We kept calling him, saying that it was time to go, but he did not present himself. So we ran to the mission for help. It took only about twenty minutes to organize a search party but it was getting dark and we found no sign of him so returned to the mission.

I asked all the children what they thought might have happened. Was Achanaki unhappy? Did they have a fight?

I knew that sometimes when children would fight, they would run away for their homes, but here in Miasal we had had no problems like that. It was different here because we had a feeling of family at the mission, and the children reported he was very happy.

We gathered around the wooden tables, silently eating in the candlelight, watching white moths fluttering around the guttering flames of candles. Not hungry, a few of the boys went into the courtyard to play soccer in the semi-darkness. In the kitchen house Amalia began to wash the dishes, and two girls hunched over a large pot of yuca, making chicha. Suddenly, the call began at one end of the mission, and the other children picked it up: "Achanaki vina huay!" (Achanaki is coming). We all ran to greet him, but the children stopped when they saw him. His clothes were torn, and blood crusted on his face where it had run from a dozen cuts and scratches. Achanaki's face was pale beneath the dirty blood, and he could not speak. I picked him up and carried him back to the eating house, for he was shaking as if very cold, and his eyes darted off into the darkness as if afraid something was waiting out there for him. My wife started to cook him hot food while we changed his clothes, and Raul washed and disinfected his cuts while his classmates watched in silence. Amalia set a bowl of hot yuca and chicken soup before him, and he ate hungrily as he pressed his body close to mine for protection. It was an hour before he could relax, but then he looked around, and we could tell he was ready to tell us what happened.

He cupped his face in his hands, looking down at the table and began his story, speaking almost in a whisper. "I had gone to defecate in a weedy place outside the garden. When I finished, I stood up to go back to work when I saw a very small and wrinkled old man, only about a meter and a half tall." A shiver went through the gathered children, for they had heard about the little people who lived in the jungle. "He was walking up the riverbank and I couldn't see his face. I was staring at him when he told me I must come with him. I asked, 'Who are you?' but he refused to answer and said, 'No one. Come with me.' When I started to leave he grabbed my hand and slapped me across the face."

"Suddenly, I was very tired and fell to the ground. He picked me up and threw me over his shoulder. Then he began to run through the forest very fast. We ran for a long time through the thick brush. I hit him many times but it did not seem to hurt him. Then he put me down and pulled me through the thickest jungle, where the thorns cut me. I was not sure where we were and cried in fear but was afraid to shout for help. Then suddenly he stopped, turned around and slapped me again even harder. This time he shouted, 'Go away. I don't want you. Go away!' I fell to the ground again, and when I got up, maybe fifteen minutes later, he was gone. I wandered around the forest for a while, then found one of our chacras and returned here to the mission."

This he told us, and many people believed him. In the Shuar community they think there are devils or little people like that one. They believe that the devils would take the children and put them inside trees where they would never be found again. In the protected darkness of their houses, the Shuar talk much about things like this and warn the children not to go into the jungle alone. I had worked in many places in the Shuar region and I had heard of but never seen such things. Superstitions are strange and not easily defeated by reason. I did not understand what had happened and I pondered what really could have happened. The wounds were obviously not self-inflicted. Someone had indeed treated him badly but I thought the boy must be making this up and decided to let things pass.

Amalia again cleaned his wounds, this time rubbing in *sangre de drago*, the red bloodlike sap of the *sangrillo* tree. The sticky sap creates an antiseptic protective barrier on the wound. Amalia put a little into a bowl of *chicha* and gave it to him to drink as well because she was concerned that he may have had internal bleeding from such rough treatment. The next morning she cleaned the wounds, and gave him more *sangre de drago* in *chicha* each day for two weeks, much as she would have treated a warrior who had been injured by a spear or arrow.

Achanaki rested much of the next day, and things began to return to normal. Several days later he was playing with his friends in the quad when he suddenly became hysterical, pointing into the forest and shouting, "He is coming again. There he is. The little man who took me!" Only he saw him, and others stared from Achanaki into the forest, unsure how to react. Then when the boy ran toward the forest the others tackled him and held him until Raul and Juan could go to help. For several days the boy's hysteria came and went, leaving him exhausted. Juan sat with him day and night praying for guidance. After almost a week he seemed improved but one of the three adults was always with him.

Then one day the children were again working away from the mission in the gardens. Achanaki was at the mission with Raul, and Juan was with the children in the gardens alert for anything unusual. The usual laughter was gradually returning to the little group as Juan joked with the boys. Then about the same time of day that Achanaki had disappeared, another boy, named Pati, went to urinate in the forest and while he was urinating, saw a little man there and he yelled to him, "Go away. Why are you here? What are you doing?" When the man caught him in his arms and started to carry him away to the mountain, Pati screamed, "The devil, the devil, he is taking me away!" The other boys who were working with him ran to help and saw the little man with Pati disappearing into the jungle. They ran after him, and although he was very fast they kept up their pursuit. After a mile or so they came to a swamp and found Pati leaning against the prop roots of a ceiba tree where the little man had thrown him. When Juan arrived the other boys were comforting him and had begun to clean his wounds. As before, Juan picked up the frightened boy and they returned to the mission.

Juan:

Now we had two children who had had similar problems. We did not know what to do, but of course I continued to pray. Each afternoon we gathered in the church to pray and sing. Pati and Achanaki were told to sit in the front row on their painted stump stools. For the first few days they resisted the prayer services, lowering their heads and trying to escape. But there is no problem that God cannot conquer. By the eighth or ninth day, the two boys were almost normal and began to participate in the prayer. Thanks to God, the boys got better. This was the first problem we had with the boys in Miasal, but the problems did not stop there; they only hid and waited for us to relax.

Another two years passed quietly. Both Pati and Achanaki were normal boys and seemed unaffected by the ordeals. Then it began again.

It started when Victoria came to Miasal from a small farm near the Peruvian border. Although she was only fourteen, an older man wanted to marry her because she was very pretty with an athletic build, perfect white teeth and black hair and eyes. Her father sent her to the school, telling the suitor that she had to finish her education. Victoria delighted in school, and the other students fell in love with her for she was a hard worker and intelligent as well as pretty. She and Amalia often worked together laughing, for they had the same sense of humor.

She had been there for several months when one night as she helped Amalia prepare dinner, she suddenly sat down by the cooking fire. Her eyes rolled back into her head, and she began to sway as she sang like a shaman does, repeating the same chanting rhythm. Amalia tried to help her up, but the girl refused fiercely, saying, "I am a jaguar. I am a jaguar." Then a few minutes later she changed and began saying, "I am a boa. I am a boa."

Amalia sent for Juan and Raul. They tried to comfort her when, suddenly, the girlish chanting stopped; when it resumed it was in the deep tone of a man's voice. The three watched and listened for almost five minutes, then the girl spoke in the man's voice, saying, "I am the shaman from this girl's home community, and I come to tell you that she must be returned immediately or this bad dart will kill her. The man who wants to marry her has sent me to return her home so they can marry, and this must be done immediately."

An hour later she seemed normal and could recall nothing. But when it happened again, Juan sent a message to her parents who came immediately. They refused to take her home but took her to another shaman, hoping to send the "bad dart," or evil spirit, away. It seemed to work for a while with an occasional relapse, but about two weeks later something happened that caused even more strain.

Over a four-day period, three more girls began to act the same way as Victoria, chanting, singing and speaking with the same male voice. Then they began to become more violent, jumping up and down, screaming in agony, even stripping off their clothes. The Salesians arranged for a psychologist to fly to Miasal. When he arrived, he went to the house where the four girls were being kept and went inside. He asked that Juan and Amalia leave so he could be alone with the girls.

They were gathered around the cooking fire, talking quietly as girls do, and he visited with them for some time. He was beginning to think that all was well when Victoria's eyes rolled back, and she began to go into her fit. The other three cringed in fear for when one began it often caused the others to do the same. This time only Victoria chanted and spoke as the shaman.

Several hours later the doctor stepped from the house. He was a little pale, and when he removed his glasses to wipe them his hands shook slightly. "Mr. Juan, I have never seen anything like this. I have seen people change voice and fall to the ground like they are dead, but I have never seen a person move so much and grimace and sing. It is a strange case." He thought there might be medications that could be given, but which ones he did not know; he promised to research the case and to send what help he could. He hurried to the airfield where his plane was waiting and flew back to Macas.

They never heard from the doctor again, but the head of the Salesians at Macas told Juan that the man reported there was nothing he could do. He thought the girls would die. Juan's pastor, on the other hand, thought it was simply a the problem of young girls growing up and of group hysteria. "It will go away soon," he predicted.

"But," Juan asked, "You have worked with children for a long time. Have you ever seen this before?"

"No," he answered honestly.

The parents of the girls all resorted to traditional means, sending them to local shamans and after several treatments over many months they seemed better but still not healed. Juan and Amalia began to have recurrent migraines from the stress and even Amalia laughed less often.

As it happened, I was in Miasal at this time with some friends and could see the agony it was creating for Amalia and Juan. One day Carlos, Juan's son, asked if we would like to meet one of the shamans and perhaps witness a jungle exorcism of one of the girls. Of course we agreed eagerly.

The shaman, Bartolo, lived several hours' walk further into the jungle. When we arrived at his house he agreed to let us stay for the exorcism. In fact, when he discovered my interest in ethnobotany, he spent part of the afternoon walking through his garden with me showing me the various plants he and his wife raised to use for medicines. He showed me what he intended to that night. My two friends and I were excited and interested but mainly thought we would see an interesting "show." It turned out to be quite a bit more.

Bartolo's wife gave us a typical meal of *yuca*, boiled plantain and a little unidentifiable meat, including a rubbery and gritty snail boiled in its shell as big as my fist. As we ate, Bartolo and the father of the girl who would be exorcised removed the center wall from the oval house, revealing the women's side. The Shuar spoke little, and their faces were drawn down in serious, concerned expressions. Beside the cooking fire, a girl of about fourteen years of age lay on the floor covered with a white blanket, her head resting on her mother's lap. She had already been given a drink of bitter *ayahuasca* and was sleeping.

Ayahuasca is central to the ceremony permitting the shaman to see the spirits and to communicate with them. Made by boiling the stems of a *banisteriopsis* vine, the black, bitter liquid has an hallucinogenic effect, and perhaps, I thought, the shaman and others *do* "see" the spirits. Bartolo sat down next to me and smiled broadly. He described what would happen during the exorcism and what we should and should not do. "I understand that you might want to take photos," he said. "That is okay but do not point the camera at my face, because my eyes get very big (the pupils dilate), and it will hurt me. You and your friends may take no more than eight pictures. Do not speak, because it will affect the spirits and they may not be willing to help the little girl."

The sun had long been gone as I stepped into the earthy

warmth of the night to relieve myself. Staring upward from the garden clearing, I smiled into a jungle sky that was totally clear, filled with bright stars in their thousands, glittering, sequin-like against the velvet sky. Night birds trilled, and quarter-sized frogs called in bell-like "tinks." A few minutes later, Carlos called me back into the house, saying the ceremony was about to begin. Inside, Carlos and I sat with my traveling companions on the visitors' bench and leaned comfortably against the vertical palm walls. Bartolo's wife lit a single candle and placed it on the dirt floor about six feet from the little girl, who had been moved to the men's side of the house but still lay under the blanket unmoving as if in a deep sleep or a trance. The girl's mother sat with Bartolo's wife, and her father knelt beside Bartolo.

Unknown to everyone I carried a little tape recorder in my shirt pocket. As the ceremony began I silently pressed the buttons for it to record. But silence filled the room as Bartolo began the exorcism. His wife gave him a bowl of the bitter, dark *ayahuasca,* and he drank it down. Then she handed another bowl to the father, who did the same. A little can sat on the ground by the girl. Carlos had told me it was tobacco leaves soaking in water. Both Bartolo and the father snorted the leaves through their noses, coughed slightly and spat them onto the ground. Bartolo began to shake palm branches over his patient and to chant an ancient, simple Shuar rhythm. I smiled, for I was recording them to enjoy later as well. Five minutes passed, and Bartolo and the father began to sway slightly. Then something happened. Bartolo suddenly stopped chanting and he whistled a tune. It was high-pitched and lilting, much like a melody I had heard at home in the United States. I leaned toward Carlos and asked, "What is he doing now?"

"Shh," Carlos warned quietly. "He is calling the spirits."

I had expected an interesting "performance," but suddenly things had changed, things I cannot explain adequately in Western terms. Within five minutes of the new whistling sound, rain frogs began to whoop. The huge frogs began first one, then another along the edge of the river below. In a few minutes more, silent lightning began to strobe through the vertical walls of the house, and flashes froze the shaman, his patient and helper in place each time. Storms there usually were preceded by wind, but it, too, was silent. I thought of the clear sky only half an hour before, and the hair raised on my neck.

As the lightning continued with such frequency, it made me think of an old horror movie when you know something bad is about to happen. Bartolo looked around him as if welcoming someone, or something, and began to shake the palm fronds more vigorously, chanting again. He leaned over and sucked the girl's forehead then sat back in obvious discomfort and vomited onto the floor. He repeated the process, sucking the evil from her neck, her breast, her arms and legs, each time retching and vomiting it out so the spirits could gather the evil and remove it. The process was short, no more than twenty minutes. Bartolo then sat back on his haunches and spoke to the father and mother, "Take her away to rest now. The evil is gone."

The parents and an older sister picked up the still-sleeping girl and returned her to the women's side, replaced the wall and sat by the unconscious child, comforting her. Bartolo sat alone, exhausted in the midst of his vomit, and I switched off the tape recorder. Ten minutes passed in silence except for the rain frogs. Slowly, Bartolo seemed to be coming out of his trance. Carlos whispered to me, "The spirits have gone." Just as Bartolo stood and stretched, another lightning bolt flashed but it was immediately followed by a thunderclap that filled the house. After the dozens of silent strobes the thunder surprised us and we jerked as if shocked by electricity. Then I noticed the rain frogs had stopped whooping. It was silent for a moment then rain began to roar down about us and continued all night.

The next morning I went outside. Brushing my teeth, I

decided to listen to a little of the tape recording and rolled it back to the beginning. The sounds were perfect, even the children talking in the background and my friends visiting with Carlos. Then the ceremony began and the chants came through beautiful and primitive. Bartolo whistled and suddenly there was nothing. Not a hiss. I thought the battery had failed but the tape still rolled. Thinking the recorder had failed I pressed the record button and spoke into it, "Test, test." The recorder spoke back, "Test, test."

I had taken four pictures, and my friends had taken two each. Back home I had my film developed and discovered the pictures before and after were excellent, but my four of the ceremony were clear film. Calling my friends I asked if they could send me copies of their pictures. "Funny thing," they said. "The pictures before and after came out, but none of those did."

I heard later that the little girl was cured, although she did have one relapse that required a second, less serious exorcism. For the first, Bartolo received a young pig and for the second he received several chickens. The girl returned to her classes at Miasal and had no recollection of the night's drama.

But the strange fits continued. While many of the Shuar sought help from the shamans, Raul and Juan sought help from God. Juan radioed his old friend Padre Luis Carollo and described the situation. Carollo agreed to come as quickly as possible, arriving at the airstrip the next afternoon. As the two old friends floated down the Mangosiza to the mission, Juan described the situation.

"I believe you," Carollo said. "Years ago, we had a similar problem in Limon. We had a girl who showed the same symptoms. The devil, you know, was the head of the Shuar many years ago, and sometimes returns to try to reclaim his powers. Do not worry though. God is more powerful."

Arriving at the school, Juan took Carollo to Victoria, who was being watched in a separate house. Padre Carollo sat on a stool beside the girl, who appeared for the moment like any fourteen-year-old. Gently, he began to ask her questions. "Tell me what happens," he said.

"One minute I feel fine, and the next I cannot control myself. It makes me very afraid."

"Do not be frightened, child. God is in control and he will not allow you to be hurt."

Juan:

Then Padre Luis and I went outside and began to pray, walking in front of her room in the gathering darkness. We would walk ten paces and then pause to pray. Each time we began a prayer, the girl would writhe in pain, screaming "AHHHHHH."

"The Virgin is coming," Padre Luis said.

"Father," I implored, "Please do not hurt her."

"Don't worry," Padre Luis said. "God is not hurting her. It is the devil inside her."

We prayed for half an hour, and the girl became as one who is dead but lay on her bed breathing slowly. "Good," the padre said. "Tomorrow no one at the school will eat breakfast. No water. No yuca. No chicha. Nothing."

We continued our prayer and fasting much of the day. Finally, the spirit spoke through the girl and said, screaming as if in great pain, "I'll go! I'll go! Just leave me alone!" The girl fell from the bed and lay face down on the floor. Moments passed as we watched her. She was breathing normally and it seemed as if she were asleep. All was silent except for the sounds from the jungle around us.

Finally, the padre said, "The evil is gone!" We helped the girl to her bed where she rested quietly. I must have looked very frightened and exhausted, for Padre Luis put his hand on my shoulder and said, "The danger has passed. All will be well." He was exhausted too but radioed for a plane to return him to his mission. We walked to the airfield, and he promised to return if I needed his help. Then he got into an airplane and left. Over the next few days the girl began to recover, although she was very thin and tired.

For Juan and Amalia the fear for the children and the tension were almost unbearable. By the end of the first month both were seized by paralyzing migraines followed by almost unbearable exhaustion, which was replaced by extreme nervousness. In another month most of the children were better, but Juan and Amalia were not. Finally, their own children said, "You must go to Quito to see a doctor." They tried to disagree, but both were so debilitated they could not. Their daughter, Maria, took charge of the school, and Carlos and Pepe arranged for an emergency flight to Macas for the next morning.

Dawn arrived with a fierce storm and low-lying clouds that lifted then fell again. By mid-afternoon it looked like they could not be evacuated until the next day, but the sunlight suddenly burned through, and from Macas their pilot son Pepe hurried to Miasal. They had packed a few meager belongings, which Carlos carried as he helped them walk to the airstrip. As they arrived, the little STOL four-seater drifted onto the grassy airstrip and rattled to a stop in front of them. Without shutting down his motor, Pepe helped the feeble couple into the plane, buckled them in and took off, all within five minutes. The clouds had begun to settle but were tall, up to thirty-five thousand feet, so Pepe flew very low, barely over the treetops, as he felt his way back to Macas. Carlos was left to fret, hurrying back to the mission for a report on the safe landing of the plane.

Two days later, at Quito, a doctor checked the pair, who were in great pain. Each had lost more than ten pounds as they could not bear to eat. Even chewing was painful. Unable to find the cause, the doctors gave them pain killers and told them to return home. "Of course, I assume you will continue to pray," the doctor said, "but for yourselves as well, not just for the children. I have a feeling that there is a bad spirit hovering around you."

Juan:

After we saw the doctors in Quito, we returned to Miasal to work, but it took quite some time for my nervousness to wear off. Although we were exhausted it was impossible to sleep through the night. Even when we could sleep, on many nights one of the girls would awake screaming that the devil was there. We would spend the rest of the night comforting her. I continued with my work, but I was weak.

I did all that I could do, but with both of us sick, the officials from the Salesian missions told me that we should not have *internos* at the mission until our health was improved. They said we no longer had enough personnel to run the mission as it had been before, even though some of our adult children were there already and others volunteered to come and help. Very few non-Indian people were willing to live in the forest so far from town or to live with the *internos*, and the Salesians could not find any other volunteers. After that school year, we stopped having *internos* for a while.

Father Raul and I often talked about what to do. He volunteered to go to Belgium, where his family lived, and see if he could find someone to come to Miasal to work in the mission with the *internos*. He was gone for a month but returned with several volunteers. With their help we were able to maintain a group of about twenty boys and girls, not as many as we had before, but it enabled us to continue to teach some children who lived far from the school. We also found a woman in Limon who loved children and was an excellent *madrecita* to the children living away from home. Most gratifying, Luis, one of our former students, returned and has stayed to teach.

Amalia gradually recovered but even today Juan has more than occasional migraines. Of the girls, none has had a lasting problem. Victoria never did go home, but married one of her classmates and lives near Miasal.

CHAPTER FIFTY-ONE

PETS

There were many kinds of pets, *mascotes* in Spanish, around the mission. Juan encouraged them, for they were an important part of Shuar family life, and almost every Shuar farm had several *mascotes*. The Shuar kept them for many reasons, mainly because, like most people, they enjoyed having animals around the house. In the jungle, however, *mascotes* served an important practical purpose in teaching the children the ways of their pet's species and how they would act in the wild. They didn't eat their pets, but did eat their pet's wild relatives. At Miasal there were always a variety of animals around just for fun. At any time there have been several kinds of turtles, two or three varieties of parrots walking around the rafters in the house, or perhaps a squirrel, howler or spider monkey. When children returned from visits home the girls often had little marmosets tucked into and peering from their shirts or riding on their shoulders. Two or three black chachalachas, a chicken-like bird, often wandered with the flock of domestic birds. Chachalachas, being somewhat territorial, usually seemed to think of themselves as the "boss chickens." Sometimes there were young white-lipped peccaries. Intelligent and pig-like, they were friendly and interesting pets but tended to root in the gardens and cause frustrating damage.

One of the great favorites was a young tapir. He wandered into the schoolyard as a little striped baby, apparently an orphan. It was unafraid and friendly so immediately stole everyone's heart as he went from child to child seeking an ear-scratch or gentle pat. This little fellow, with its pig-like body, short, elephant-like trunk and the beginnings of a horse-like mane, ate bananas from everyone's hands and wandered around as if he had found home. In fact, he had. He was named *Gordito,* (chubby).

As Gordito grew, he became even more tame and friendly. Although by the time he was an adult he weighed more than five hundred pounds, he was always gentle and never pushed anyone or destroyed even a small garden plant. No one considered keeping Gordito penned up, so he wandered about freely, sometimes stopping by the school several evenings in a row, then disappearing for a week or more at a time. Although he spent most of his nights at the school he also dropped into other farms, always expecting a handout and a back scratch. Although tapir meat was a favorite among the Shuar those in the surrounding community realized that he was a pet and didn't shoot him. Juan's daughter, Patricia, however, felt Gordito needed to be marked somehow, so just to be sure he was recognized as a *mascote,* she kept his mane well-trimmed.

A typical visit began with Gordito sauntering into the yard. Amalia would run out to scold him after one of the dogs pestered him and he bit back. When the dogs would retreat, Gordito would shuffle to the kitchen where his humans always seemed willing to peel a few *platanos* or bananas for him. On a typical visit, the tapir would eat peeled *platanos* from Patricia's hand, while Carlos pulled ticks from his back and threw them onto the ground where the chickens and chachalachas scrambled to eat them. When Carlos would begin scratching Gordito's belly, the tapir arched his back, closed his eyes and lifted his back left leg in pleasure.

After eating his fill, Gordito would usually visit another *mascote,* a spider monkey. The monkey was raised from infancy so could not be returned to the forest. It turned out to be such pest, in fact, that it was kept tethered to a pole, but could climb about freely on a little tree by the house. Whenever the tapir would appear, the two had a wonderful ritual. The tapir stretched out on its stomach and spread its legs comfortably. Eagerly, the monkey ran to it and sat on the ground beside it then began to pick off the remaining ticks. The monkey pulled the ticks off with its teeth then ate the blood-filled insects with the delight humans showed as they ate sweet grapes. The tapir gradually rolled as the monkey moved around its body and eventually the big beast would be upside down. All the while, the monkey continued to pluck ticks from every conceivable crevice. Bored, the tapir began to gnaw loudly on a big, hard branch, the crunching noise sounding like the teeth were breaking in its jaws. Sometimes the tapir would spend the night, snoring lightly with the tethered well-fed monkey sprawled upon its back.

CHAPTER FIFTY-TWO

CHRISTMAS
CELEBRATIONS

By the mid-1990s the school had regrown and other teachers came to help. The school had about seventy *internos* again, and another twenty-five students who came for the day. Life had become a little easier for the Arcos family as others joined in the work and fun of life with children in the jungle. Holidays became more elaborate as more adults took various parts and added their own sense of creativity.

On December 24, 1998, Christmas vacation began with a field day in the school plaza.

Juan and Raul joined the other teachers as they gathered the eager children about them. They divided the laughing and chattering children into two teams, ranging in age from six to fifteen, and lined them up for a relay race. One of the teachers set two gallon-size plastic buckets on the sandy soil about fifty feet from the two lines. By each line of eager children, a larger bucket held water and a gourd dipper. Raul stood at the front of the line with his arm raised. "Ready. Set. Go," he barked with a huge grin. The first child took a mouthful of water and ran to the smaller bucket, spat the water into it, then returned to the line where another child did the same. This continued, accompanied by loud cheering and laughter, for about ten minutes until one team filled its bucket.

Then it was time for a *sirvatana* (blowgun) contest. One of·

the teachers took the *sirvatana*, loaded it with an unpoisoned dart, and took aim at a bunch of *platanos* perched atop a small log about fifty feet away. The dart hit one of the unripe *platanos* and passed halfway through. Everyone cheered. Then the children took their turns. Some of the darts hit the *platanos* but most went flying into the sand below the target.

Field day over, everyone went their separate ways for a while. Some of the boys began playing barefoot soccer with a deflated ball while the girls broke into little groups of three and four and began strolling around the plaza, giggling and watching the boys. Some of the adults went to the community center to clean and prepare it for the night's "cultural activities" (a talent show). The day had been sunny, so the little solar panel donated by a thoughtful visitor would provide an hour or two of fluorescent light from a single bulb and run a tape player that would also serve as a PA system.

After an early dinner, at seven o'clock people gathered at the community center. All afternoon people had been arriving from the area around the mission. Most of the men were dressed in white or blue shirts and the women in faded cotton dresses to the knee. As protectors, the men carried themselves and their weapons; the women carried aluminum pots of *chicha* or plastic bottles of *chicha* capped with a banana. Most of the women led a child and carried another, wrapped in a bright-colored wool shawl from which the curious-eyed babies watched everything. The school's boys dressed in their school uniforms, white shirts over dark blue or khaki green pants. The girls mainly wore white blouses over straight blue skirts, but a few wore the stylish blue jeans.

When Juan and Amalia arrived, Juan was given a seat of honor in the front row, for he would be one of the talent judges. Amalia joined her friends and began to pass bowls of *chicha*, laughing and joking. The other judges included Helmut (the German husband of Juan's daughter Patricia), a visiting nun, a local shaman and a man wearing a traditional palm and feather corona, shorts and a blue T-shirt that proclaimed, "I'm proud to be an Oaklander." As the night sounds revved up to full volume, so did the excited voices rose inside the little building. Sometimes in community meetings everyone would sweat, but on this night the air was cool and a breeze blew through the building, raising the already high spirits of the audience. When it was time to begin, the head teacher drank a quick bowl of *chicha* and spoke into the microphone, making preliminary announcements. He held the microphone very close to his mouth, which caused his words to slur somewhat but gave him more volume as he tried to speak above the noise of the audience, which mostly ignored him.

Only two of the performers were young; the rest were in their mid-forties. The first performer was a little woman in her mid-fifties and four feet ten inches tall. She was dressed in semi-traditional style, with an *itip* skirt of bark cloth. The audience quieted a little as she stood in the middle of the stage. She then began to sing a traditional women's song in a very high-pitched almost melodic voice. The audience howled with laughter, but she ignored them and continued to sing. The next performers were three men, also dressed traditionally, who sang as they danced around the stage while one of them beat a small *tuntui* drum with a tanned squirrel skin as the playing surface. The audience never stopped laughing. Four other performances followed, and each was heckled by the gathered Shuar. Then, as the light and the sound system began to fade, the master of ceremonies made another announcement and the performers came out and each did their acts again.

All the time, women kept passing bowls of *chicha*, and the crowd became rowdier.

About nine o'clock just as the prizes were being awarded, the power failed, and everyone began to file out of the community hall and across to the church. They stood outside the door, quietly talking, and waited for church to begin. Little clumps of men joined and separated, the new arrivals always shaking hands all around. In the darkness one boy of about ten, dressed in red jogging shorts and a blue T-shirt, rang the church bell—two short claps, a series of fast claps, then three short ones, with a slight pause between. The door to the church opened, and the waiting parishioners filed in silently. The only light was from a single solar-powered bulb on the ceiling and one candle on the altar, but the two gave a surprising amount of definition to the shadows.

The children took their usual places atop stump-stools, carved in hourglass shapes and painted red, blue or yellow. Boys sat on the left and girls on the right, with younger children to the front and older to the rear. The adults gathered round the perimeter of the church in the same pattern, men to the left.

Outside, the frogs called and other night songs mingled with the sound of the Tsuirim River rippling over its rocks. In the community center it had been too noisy to hear them. Now it was silent in the church, except for two barefoot two-year-olds playing at the door, who clumped childlike across the room to give their mothers hugs then ran back to the door. All the parishioners stood serious-faced and ready for the service to begin. A latecomer arrived, and as he passed he shook hands with each man until he found an empty space and turned to face the altar, waiting expectantly.

Juan and Raul sat at a white-cloth-covered altar in the front with an older student between them. Raul began the service leading the Lord's Prayer in Shuar. The people smiled as the beautiful, familiar cadence filled the room. Then the student stood and, in a strong voice, gave a reading from the Bible. As he finished, Juan smiled at him approvingly and the boy returned the smile as he left the table and took a seat with the older boys.

Raul, as the priest, led the service. His long white hair and beard made him look like Father Christmas and had given him the nickname of "padre hippie," which the children used when he was out of earshot. A simple white headband held his hair back, and his white shawl and cassock with gold thread decorations glowed softly in the low light.

This church, or "hall of meditations" as Juan called it, was elegant in its simplicity. It was a round building, about fifty feet in diameter. A single support pole about eighteen inches in diameter rose in the center. The lower half-walls, made from chonta and bamboo were seven feet tall. The top five feet was divided into openings with decorations and pictures depicting the life of Christ. Behind Juan and Raul, several decorations hung on the wall

To the left of where Juan and Raul stood hung a painting of a Shuar family by a waterfall. To the right of the painting were a large basket, then a lance and a *sirvatana* set vertically. The center of the wall rose to about fifteen feet, and at the highest part hung a painting of the rising Christ, but the image was of a Shuar warrior, his arms outstretched and ascending as a waterfall cascades behind and below him. Below this significant picture was a Shuar dance belt, and below that a traditional orange toucan feather corona. At chest level, below the corona, hung another basket, this one with a lid, for it contained the communion wafers. To the right was another basket that matched the one on the left and another painting, this one of the Madonna and child, depicted as a Shuar woman with her baby.

Beside the *pau*, or center post, a tall *chimbi* stool held a blue plastic bowl for donations to the poor. A hand-lettered sign above it read, "Vimosnas, enfermos, jaa, yaintal" (for the poor and the sick). On that night, the sign was upside down. Above the "poor bowl" hung a framed copy of the poster explaining Catholicism to the Shuar in terms of their legends.

When a guitar began to play, the thirty gathered children followed, clapping in rhythm. Then they begin to sing. The words were in the Shuar language, and with the high voices of the children it sounded chant-like, a beautiful, soothing sound that pulsed through the room. The children sang two more hymns, their lovely high voices lifting spirits and making their parents smile.

Toward the end of the service, Juan passed the blue bowl for donations, collecting only a few thousand sucres (twenty-five cents), for the parishioners *were* the poor, at least in terms of cash they held. After church, people returned to the community hall for more *chicha,* food and conversation well toward the dawn.

CHAPTER FIFTY-THREE

EARTHQUAKE
AND THE
VANISHED RIVER

Juan:

The Andes are always grumbling about something, and *terremotos* (earthquakes) are fairly common. But in 1994 we had a very large one. About nine in the evening, we were already asleep, as is normal. The houses began to shake and move almost a foot in each direction as if a forest demon were shaking them. Two foreigners were here visiting and were, like us, very much afraid. We gathered the children and ran to the center of the schoolyard, away from the forest. Even the giant trees shook violently as if the wind were blowing, but the air was still. People who had run to our house for help joined us in the clearing when a nine-inch-wide crack opened through the center of the house. They panicked when water began pouring from it and flowed through the house. All the children were safe, and none of the buildings fell. But we spent the night huddled together in the middle of the schoolyard, praying, as aftershocks continued.

In the dawn light Juan surveyed the damage. All the houses, though damaged, still stood, and the damage in his house was slight, for the crack had resealed itself. The real surprise was the Tsuirim River. It was gone. The day before, the river was filled with rocks of all sizes up to a foot across.

Now they too were gone, shaken down into the sand by the earthquake. Only a few pools of water were left, quivering in the small aftershocks or from the movement of confused, trapped fish.

The children were eager to gather the fish, but they did it with great care, for Juan knew the river would return, and when it did it would be a foaming brown killer. When the earthquake shook the earth, whole mountainsides of trees, rocks and mud fell into the valleys, forming dams fifty and a hundred feet high. The streams continued to flow into the valleys, and lakes grew behind the dams. Juan knew the dams would gradually weaken until finally one by one they would give way and pour from every valley for miles around them. Even the Mangosiza, which is a large river, had already backed up, flooding the airstrip. They were cut off from any aid, and it would be a month before the airstrip would be usable again. The foreign visitors were put into a *canoa* and carefully taken downstream to Porto Morona, where they could take a bus back to Macas. The trip took four days instead of the usual one, for the river had become as the Zabalo had been for Juan when he visited Tukup, choked with fallen logs.

Meanwhile, at Miasal, each day Juan watched the Tsuirim nervously and told the children what to do when the floodwaters came. They had to be prepared, for anything in the path of the floods would be ground to pieces.

About noon on the third nerve-wracking day, Juan heard a loud rumbling as if a thunderclap were rolling downstream. "Run!" Juan shouted, as he, Raul, and Amalia led the children to the highest ground and nervously counted them to be sure everyone was there. Then they waited and prayed. Only a few minutes passed before a twenty-foot-tall wave crashed down the valley.

Juan:

It was filled with trees, rocks, and dead things and made the most horrible crashing and roaring sound. But the children were safe and unafraid. In minutes, the river rose twenty feet, and in an hour it flowed within six feet of our houses and the school. But although it roared and gurgled at us, we were all safe, and not a building was lost.

After this final violence, life returned to normal. Many of the mountain valleys were totally changed. Always steep but once covered with trees and undergrowth, many of the slopes were stripped bare, so for months, whenever it rained, the rivers turned dark with mud. Then gradually they healed and again protected the land.

CHAPTER FIFTY-FOUR

FISHING
FOR PIRARUCU

Juan's son, Carlos, had two homes—one at Miasal with his parents and one in Macas with his family. Because he often brought tourists to stay at Miasal, to hike in the jungle and meet his and Juan's Shuar friends, Carlos was busy. Still, whenever he could he took time to help, often going with other Shuar to catch fish. One night he went fishing and had an adventure he wouldn't forget.

Carlos and several friends were night fishing in a deep and quiet lagoon, sipping *chicha*, smoking and casting out nylon lines baited with smelly meat, for they were after the giant catfish. Their lines were anchored to foot-long lengths of palm wood. As the men lounged in the two *canoas*, they jiggled the lines from time to time, more for something to do than to tempt a fish. Although the night was passing slowly none of the men minded for they were with friends, laughing quietly periodically and dozing. About 2 in the morning, all feeling of quiet disappeared as Carlos leaned forward, straining to hear in the darkness. "Listen," he said. "There's a *pirarucu* in this lagoon." The others listened and agreed as they heard a loud slurping sound floating toward them from the center of the lagoon.

What a catch that would be for the night! *Pirarucu (Arapaima gigas)*, largest freshwater fish in the world, could grow up to ten feet long and weigh four hundred pounds. Its body was covered with big, tough scales that Shuar dried and used for nail files, or fastened to dresses and dance belts for the pleasant clicking sound they made as they swayed. What's more, the meat was sweet and delicious. So as the fish slurped again, the hunters changed their tactics. Carlos baited one of the huge, seven-inch-long hooks with one of the ten-inch fish they'd caught earlier in the night. In the other *canoa* another man did the same, then they pushed the *canoas* silently toward the slurping sound. Primitive fish, the *pirarucu* breathed by taking air into a modified air bladder, so the men listened for the sound of the fish breathing and stalked it. When it ate, the *pirarucu* would swim to smaller fish and rapidly open its mouth, vacuuming its prey right into the waiting maw. So the two men threw their baited hooks well over the *pirarucu* and slowly pulled them toward the canoa, creating the illusion of fish swimming.

As Carlos's baited hook almost reached the *canoa*, a huge ripple raced after it and Carlos felt a powerful tug. He pulled hard to set the hook, and the line ripped through the water. Suddenly the *canoa* leaped forward as the fish pulled it to one side of the lagoon, paused, then spun the boat about and pulled it back to the other side of the lagoon. At the bow of the *canoa* Carlos held tight. He began to tie the line to the front of the boat then remembered the stories he'd heard of *canoas* being swamped and capsized when a *pirarucu* dove into deep water. Instead of tying off the line he braced his legs and leaned back against the force. No one had thought to bring a harpoon but Carlos had his rifle, which one man loaded then held poised at the gunwale to shoot the fish when it rose for air. But the fish was too fast. Back and forth the *canoa* went for more than an hour. Then, as dawn was lighting the sky, the fish surfaced and paused, exhausted. A gunshot echoed across the lagoon, and the water foamed for a brief moment as the fish thrashed and convulsed, then lay still.

At one hundred pounds and about the size of an eight-year-old boy, the fish would feed the children at the school for several days. The exhausted men hoisted the fish into the *canoa* and marveled. What would it have been like with a truly large *pirarucu* four times that size?

CHAPTER FIFTY-FIVE

CHALLENGES OF THE NEW CENTURY

Juan:

The Shuar are very well prepared to defend themselves against sickness. It has been many years since any of the children have suffered my brother's fate and died from whooping cough because now the children are vaccinated. Most people are within a few miles of an airstrip if they need medical help.

The biggest problem now is alcohol. Before, the people did not drink very much. Sure, they made their chicha from yuca, because the yuca is life, but chicha cannot be compared to liquor found in the towns.

Most of the Shuar still live in the jungle, where they have always taken care of themselves. Now many who live in towns have lost the skills to do this. It is a positive thing that many are learning and are in school so they receive better treatment as citizens. But now I am old and somewhat of a pessimist as I worry about my friends. When I was a child the Shuar community was a virgin. It was innocent. Now it is very different.

What Shuar goes to the waterfalls? What Shuar drinks ayuhuasca? Very few. The shamans will drink it for their cures, but more people now trust doctors. Part of the reason is that the shamans have changed very much also. In the past a person became a shaman because he was called to the work by the spirits. Now a man becomes a shaman only to make money. A cure may cost a month's earnings, or the shaman may charge a cow or a dozen chickens. Many say that if they are to perform a ceremony they must be given a girl or a woman.

In the past, the Shaman would prepare for months or for years to learn a ceremony. As the the time for the ceremony approached they would not eat and they would not speak. They would spend all their time finding spiritual darts with which they could perform cures, and they were always working to improve their character and their spirit. During a ceremony they would, for example, bring in the sick person and would drink natema (ayahuasca). After drinking the natema they would be able to see what was causing the sickness. They understood. They would then put a dart or something into the affected part or suck the evil from that part. They would be able to tell if it was a curse that was causing the problem of if the problem was a physical one that could be solved by taking certain herbs. They would then cure the person. Now they say, "Bring the liquor. Liquor. I cure with liquor." Then they sing and perform their ceremonies drunk. Natema and liquor are not the same. They are distinct. At least a person who is using natema can function. This is what is changing the Shuar community.

First I would like to say that education during childhood is very important. After God and my parents, who were very good people, I need to thank the Salesians, especially the Salesian teachers. They were the first people after my parents who planted a good seed in my heart. Father Conrado Darde, the Spanish director of the mission of Gualaquiza when I was young. The second was Antonio Giardini. He was an Italian who was about seventy years old. Later Senor Solis worked at the school and taught us how to work. After him came the two teachers Luis Vosa and Jose Peter. These were my guides. They taught how to love God, to work hard, to follow the good path. It was with their guidance that I was able to work as a missionary. I think that the Christian lessons are important ones, and I have tried to follow them.

Today it is still common for a man to have several wives, especially among the Achuar, but this is changing. Instead of having several wives that he cares for and protects, a man might have one wife and several lovers at various places. In the case of lovers he might accept no responsibility for the children or care of the woman. There are divorces, but the priests try very hard to keep this from happening since it sets a bad example, and the fathers then have no contact with their children. Even teachers at the rural schools can fall in love with their female students and use them for a while before leaving the schools and returning to the city. Women, too, fall into a trap and marry a man just because he has money, or seems to.

It is very hard to make money in the selva. There is a small market for *artesanias* (handicrafts), and Juan's daughter Maria comes to the mission to teach the students how to make baskets, *shigras* (woven mesh bags) and traditional jewelry from seeds and insect wings. They make *coronas* (crown-like head gear) in the old style. Some are in the shape of the animal from which they are made—a squirrel, a bird or even a monkey. The most prized *corona* is the orange-feathered *tawasap* made by the Achuar from the vent feathers of dozens of toucans, very beautiful but also very expensive.

Since the late seventies, there has been more interest in teaching the children Shuar myths and legends, which keep alive a sense of pride in their culture. One of the popular aspects of the radio school is the program broadcasting Shuar and Achuar news, cultural events and the telling of these ancient stories.

Chicha continues to be important as a food and for celebrations, but *cerveza* (beer) has taken on more significance. Fiestas, once a time for celebration and good-natured drunkenness, have taken on a new character. There are actually more killings than in the past in many places, and the killing is more indiscriminate, by knives and guns and poison. Juan says, "The *selva* is very large and it is easy for a body to disappear." Even politics has become more dangerous as the Shuar fight over their various candidates. One group, an offshoot of the Shuar Federation, believes that violence is the only way to get things done. At Miasal, the past few years up to the publication of this book have been relatively quiet, but that could change even tomorrow.

The Shuar had always used *tsantsas* to gain spiritual power. Now some have turned to creating the shrunken heads for economic power, making them from the heads of sloths and selling them to tourists as human heads. Recently the Shuar community was shocked when it was discovered that two young men who needed money could find no sloths, so killed their own grandmother, made a *tsantsa* from her head and sold it to a tourist.

Miasal's school is completely operated by the Shuar of the district. Raul (at sixty-three) and (Juan at eighty-two) continue to act as the religious leaders of the area and to counsel the leaders when they request it. Raul, in forty years of service and having walked thousands of miles to serve the needs of the Shuar, had worn out his hips. By 1999, he could barely walk enough to carry on the church services, but he still did it with great joy and with great pain. He never sat but used instead a tall "leaning stool" with a high back where he could at least take most of the weight from his hips, and so his knees bent very little. In October of 1999 the Salesians sent him home to Belgium for hip-replacement surgery, which has been successful and has given him a renewed energy. His hearing went some time ago, and he had been feeling more and more isolated from his friends and parishioners. Now, hearing aids in each ear have reconnected him. Sometimes he smiles as he hears the children say something about "Padre hippie." He now spends part of his year at Yaupi but lives most of the time at Miasal, helping where he can.

After more than sixty years of work for the Shuar and for God, Juan and Amalia now live on the piece of land that belongs to her as a Shuar. It is four blocks long and wide, about seventy hectares (approximately 170 acres). They bought the property from a friend almost twenty-five years ago, but the man's family is angry now and wants it back.

Patricia Arcos had lived in Quito for several years but returned with her German husband, Helmut, and their children. She wanted to be involved in her parents' work, but equally she wanted her children to have the same kinds of memories of her parents and the jungle that she treasures.

Although after several years Helmut died suddenly Patricia continues to live in the house that Juan built for her grandmother, Masuink. The children gather round Juan and Amalia each day or help in the kitchen, adding their laughter to the busyness of the days. Each Sunday Patricia invites local Shuar mothers and their children to a "play group." Her children have plastic toys from the city as well as ones that are typical Shuar, and she has taught them to share with the other children. The five or six children usually play together without fighting or squabbles.

Helmut, Patricia's elder by at least twenty years, was a balding, thin-bodied man, always busy thinking of how to make things easier and more comfortable. In Germany Helmut was a printer and a mechanical engineer and who knows what else before he came to Ecuador more than twenty years ago. Using log rounds, he laid a beautiful floor in their home, and in the gathering area he installed the solar lighting given to the school and to the Arcoses; he was a good father, playing with the children constantly. He was also an atheist who hated even the very concept of God. Juan accepted this, but over the years he and Helmut had some interesting discussions.

By 2001, Patricia and her sister, Maria, had taken over much of the day-to-day work at the school, which no longer has *internos* but retains about seventy day students. Various Shuar take turns acting as president of the school. Maria teaches handicrafts and personal development, while Patricia has taken special interest in the "distance learning" program, which provides correspondence courses beyond elementary school. The program has proven to be very successful under her guidance.

Patricia continues to work for Shuar security much as her father did over the years. Recently, she was called to a downriver community with the president of Miasal. The people there were fighting and on the verge of starting another vendetta. Like Juan, she went as a peacemaker. Incredibly, despite the fact that she is a woman, they listened and the fighting was prevented.

One of the teachers at Miasal thought he would like to be a priest and to carry on Raul's work, but he had a girlfriend. Raul and the Salesians appreciated his interest but told him that he could not be a priest. The Shuar community asked, "What's the problem?" for they still do not quite understand Padre Raul's lack of a wife. Of course, Juan counseled the teacher that he could be a lay missionary and do great good, especially if his wife wanted to work with him. The man continues to teach at the school and may someday take up for Juan and Amalia.

Juan:

> Well, this is the way it was and I tell this because, should some young person read this, he should know that the life has been and can be very difficult. But it has been rewarding. Right now we need many missionaries and volunteers who would be able to commit to a life in the forest or even to two or three years of living in the Shuar communities helping the Shuar. There are few things that would improve their moral force more than working with the Salesians. It takes a special type of person to work in the forest because they are isolated and the life there can be very difficult. There are no televisions, or luxuries.

The hospital in Sucua continues to provide free service to the Shuar, and the Shuar Federation airplanes are free for those who need emergency medical care. Most make proper use of it. In recent years, however, there have been more than a few abuses. People have pretended to be sick and took a free plane ride to Sucua for treatment but then went shopping or carousing. Now if a person is flying on a medical emergency a doctor meets them at the airstrip. If they are not sick, they are put back on the plane and returned to their home.

Over the past four decades the other air service provided by the Salesians, Aero Misionario, has saved many lives and brought people to and from the jungle. Unfortunately its services are to be cut back dramatically, for the Salesians can no longer support it. The Ecuadorian government promised subsidies, which have never come. Now a Shuar will have to pay for any flights, and since they have little cash in the jungle, the old trails may become busy again. At least the *tigres* are no longer dangerous, for they have become very scarce.

Still, planes do continue to fly for the Shuar Federation, providing transportation to and from dozens of grassy jungle airstrips and delivering various goods. The life of a jungle pilot is dangerous; in twenty years eight planes have been lost, one of which was never found. In 1999, a plane leaving Miasal's airstrip lost power and was about to crash in the Mangosiza River. One of the passengers, an Achuar man, actually leaped from the plane into the river. The pilot broke his leg and crushed his knee but the other passengers were unhurt. Even after his hundred-foot leap, the Achuar broke only his arm. Parts of the plane still lie scattered at one end of the airstrip, but most of the debris has been recycled at various Shuar farms. Pepe Arcos, still a pilot, crash-landed his plane in 2000 and was seriously hurt but survived. After weeks in the hospital he was released but not cured, so he returned to Miasal where Amalia took up his care. Through her knowledge of natural medicines Pepe regained his health and is flying again.

The little city of Puyo boasts an indigenous university. Most of the leaders of the Shuar communities have passed through this university. Some critics point out that the education there is marginal, but it has produced graduates who are committed to serving their people instead of merely seeking their own fortunes. Many of those students received their start at missions like Miasal, and without this education many things would be different. Most of the Shuar are at least somewhat literate and, in addition to their native Jivaroan, speak Spanish, which is still a major requirement for gaining the rights of citizenship.

Carlos Arcos married and had four children. His non-Shuar wife was uncomfortable in the jungle, so he maintained a home in the frontier city of Macas. His children were good students at the local schools there and occasionally went to Miasal with him. He continued to develop his ecotourism business, bringing visitors to stay at a lodge he built near his parents' home. Ecuador, however, developed severe economic problems. In 2000 the nation abandoned the sucre because inflation had become so high. One dollar had been equal to 140 sucres in 1986, but by 1999 one dollar was equal to 25,000 sucres. 1n a process dubbed "dolarizacion," the U.S. dollar became the Ecuadorian currency and a slow improvement is taking place. Unemployment is still high, as are various crimes, including kidnapping. As a result, the flow of tourists became a trickle, and Carlos's business withered.

In the summer of 2001, while at his home in Macas, Carlos became ill with hepatitis. At the Sucua hospital the doctors could not help, and he was so weak they expected him to die. He returned to Miasal where he moved in with Amalia, who took over his care as she had for Pepe the year before. Carlos improved and seemed to be out of danger through his mother's use of a natural medicine regime. He recovered some of his energy and took up new work. Because airplane flights are so expensive, he rebuilt an old boat motor and began constructing a large *canoa*. When the Mangosiza rose high he planned to transport people from Miasal to Porto Morona, where they could take an eighteen-hour bus ride to get to a city. When the river was too low for navigation he would, himself, return to Macas to be with his family.

But he had hepatitis B and it began to affect his liver. He died in October of 2002. Juan and Amalia were devastated, but life went on.

Juan:

My greatest challenges have not been from the jungle itself. They have come from people. It was, as you can expect, difficult to help keep a naturally belligerent people together, especially when they seldom trusted even their own family. We realized that conversions were often real, and the people became good Christians. Sometimes, however, they were conversions for status or for material property. My family has been a continual blessing, but it was often difficult to feed and provide for all ten of us on the small salary we received from the government as schoolteachers. But the thing that has been most trying for me has been to overcome the long memory of the church, as represented by the priests and nuns. Many were wonderful humanists, but many also loved the Shuar in the abstract. The Shuar, in their thoughts, were God's children, but they were "Jivaros," savages, in reality a lower type of human.

Well, my wife was exhausted from many years of working constantly with many children. She was the mother of eight children and the spiritual mother of many students. She was always caring for the children when they were sick and giving them medicine and giving other help with natural medicine. In the end she worked fifty years as a missionary and she had become exhausted, especially after the problems that we had with the girls in Miasal. It was because of this that she had to take a break. I told her that she should stay in the house for a while and that I would work the mission until she was rested and thought that she could return to work. I am now eighty-one years old, but it is not a problem because we have a number of Shuar leaders who are able to help me. I will continue here in Miasal doing what I can until I see the end of the mission.

May God bless you and keep you safe and happy all of your life, as He has throughout mine.

Now I would like to end with this Psalm that has sustained me in many of our most difficult moments.

> We do not have sadness.
> We do not have solitude.
> Because you are, Lord, in my happiness.
> I always have your friendship.

We do not have, Lord, the night.
We do not have, Lord, the darkness.
Because you shine your light in the shadows,
There is no night, you are light.
We do not have, Lord, sadness
We do not have, Lord, ingratitude.
Because you triumph, Lord, in life,
You have, you give.

We do not have, Lord, the abysses,
We do not have, Lord, the immensity.
Because you are, Lord, the path,
And the life, the truth, Amen.

THE END

LANGUAGE NOTES

In Spanish and Shuar one pronounces all the letters.

A: *ah* as in part
E: *a* as in date
I: *e* as in seem
O: *o* as in boulder
U: *oo* as in coot

Ie: as in *Ya*le
Au: as in *cow*

H: generally silent. *Hogar* (home) is pronounce "ogar"
J: pronounced like an h. *Junto* (together or close together) is pronounced "hunta."
Ll: pronounced like a y. *Llama* (name) is pronounced "yama."

GLOSSARY
AND NOTES

aak (ahk): A simple shelter often built by hunters or travelers through the jungle. See the appendix for a drawing and explanation of how it is built.

agouti (agooty) (*kayuk or yunkits* in Jivaroan) (Dasyprocta variegata): A brown nocturnal, ground-living rodent with small ears weighing eight to ten pounds. Its main food is fruit, leaves and roots. Its legs are rather long for its body so it moves with a curious jumping motion, not unlike a deer pronking (jumping with all four legs into the air at one time). Normally, they have two babies at a time. The jungle is dangerous, so these young must be immediately able to care for themselves. However, they usually remain with their parents for as long as twenty weeks. Jaguars often prey upon them, as do the Indians.

achiote (ahchyotay) (Bixa orellana): A relative of paprika. The seeds are orange-red, oily and hidden within a rather spiny-looking husk about three inches long. To use it one cuts the husk open, rubs a bit of the red innards onto a finger and applies the paint directly to one's body. Both men and women use it as a makeup and war paint. Or the oily seeds can be spread out on a banana leaf and allowed to dry. Then they are rubbed into powder and stored in a small gourd for use later. Teenagers use achiote to cure skin blemishes and sometimes it is used as an insect repellant.

Achuar: A closely-related tribe to the Shuar. One of the five tribal groups that speak the Jivaroan language. The others are the Shuar, Aguaruna, Huambisa and Mayna.

armadillo (armadeeyo) (*shushui* in Jivaroan): One of several American mammals with bony plates in the upper body skin, which provide excellent protection. These many small plates, fit closely together, and although the plates are hard and stiff, they are jointed to provide flexibility, so the animal can curl itself into a ball porcupine-like, to protect its soft lower parts, even tucking its head and feet safely out of harm's way. Although they sometimes eat berries and bird eggs, the armadillo's food is mainly insects, earthworms, spiders and land snails, which it laps up with its long narrow tongue, anteater-like. Because it has only small teeth placed well back in its mouth, it cannot bite in self-defense. The bony plates provide its main protection although at the first sign of danger its scurries into its burrow. A fairly sizable animal, the armadillo grows to two feet and fifteen pounds. Interestingly, the female usually gives birth to identical quadruplets, always of the same sex, for they are from the same egg. From time to time the Shuar contract leprosy from contact with the armadillo, for they are the only known animal host of the bacterium that causes it.

ani (ahny): A crow-like member of the cuckoo family that lives throughout South and Central America. Black and large, there are two varieties, the smooth-billed and the groove-billed, which has a larger beak. Both are predators on other birds' nests, often laying their eggs in a host's nest in typical cuckoo fashion.

anyango: Leaf-cutter ants, which are eaten as a special food.

At certain times of the year the ants begin to swarm, the males and females swirling from the hills.

You have to get up early in the morning to catch some ants. But, you must also make preparations in the early evening before. When the Shuar hunter notices that a particular anthill is becoming active with winged ants ready to swarm, there is great excitement in the house. In the late afternoon, the hunter circles the entire hill with a series of small dish like depressions, each about eight inches across and several inches deep. Then, the hunter builds a small wall from sticks and leaves woven together to create a miniature barrier about a foot high, also around the entire hill, which might have a diameter of thirty feet or more. In the evening, the family makes torches and attach's them to sharpened sticks.

Rising early next morning, the hunter is at the anthill by five o'clock. Before dawn he lights the torches and sets them beside each of the holes. When the ants see the light in the darkness they fly out and begin to circle the torch flames like moths around a candle. Within minutes hundreds or thousands of the winged ants are circling the torches, scorching their wings and falling into the dish-like holes. Handfuls of the nutty, high protein and somewhat oily food are eaten on the spot, but most of the ants are carefully gathered into palm baskets and carried home. Some will be dried in the smoke over a fire for eating later and some will be roasted in a skillet and eaten immediately.

bagre (bahgray in Jivaroan) catfish: In the Amazon there are many varieties, some reaching amazing weights—hundred pounders are common. One of the favorites at Miasal is the *dorado*, or "golden one." The redtail catfish is one of the most colorful and is also known as the macaw fish because of its striking orange-red fins and tail. *Piraiba*, or *filhote*, are largest of the catfish, almost as big as the *pirarucu*. They can easily crush a leg or sink a boat. There have even been reports of giant catfish capturing swimmers and dragging them underwater for a meal. One of the smaller members is the poison catfish. It lives in rivers and even in ponds that are drying after a river has flooded the forest. All have long "whiskers" that they use for finding their prey in the often-milky waters. Indians often use two hundred pound test nylon line with a wire leader.

barbasco (barbahsco) (*Lonchocarpus*): The juice of a specific low plant or a thick vine. Crushed, it produces a milky substance that contains large concentrations of rotenone. When a basketful of the oozing fragments is dragged through the water, it paralyzes fish. They float to the surface and can be easily caught. People handle the juice without problems for it seems to have an effect only on cold-blooded creatures.

bark cloth: For hundreds of years, bark cloth was used to make free and comfortable clothing, especially the skirt-like *itips*. People today seldom make bark cloth, but choose what they perceive as the more prestigious cotton or hot nylon.

bocachica (bocacheeka): A larger fish, up to fifteen inches in length. It has large fleshy lips that have given it the name, which means "mouth of the girl." When Shuar sit to a meal of *bocachica* they usually pick up the head and suck the sweet lips off first, as they are considered the best part. The white meat has an excellent flavor, but it is difficult to eat because it contains dozens of needle-sharp bones.

canoa (cahnoah) or dugout: A boat in the shape of a canoe, generally shaped from the trunk of a single, large tree.

To construct a *canoa* is very difficult and time-consuming, although it is much easier today because of chainsaws and metal tools. The craftsman first cuts a big log with the diameter of at least four feet, then painstakingly cuts it into the general shape he wishes. Most use an ax, but if a chain saw is available it makes it easier to remove the inner part to form the passenger "cabin." Building a cool fire with green leaves added so he can control the heat, he slowly burns away the excess wood then cuts away the charcoal with his machete or ax. This can take many days or even weeks, as he will only work a few hours each day. As he sculpts the boat, he is careful to maintain the balance of the craft so it will not tip when placed into the water. As he nears the end of his work he builds another fire, this one under the *canoa*, again adding green palm fronds to keep the fire from getting too hot and burning his creation. The heated wood becomes somewhat flexible so the man forces increasingly larger pieces of wood into the opening. This gradually stretches and shapes the *canoa*, at the same time killing any insect larva hiding within the wood. The final jobs are two more burnings and scrapings to polish inside and out, for comfort and so the boat slips through the water smoothly. A well-built *canoa* can last twelve or fifteen years and is an invaluable resource to the hunter and his family, so is worth the time and energy.

As the canoa nears completion the builders heat the wood to soften it for shaping and to kill insect larvae within the wood.

capybara (kahpybahra) (*unkum'*) (Hydorchaeris hydrochaeris): This is the largest of the rodents (up to 100 kg/250 pounds and four feet long), and looks like a giant guinea pig. As they spend much of their lives in and around water, their feet are webbed, and they are strong swimmers. Primarily night travelers, they can also be found during the day, feeding along the shore on water plants. A hunter in search of *unkum'* sniffs the breeze for their strong scent and listens carefully for sleeping animals, which snore loudly. They are generally peaceable within their group but when they fight they make a loud "kaa'k, kaa'k" that can be heard several hundred yards away. They "talk" as they move along. This helps them to keep contact in the thick jungle near the rivers. When one of the group becomes separated they notice immediately and begin to call "fui', fui', fui'" until the lost one rejoins them. When startled it makes a click noise as it runs into the water then uses its webbed feet to swim away to safety. But while the meat is edible, the Shuar seldom hunt *unkum'* for themselves as it has a fishy taste. Its main use is for dog food.

ceiba or *ceibo* (saybah or saybo) (*Ceiba pendandra*): Also known as the silk-cotton tree for the seed-fluff that floats from it at various times of the year. A type of emergent tree generally recognized as the largest tree of the South American rain forest. It often reaches heights of 150 to 200 feet and has huge buttress roots thirty or more feet tall. It is also called "kapok." Early life jackets were made by stuffing watertight plastic bags with the light seed fluff. The Shuar use the fluff from the seeds to wrap around their *sirvatana* (blowgun) darts, making an airtight seal so the darts travel farther. Each quiver that holds the darts has a small gourd filled with the fluff, which the hunter plucks out and wraps around the darts as needed. To many the ceiba is the quintessential tree of the rain forest. This is the tree in which Juan and his friends on evening at dusk saw more than two hundred pairs of macaws roosting.

chacra (chahkra): A small garden plot, generally two to three acres. It is cut from the jungle using the ancient methods of "slash and burn," where the trees are cut, allowed to dry, then burned. Crops are planted in the ashes, which add nourishment to the poor soil. Generally the farm is abandoned after two to five years then allowed to return to forest. Meanwhile another *chacra* has been prepared nearby, or at an extension of the old, soon-to-be-abandoned farm. Sometimes these *chacras* are a long distance from the main house, making it necessary for the farmers to camp at the garden from time to time. It is hard work today but even more so before metal axes were introduced. The original axes were dull stones in a handle, which the user simply used to batter his way through the wood.

cicada (sikayda): A large-bodied insect with clear lacy wings. They eat mainly plant juices and can pierce even thick bark to get to it. When ready to mate the males begin their trilling, remarkably loud call. On each side of the abdomen of the male there is a small, thin and very elastic plate. A miniscule muscle is located below this plate, and when the muscle contracts it causes the plate to buck, which makes a click. It clicks again as the plate is released, and because the cicada can contract the plate hundreds of times a second the call is like a continuous buzz that attracts willing females.

colono (cohlohnoh). Spanish for colonist: Most in the rain forest of eastern Ecuador are whites or part-white settlers *(mestizos)* who move to the *selva* in response to the government's promise of free land. Most of them were simple hard-working people but many were not. They often did not respect the Shuar and persecuted them whenever they came into contact. Since the Shuar hate to be looked down upon this has caused much trouble over the past five hundred years in which the two cultures have been in contact. Much as did the pioneers in the United States, they often do not think of the forest as a living thing of wonder. It is merely an obstacle to what they want to do with or what they want from the land.

curare (coora'hray): The poison into which the blowgun darts are dipped, creating a shiny black varnish on the sharpened end. Each man makes it from his own particular more or less secret recipe, using the roots, leaves or stems of various plants. Curare acts as a muscle relaxant and paralyzer, but while it is a strong poison it usually takes several darts to immobilize a monkey, which falls from the tree and dies from the fall. Apparently the blowguns and poisoned darts were commonly used in fights against the white people but not against Indians, where they used machetes, spears and guns. If a man is injured by a poisoned dart he may cut the wound deeper and wider then rub rock salt into the cut several times while drinking cupfuls of salted water.

drip tips: The long and rapidly tapering, generally twisted end of many rainforest leaves. Because there is so much moisture in the forest, a leaf that is continually wet will harbor mold. It is essential that the water be removed quickly. Most of the leaves are at least somewhat waxy, which enables the water to slide easily over the leaf. Surface tension on the waxy surface keeps the water in droplets, and the tapering, twisted leaf pulls them toward the tip where they form a larger drop that falls away. In a few hours the water is gone and the leaf is dry, making it less susceptible to parasites and moss that might damage it or prevent photosynthesis.

Emergent: The tallest trees of the rain forest, often more than 150 feet tall and draped with lianas. They grow widely separated from others of their species, often as much as a half mile apart.

epiphyte (epifight): Plants that grow on other plants. Most apparently do no harm to the host plant, using it instead for support. The longer the host lives, the better it is for the epiphyte. Scientists have recently discovered that they assist the tree's food-gathering work by creating a thick humus on the host's branches and they quickly send roots into the food mat, adding more possibilities for food production.

internos/internas: Boys and girls who live at the school as boarding students.

liana (leeahnah): Woody vines. Most of these start their growth at the top of a tree. Many of the tiny seeds have a sticky coating that makes them adhere to a bird's foot. When the bird lands on a branch, the seed rubs off in the epiphyte mat begins to grow, often a hundred and fifty feet or more in the air. Other seeds are hard. The thick coat is slightly rubbed off while in the bird's gizzard and so is not digested. When the bird defecates on a branch the seed stays on the branch and quickly begins to sprout. The liana grows downward until it touches the ground, where it puts out roots. Not only do the roots help the liana but they further stabilize the tree. Many emergent forest trees are totally covered with lianas, and because the lianas often grow from tree to tree they tie acres of forest together so a wind through the forest causes the entire canopy to sway. If one tree falls it often pulls down several others because of the lianas' connections. But this is not necessarily death for the liana for they will grow along the ground until they find another host then climb it. Some lianas are among the oldest plants in the jungle.

Monkeys: spider monkey: These creatures live primarily in the trees and seldom come to the ground. They can live twenty-five to thirty years. They get their name from their very long arms and legs and the thin prehensile tail. They are sixteen to twenty-one inches long and weigh about twenty pounds. howler monkeys: There are two species, red and black, with the black being most common near Miasal. Large monkeys, they weigh from nine to twenty-two pounds. They are diurnal so hunters can more easily find them by watching for movements in the high branches as they pull off leaves or fruit. They also have a loud challenging call, created by a combination of a lower jaw with a special angle for broadcasting the noise and a huge sounding chamber in their throats. Shuar follow the calls then watch for the movement of branches or the sound of urine or feces dropped by the monkey troop. The females and young are brown. Because the Shuar never want to kill the alpha male, which has most of the family's protective wisdom, the coloring helps in selecting an animal to shoot. Most often the people use blowguns to hunt monkeys, for they are silent and with luck a hunter can shoot two or more before the troop discovers they are in danger.

Names: Many Shuar have two names—a Christian name such as Pedro and a Shuar name such as Tukup, or Patricia and Yaanua.

nutria (newtreeah) (uyu in Jivaroan) (Myocaster coypus): Similar to a muskrat but unable to withstand cold weather, the adult is brown, about fourteen inches long, not including the tail, which is twelve to seventeen inches long, round and hairless. Prominent whiskers, about four inches long, are so numerous it looks like it has a beard. To keep its three layers of hair waterproof it has glands near the corners of its mouth, which produce oil to rub into its hair. An adult's average weight is sixteen to eighteen pounds but they can grow to twenty-vive pounds or more. The mammary glands are located unusually for a mammal in that they are high on the sides of the nutria. It's not unusual to see babies nursing as a mother swims. Prolific animals, they mature at five and a half months of age and females can have two litters each year, breeding virtually any month and breeding within two days after giving birth to a litter. Because they live in communal burrows (often with one male and three females plus young), and because they often over-harvest their favorite foods, they can quickly devastate an area.

Although awkward and vulnerable on the land, they often travel inland to feed on preferred foods like the Shuar's crops. Many consider the nutria to be vegetarians, but several Shuar confirm that the animals also eat fish, as described in Juan's story of how on a trip they used a fishing nutria to obtain food for themselves.

Oriente. (oree-en-tay): Another name for the rain forest. Also *selva*.

Oropendola: The Montezuma oropendola is a rather large (eighteen to twenty) black bird with a bright yellow tail. Its bill, too, is dark but the tip is bright scarlet, as if dipped in blood. For safety, they cluster their colonies a hundred feet and higher in the trees. They build oriole-like nests, often four feet long, weaving them from palm and other fibers. The male's song is unforgettable, a sort of wheezing gurgling and popping sound, not unlike dripping water falling into water. When delivering the sound, a mating call, to a female, the bird may even somersault around a branch.

otter, giant river otter (Pteronura brasiliensis): Very rare because their skins are much treasured. Almost five feet in length, they are dramatic and playful river inhabitants. But they are ravenous. It is thought that a pair of otters may eat three tons of fish in a year. Because they are competing for the fish that the Ecuadorian fisherman (*colonos*) are after, *colonos* will kill them on sight with machetes or rifles.

paca (pahcah) (*kashai* [kahsh-eye] in Jivaroan). (Agouti paca): A brown animal with four rows of white dots creating lines that run from one end of its body to the next along its 40 pound body, which can grow to almost three feet long. It has large cheeks, that resonate to make loud calls of various types. Excellent swimmers, if endangered they try to run to water for escape. They live alone, typically feeding on plants at night. Young pacas are common pets with the Shuar, and a traveler might often see children with one tied on a palm fiber leash.

paiche or pirarucu (paeechay or peeraroocoo) *(Arapaima gigas)*: The largest freshwater fish in the world. Once it was common to find specimens more than ten feet long and weighing four hundred pounds, but over-fishing has decreased their number and size. Called "living" fossils, they belong to the bony-tongue family of fishes. Its tongue is about five inches long, bony and rough. The Shuar often use its rough surface as a rasp to smooth wood. They have both gills and a primitive lung that has been adapted from its swim bladder,which enables them to survive even if the river subsides and leaves them stranded. The *pirarucu* likes to live in lagoons, which have low oxygen levels, so the fish rises to the surface to gulp additional air. It is this gasping sound that the Shuar hunter points his harpoon toward. Sometimes the fish is trapped in a dry riverbed. When this happens it merely finds a burrow in the mud, curls up into a ball and aestivates (like hibernation) until the river floods again.

One night on a fishing expedition, Carlos, Juan's son, and his friends had a hooked paiche pull their loaded dugout back and forth across a dark lagoon for several hours before it tired and they could kill it. The fish is silvery and covered with scales up to three and a half inches long, each with a dark diamond-shaped portion that is thick and tough, effective protection against caiman, freshwater dolphin and any predatory fish. Once they are adults, only the metal-tipped harpoons or shotguns of hunters seem to endanger the fish. The dried scales are used to make a decorations on dance dresses or belts, for they "clack" together with a pleasant sound. Because the oily flesh is delicious both dried and salted, the *paiche* has been fished to extinction in many places where they once were numerous.

palmito: The furled new leaves at the tip of a palm tree. The most prized is from the chambira *(chonta)* palm. It has a mild flavor and can been eaten raw or cooked, served in a salad or boiled and served like spaghetti. In the U.S. it is pickled in acetic acid and sold as "hearts of palm."

paramo. The grassy plains of the Andes above treeline

patacones (pahtahconays): A dish similar to round French fries, made by slicing plantains *(platanos)* and frying them. Partway through the cooking process the rounds are pressed flat, often using an empty Coke bottle, so they become crispy.

peccary (pekary) (*paki* in Jivaroan*)*: These animals are in two varieties, white-lipped, which travel in groups, and the more solitary collared variety. This is a wild pig, a variety of which lives as far north as the southwestern U.S. They are extremely agile despite their ungainly shape, and can be dangerous to hunt, especially the white-lipped variety. They have a very strong odor that clings to the plants as they pass through the jungle, making it easier for hunters to find them. If a hunter approaches the band they usually will not run at first but will click their teeth together as a warning, which sounds like two pieces of bamboo being struck. If the hunter shoots one of the pigs he is alert, for though most of the time the herd runs, sometimes it charges the hunter. Tukup told how he had been treed by a family of *paki* and that they actually stayed under the tree, dozing and waiting for him to come down. He stayed in the tree overnight.

pilche (peelchay) (calabash): The round green gourd-like fruit of a small tree. A form of calabash, it is quite round and varies in size from as large as a cantaloupe to as large as a basketball. When dried and the seeds removed, they make excellent containers for food. For the Shuar it is the traditional bowl or "canteen" for serving *chicha*. *Pilche* is easily grown from cuttings.

piranha (peeranya) (*pani* in Jivaroan): Black and red varieties exist, with the black being the largest. Most of the time the piranha eat fruit, and when a ripe fruit falls into the water the place swirls with the sharp-toothed fish fighting for it. Black piranha can grow up to a foot long, and their meat is tender and mild-flavored. The Shuar usually save the jaws and use the sharp teeth to notch their blowgun darts, so they will easily break off in a hunted animal. Red piranhas are smaller, bluegill-size fish that prefer to travel in groups. It is they that have the reputation of killing an animal in the water and cleaning its carcass to the bones in only a few moments. Red piranhas are most dangerous, however, when they are caught in a shrinking pool as the river that has flooded into the forest returns to its channel.

plantain (*platano* in Spanish and Jivaroan): A member of the banana family. The fruit looks like a banana but is not sweet; in fact the flesh is rather woody and is inedible until cooked. The flavor is quite bland so the eater usually dips the fruit into salt or a garlic-salt and pepper mix, or makes round *patacones,* which are much like French fries.

rio (reeo): River in Spanish.

s*angre de drago* or *sangre de draco* (sahngray day drahgo or sahngray day drahko) (dragon's blood): Made from the blood-like sap of the *sangrillo* tree, it has many uses. It is very effective used as an antiseptic, its stickiness closing a wound and preventing further infection. But it can also be taken internally and is also used as a cure for ulcers, internal bleeding or to help cure wounds from arrows or spears—seven drops in *chicha* three times a day for a week is a normal dose.

sangrillo (sahngreeyo): An emergent tree whose sweeping roots have the texture of human muscles. A cut in the tree begins to ooze large quantities of sap immediately that, when boiled,·

turns blood red and is called *sangre de drago* or *sangre de draco* (dragon's blood). Painted on a wound, it has an antiseptic quality and seals the cut against dirt.

selva (saylbah): Another name for the rain forest. Also *oriente.*

Shuar (Shooar): The name that the tribe gives itself and which means people, man or men. Foreigners who first came were aware of their ferocious and warlike nature so called them "Jivaro," the fierce people. The people do not like to be called Jivaro as they consider it an insult and an ethnic slur.

sirvatana (seerbatana): blowgun. Also *bodequera* (bodaycayra) in Spanish.
    See the appendix for an explanation of how it is constructed and used.

tapir (taper) (*pama or danta* in Jivaroan): The largest of the mammals in the rain forest. Because there is little light at the forest floor there is little ground vegetation or grass and what there is is often deficient in minerals and vitamins, so large herbivores have a limited choice of food. Tapirs weigh from 200-250 kg (500 pounds) and have a body like a pig, three toes on each foot (with each toe being shaped like a horse's hoof), a skimpy mane similar to a horse and a longish nose like a short elephant's trunk. In fact, they are pachyderms, and their closest living relatives are elephants and rhinoceri. They are a favorite prey for *tigres*, which kill by crushing the skulls of their prey. The skull of the tapir is very thick and tapered toward the top, making a killing bite more difficult. They love water and are powerful swimmers. Shuar hunters talk about seeing a tapir being attacked by a *tigre*. The tapir immediately turned and ran into the jungle with the *tigre* on its back. Unable to dislodge the roaring cat, the tapir leaped from a cliff into a stream below. The surprised and soaked *tigre* was so confused that the tapir easily escaped. Sometimes a Shuar obtains an orphan tapir, still with its mottled stripes, and takes it home. They make good pets and tame easily, soon eating bananas and plantains from the hands of family members. Sometimes they become food for the family but a surprising number remain as pets throughout their lives. To mark one as a pet the family trims its mane, so other hunters will realize that the wandering animal belongs to the nearby family and should not be shot.

tigre (teegray): The Spanish name for jaguar. These large, spotted cats were once numerous in the Cutucu Mountains and very dangerous as they had no fear of humans. Now they have been hunted so hard that they are seldom seen and have a healthy fear of people. Shuar traveling through the jungle usually had to take two warriors for each child or woman, sleeping at night with the vulnerable one between two warriors. With dark patterns over its body in rosettes and a body the color of dead leaves in sunlight, the *tigre* can watch without being seen. They eat about any kind of meat and when they find a stagnant pool with trapped fish they often leap in with claws flailing, throwing fish onto the shore. It has even been reported that they will sit quietly by a stream with their tail dangling in the water to attract fish which they then pounce on.

toucan (tookan) (*tsukana* in Jivaroan): These are killed both for food and feathers. The most prized feathers are orange and from the vent area. The feather *coronas*, or crowns, that are most prized are the ones made from those achiote-orange-colored feathers.

tree fern: Ferns that grow to the size of trees. They reproduce in the same manner as ferns, by microscopic spores. Scientists believe they are a very ancient form, even predating the age of dinosaurs. The Shuar call them "monkey tails" because the opening leaves are curled and look like many hairy monkey's tails on the top of the tree.

varzea (vahrzayah) flooded forest: At various times of the year, during "winter," the rivers rise forty and fifty feet, flooding back into the forests. Fish swim through the flooded forest like flocks of birds soaring from treetop to treetop, plucking fruit from the submerged limbs. The tambaqui fish in particular are well adapted for this as their jaws are broad and studded with razor-sharp teeth to attack even the hardest nuts. Their favorite seems to be the high-protein nuts of the rubber trees. As the river falls the fish migrate back to the river, unless the Shuar have placed bamboo fences across the tributaries, which capture the biggest fish and let the smaller ones pass through. Shuar then come to the fish corrals daily to spear what they need to feed their families.

When the river floods into the forest it aids in a complex system of cross benefits. The flooding of the forest provides much-needed silt and fertilizer to the mineral-poor land. Most of the Shuar live near the rivers for this is the place where the most fertile soil can be found. In turn, when the river floods again it carries some of that fertile soil back into the also-poor waters of the river, enriching them. About two percent of the Amazon Basin may be in *varzea*

BIBLIOGRAPHY

[1]   *Adaptive Responses of Native Amazonians.* Edited by Raymond B. Haines and William T. Vickers. New York: Academy Press, 1983.

[2]   *Native Peoples and Economic Development.* Edited by Theodore MacDonald, Jr. 1985. Cambidge, MA: Cultural Survival, 1985.

[3]   Chapter 4A. Ethnic Groups and Languages, "*Countries of the World.*1991.

[4]   Harner, Michael J. *The Jivaro, People of the Sacred Waterfalls.* Berkeley, California: University of California Press, 1984.

[5]   Plaskin, Glenn "Secrets of the Centenarians," *Family Circle Magazine* p. 36 January 2001. New York: Gruner + Jahr Publishing,

[6]   Descola, Philippe *Spears of Twilight.*New York: The New Press, 1993.

[7]   "Geophany" (soil-eating), *Hutchinson Dictionary of Science,* 01-01-98, (available on the Internet)

[8]   Howe, Robert, Personal journals from trips to Ecuador, 1984-2001.

[9]   Smith, Nigal H. *The Amazon River Forest, A Natural History of Plants, Animals, and People.* New York: Oxford University Press, 1999.

[10] Terborgh, John *Diversity and the Rain Forest.* New York: Scientific American Library, 1992.

[11] Rachiowiecki, Rob *Ecuador & the Galapagos Islands.* Oakland, California: Lonely Planet, Travel Survivor Kit, 1992.

[12] Hames, Raymond B. and Vickers, William T., Editors *Adaptaptive Responses of Native Amazonians.* New York: Academic Press, 1983.

[13] Forsyth, Adrian and Miyata, Ken *Tropical Nature: Life and Death in the Rain Forests of Central and South America,* New York: Touchstone, 1984.

[14] *Introduction to Leprosy.* Available on the Internet: www.raex.com/-bbeechy.

[15] *Mundo Shuar, Series C, La Cocina* Cesar Bianchi, Centro de Documentacion, Investigacion y Publicaciones, Sucua, Ecuador, 1978

[16] ibid, vol. 5

[17] ibid, vol. 11

[18] Bianchi, Cesar *El Shuar y El Ambiente.* Quito, Ecuador: Abya-Yala, 1988.

[19] Stoll, David *Fishers of Men or Founders of Empire?* London, England; Zed Press, 1982.

[20] Crompton, John *Ways of the Ant.* New York: Nick Lyons Books, 1988.

[21] Service, Elman R. *Profiles in Ethnology, Revised Edition.* New York: Harper and Row Publishers, New York, 1971.

[22] Clark, Leonard *The Rivers Ran East.* San Francisco: Travelers' Tales Publishers, 2001.

[23] Dalton, Stephen, Bernard, George and Mitchell, Andrew *Vanishing Paradise, the Tropical Rainforest,* New York: Overlook Press, 1960.

[24] Cousteau, Jacques-Yves and Richards, Harry *Jacques Cousteau's Amazon Journey.* New York:,Harry N. Abrams, Inc. Publishers, 1982.

[25] Tierney, Patrick Darkness in El Dorado. New York: W.W. Norton and Company, 2000.

The Shuar and their Homelands

While the Shuar live in the Amazon rain forest—one of the most heavily forested places in the world—their land is poor by farming standards. Most of the minerals are tied up in the plants, including the giant trees and epiphytes that hang thickly on them. To farm, which they must to provide sufficient food, the Shuar cut openings in the forest, burn the debris and plant in the thin soil—classic "slash and burn" agriculture. Unlike many forest peoples, however, they tend to stay in the same areas, cutting and farming in a relatively small area, abandoning the farm to regrow forest and returning to cut and burn a generation later, once its fertility has been replaced by the growing forest.

The Shuar were never conquered by the Spanish. One reason was their pugnacity but another was that they did not live in villages, which could be easily surrounded and burned. Now, because there is less warfare, people are settling along the edges of airstrips in villages called *comunas*. Some *comunas* have even formed around soccer fields. People today can enjoy the benefits of living together and the conveniences of "civilization."

It is common for people not acquainted with the jungle to think that it is mile upon mile of dense vegetation, tangled and impenetrable. In fact, that mostly occurs where the people have slashed and burned then abandoned the site, where trees have fallen to create a light gap or along the sun-filled edges of streams and rivers. In most of the virgin forest there is a cathedral-like dusky openness, for the giant trees and the epiphytes on them create a dense shade where a thin layer of smaller plants and young of the giants languish, patiently waiting their turn to grow when the large trees die and fall. Most of the bulk of the vegetation in the rain forest is in the canopy, and when a tree crashes down, it quickly rots, releasing its vital minerals into the soil. With the heavy shade there is little grass and therefore only a few large animals for hunters. The tapir is the largest animal, and with delicious meat it is a favorite game when it can be found. In other instances howler and spider monkeys or a half dozen varieties of large rodents, from agoutis and pacas to the capybara (a sort of giant guinea pig), make good hunting.

The rain forest is, indeed, a place of rain, often two hundred inches a year, sometimes falling so hard that it swamps *canoas*, but it seldom rains all day and on many days a sudden and violent shower will be followed by clear skies. Nights are usually clear. Without light interference from cities, the stars are bright and fill the sky with uncounted numbers. Days can be extremely hot, and when crossing a clearing travelers often feel that their brains will boil. But there is a remedy. Step into the forest and the temperature can be twenty degrees cooler than in the sun.

Jaguars, or *tigres*, are the largest carnivores. In the past they were more dangerous than today, for they are intelligent and have learned that men carry guns that can kill from a long distance. When the Shuar traveled through the forest in the past it was common to have three or four warriors in the party to protect the camp at night. Juan told the authors how people traveling with children or women would have two men per child or woman. They slept on each side of the vulnerable ones—on many occasions a *tigre* would slip up to the *aak*, and reach in to pull out and carry away a small sleeper. With persistent hunting, the *tigres* have become very shy and are no longer much of a threat to travelers. The Shuar and other tribes often had superstitious beliefs about the *tigre*. It was widely believed, for instance, that a powerful shaman could change into the form of a *tigre* and roam the forest. So a night *tigre* might be the true animal, a shaman in animal form or a vengeful group of warriors on a night raid.

The Shuar, or Jivaro as they hate to be known, are indeed a powerful and often warlike people. Even in the modern world, although vendettas are rare, the people are careful to protect their image. Any slight that seems to indicate that they are being taken advantage of or thought of as less than powerful can create an "incident."

They became famous as the "head-shrinkers of the Amazon" for their custom of cutting off the head of their enemy and making a *tsantsa,* or shrunken head, to capture the powerful spirit of their enemy for themselves. They slit the back of the head to remove the skull, then carefully sewed the eye-holes, ears and mouth shut so the spirit could not escape. Over a period of days or weeks the warrior would pour hot sand into the head until it had shrunken to about a fifth of its original size. The *tsantsas* were valuable but they were also a danger. Even the "big men," the most powerful of warriors, kept them only a year until they were disposed of, often buried with ceremony. In reality other tribes captured and shrunk heads in the past; the Shuar kept the custom much longer, perhaps until the early 1950s.

A Shuar home is built much the same as in the distant past. It resembles an oval fort, and that was how it was used for many hundreds of years. It is divided into two parts, the men's portion and women's, which is also for sleeping and family activities. Visitors are seldom invited into the women's portion, called the *ekent.* They still serve *chicha*, a drink made from masticated and fermented *yuca* (manioc). Depending on the age of the *chicha* it can be nonalcoholic or very strong, but visitors are expected to accept the offering. When a woman offers the *chicha* she sieves the fibrous liquid into a *pilche* (calabash) bowl with another *pilche* gourd that has holes punched into it. Before she offers it to a visitor she wipes the rim of the bowl with her fingers and licks her fingers to prove that it has not been poisoned. Women are acknowledged only slightly, and if an insect lands on the bowl the visitor simply holds the bowl up for the hostess to remove the little swimmer.

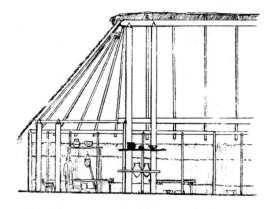

A side view of the ekent, the woman's side of the Shuar home, used for cooking and sleeping.

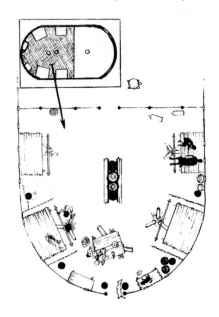

Top view of the ekent.
(Both drawings courtesy of Abya Yala, Qvito Ecuador)

Because of their warlike lifestyle few men died of old age. Because of the shortage of men it was common for a man to have three or more wives. If they were sisters, which was often the case, they lived in the same house. If they were not related, the man was responsible for creating a house and farm for each of them.

It is interesting that they were so warlike, for the Shuar concept of the afterlife was horrifying. In his book, *The Jivaro, People of the Sacred Waterfall*, Michael Harner gives an excellent and complete description of their beliefs. Basically, when a person dies the Shuar believe that he repeats his life, with all its joys and terrors, but throughout that time the person is in a perpetual state of hunger. Even today Christian Shuar, thinking they are about to die, will call for food so they can eat as much as possible before death, just in case. The Christian concept of life after death is definitely more appealing. Children who died were believed to change into little birds, and there was little ceremony about the disposal of their bodies.

There are no "chiefs" among the Shuar, only the *Kakarams* or "big men," the greatest warriors and killers who had created the most *tsantsas*. Tukup, who is an old and valued friend of Juan Arcos, is among the greatest of the "big men" still living, although he is now a Christian. In the distant past it is said that a war party would prepare all night for a raid, then send an emissary to warn the other Shuar that they were going to be attacked. Others did not receive that respect: When war parties were planning to attack whites or non-Shuar, there was no warning emissary. When a "big man" died, the Shuar believed that he changed into a *tigre* that roamed the forest and continued to harass his enemies, so even his death was no assurance of safety for those enemies left behind.

Waterfalls are the places where spirits dwell and where a Shuar can go to seek a vision or to find a spirit helper, an undying *arutam* soul. Young boys, often as young as six, and men may go there for a vision, or if a young man is having problems "growing up" he may be taken there for a lesson in self-discipline. When a man has a vision he tells no one, but his life has changed forever, and for the better. He carries himself more confidently and speaks with greater power, which gains him the respect of others. Even with the terrors that sometimes come with the vision it is a valued part of the Shuar life, for with it a man gains intelligence and strength and cannot be killed by either physical violence or even by sorcery.

Even with the advent of modern medicine the shamans are busy. The Shuar never blamed every illness on "bad arrows" sent by an evil shaman and they did have a good understanding of contagion, most likely a "gift" from the Europeans who brought so many deadly diseases.

From 1937 to 1952 the Leonard Exploration Corporation and the Royal Dutch Shell Company prospected for oil. In the mid sixties, Texaco-Gulf as a consortium led other companies in oil exploration and production. There was an oil boom, especially in the northeastern part of Ecuador, and as roads were built to manage the oil, *colonos* began moving into the jungles and bringing a different kind of agriculture. By 1974, twenty percent of the population of the Amazonian region was white *colonos*. The rapid colonization caused problems with the native populations, many of which Juan has described, and forced the Shuar from their traditional lands. Now the Shuar are trying to work within the system to request, and demand where necessary, their land rights. The government has been slow to survey the lands they've given to the Indians, and this has caused some land-claim problems. The government tends to lean toward supporting the *colonos* against the Indians because the Indians require more land for their subsistence agriculture than the *colonos* do for their more settled type. This ignores the fact that the Indians' agriculture is sustainable and the *colonos* is not. In many cases the Shuar land is slashed then not burned, but rather the plants are left to rot, which improves the land. *Chacras* (farm plots) are small, and a Shuar family might have two or three *chacras* in various stages of production or abandonment. After a few years, a *chacra* is abandoned; the forest regenerates and the lost nutrients will be slowly replaced by natural forces. The plot might be reused once in each generation.

To protect their rights, there are several Shuar organizations in the twenty-first century, the largest and most influential being the Shuar Federation. This organization began as a response to the threat from the Ecuadorian government to take their land, for the government policy is that any unused land belongs to the Ecuadorian government. When a land shortage developed in the highlands the government began to encourage the mountain people to go to the jungle and homestead farms. The land is a "productive asset" and as such it must benefit not only the owner but also the community and the nation. To prove that they were using the land, the Shuar were being forced to use the same farming techniques as the *colonos*, techniques that did not work in the jungle.

To make sure that the Shuar lands met the standard of being a productive asset the Shuar Federation began to loan money to cooperatives in various areas to encourage the Shuar to cut pastures and raise cattle. The *Radio Federacion* was an agency of the Shuar Federation whose purpose was to educate the people. The well organized radio broadcasts may have made the Shuar for a while the most literate indigenous group in South America. The Shuar Federation in the 1980s was one of the strongest of the indigenous organizations. Its power may have waned since that time when it united more than 150 centros (communities) and at that time represented more than twenty thousand Shuar and Achuar, but it continues to be a powerful force in the lives of the Shuar and Achuar people.

Other organizations, however, have increased their influence as they advocate a more violent approach to solving problems with the Ecuadorian government or with *colonos*. Like most of the indigenous people in South America, the local white governments continue to take advantage of the less-educated people. For a while in the seventies, the Shuar seemed on a strong track, making education and bilingual (Shuar and Spanish) training a part of their lives. Today it is unclear what direction they are taking, and the children receive only a rudimentary and inconsistent education. But they remain a proud and unbending people. If you see a man standing on the corner of a street in Quito you can recognize him as a Shuar by his proud bearing.

BLOWGUNS
(*BODEQUERAS* OR *SIRVATANAS*)

Here are the instructions, as given in book 6 of Mundo Shuar by Cesar Bianchi

1. Obtain two pieces of palmwood, straight and dry, about three meters long and 4.5 centimeters thick. One is an extra in case you discover the first is malformed.
2. Prepare another piece of wood in a "Y" shape about 50 centimeters in length. Split it carefully in the middle of the forks and insert a machete into it, creating a drawknife.
3. Drive two green posts two meters long into the ground and two meters apart. Use your machete or an axe and split them. Put a stone into the bottom of each of the splits to keep them open.
4. Lay one of the palmwood pieces into the split posts and carefully remove the bark and any branches, creating a long and smooth pole. Do the same with the other pole. When you are finished they should each be about 3 centimeters wide and 2-3 meters in length. From one end to the other they should be as exact as possible.
5. Slowly heat each pole over a fire and when the wood is softened bend it carefully until the poles are perfectly straight. Set one pole aside.

6. Rasp the outside, using the dried tongue of a pirarucu or a store-bought file until the pole is perfectly smooth.

7. With your machete, carefully split the pole so there are two pieces.

8. Lay one half-piece into the post again and carefully cut a groove from one end to the other, then use wet sand in the groove and another long pole to smooth the groove and deepen it. Do the same with the other half-piece until the center is very smooth and the two sides match perfectly.

9. Wrap the two matching pieces tightly and hold them to the sun. There should be no light showing through. If there is, continue sanding. Then unbind the pieces and lay one back on the post with the groove upward.

10. Cut pieces of wood the same thickness and place them at intervals along the top of the groove but so the groove is open. Then lay the other on top and bind them together again so the pieces act as spacers with slot openings between. Now push the sanding pole back through the opening and move it back and forth as you pour sandy water through it. The excess water, sand and sawdust will go out of the slots. Continue this until the bore is completely smooth. Remove the spacers.

11. Bind the s*irvatana* at three or four places and shape the outside so it is completely round, and tapering toward one end. Move the bindings as needed but keep the two pieces very tightly together.

12. Cut a very straight piece of bone about 2.5 centimeters in length and rasp it until it fits tightly into one end of the bore. If need be you can use beeswax to make it fit tightly and make a good seal.

13. Cut four or five grooves all the way around the *sirvatana* and bind the pieces together tightly at each of these grooves.

14. Gather the bark of large *kanku'm* vines, boil it until soft then while it is still hot use your machete or knife to cut

it into long thin strips. Begin at the thin end and tightly wrap the length of the *sirvatana*. This will give protection to the weapon as well as help make it airtight.

15. Heat the black wax from the stingless bees or any other wax and rub it into the wrapped vines. As it cools put on another layer. Continue until the weapon is smooth. Use a heated machete to help spread and polish the wax.

16. Cut the bark from a thick yuca stem and use this to further smooth the outside of the weapon.

17. Install a sight about a handspread width from the mouthpiece. Add more wax and to this, across the top, press the white, arched tooth of a squirrel or young paca or agouti, to protect the sight and so it can be seen in lower light.

18. Good hunting.

Aak

When traveling through the forest or at a waterfall seeking a vision the Shuar often build a simple lean-to type of shelter, called an *aak*. Most are simple one-night shelters.

Cut a straight pole about 2.5 meters long and with a small crotch or "Y" at the top. Then cut a second about one meter long and straight. Sharpen the longer pole and push it into the ground tilting it at about a sixty degree angle. Cut eight or nine other straight poles about five or six meters long, remove the branches and sharpen one end. Drive these into the ground. While one person holds the smaller (one meter) pole in the crotch of the first, lean the other poles so they rest on the support. Cut palm fronds and lay them over the framework in several layers. This forms a somewhat triangular-shaped shelter. If one is going to a waterfall to seek a vision, or taking *ayahuasca* to obtain a vision, the shelter might be larger and more rectangular with three supports instead of the one as it will be used for two or three days or more.

Tukup

It's difficult to tell Tukup's age—somewhere between seventy and ninety most likely. But you wouldn't know it from his appearance. He has the stamina and physical power of a man forty years younger. One of the last of the *kaka'ram* (warriors), he is now a Christian. In addition to being a *kaka'ram*, he is also a *uunt* (big man), who is head of the community of Tukup, and a shaman. To the Shuar and the Achuar he is the epitome of power. He has been reported to have killed almost a hundred men in war, but the real number is probably not known even to Tukup. Still a powerful partisan, he is a supporter of the Shuar Federation, but only so far as it does not infringe on his power or what he considers to be his rights. If you are his friend he is the most loyal of friends. If you are his enemy, he is still the most powerful of enemies. Known throughout the Shuar and Achuar territories, for he lets both groups believe he is one of them, his name is a threat even to misbehaving children: "If you do not behave, Tukup will come and take you away." Tukup is a master of "speaking properly." To the Shuar it is said that a man must speak directly and clearly, not to "beat around the bush," and with force. He must never joke or lie in a negotiation. If you are angry you must not show your anger in the original discussion for that would be seen as aggressive and therefore show that you are dangerous.